TRANSFORMATION ETHICS

Developing the Christian Moral Imagination

Thomas R. McFaul

University Press of America,® Inc.
Lanham · New York · Oxford

Copyright © 2003 by
University Press of America,® Inc.
4501 Forbes Boulevard, Suite 200
Lanham, Maryland 20706

PO Box 317
Oxford
OX2 9RU, UK

ISBN 0-7618-2456-1 (paperback : alk. ppr.)

Dedicated to the memory of
Shirley A. McFaul

Contents

Acknowledgments   vii

Introduction   ix

Section I: Foundations of Transformation Ethics

     Chapter 1   Transformation and the Frameworks of Moral
                  Reasoning   3

     Chapter 2   Theological Origins and Historical Settings of the
                  Four Frameworks   21

Section II: Moral Imagination and the Four Frameworks

     Chapter 3   Faith and Love   43

     Chapter 4   Moral Law   65

     Chapter 5   Character   89

     Chapter 6   Justice and Liberation   109

Section III: Moral Imagination and the Transformation Framework

     Chapter 7   Transformation Ethics: Combining the Strengths
                  of the Four Frameworks   141

     Chapter 8   Capital Punishment   157

     Chapter 9   Genetic Modification   175

     Chapter 10 Homosexuality   195

Index   223

About the Author   233

Acknowledgments

Numerous persons have contributed in very significant ways to the preparation of this book. First and foremost, credit goes to the many undergraduate and graduate students who provided valuable criticisms, observations, and constructive suggestions during the many years I have taught a broad range of Ethics courses as varied as Christian Ethics, Comparative Religious Ethics, Philosophical Ethics, Technology and Ethics, Bioethics, Business Ethics, Urban Ethics and Religion, and Studying the Future. All of these courses in one way or another have embraced both in theory and practice the most important aspects of ethical beliefs and behavior described in this book. While it is impossible to recognize by name all of these students for the shared gift of their insights, for more than three decades they have been, and will continue to be, my main mentor.

In addition, I have benefited tremendously from suggestions made by Rev. Jane Eesley of Community United Methodist Church in Naperville, Illinois and Dr. Howard Mueller, Chairperson of the Religious Studies Department at North Central College, also located in Naperville. Both of them took time out of their busy schedules to read all or portions of earlier drafts. I trust their judgments implicitly and relish their friendship. I never cease to be amazed at their keen ability to go below the surface, uncover core issues, and move forward the process of critical thinking.

Finally, my family deserves special mention because without their continual encouragement and support none of this would have been possible. Any shortcomings of this book rest entirely on my shoulders.

Thomas R. McFaul
North Central College
June 2002

Introduction

The purpose of this book is to develop a new and imaginative framework of Christian moral reasoning for the twenty-first century. As we move deeper into the new millennium, our world confronts many pressing moral dilemmas that beg for resolution—from environmental destruction to global terrorism to persistent inequalities. For the approximately two billion Christians who inhabit the planet, there exists an urgent need to join with others in helping to steer humankind away from the potential perils that lurk in the shadowy corners of the present. Little doubt exists that dramatic transformations await us in the future. The only real question involves the direction they will take. Christians can play a major role in determining where we will go and how we will get there.

We begin by defining our terms and laying out the assumptions that guide the writing of this book. Despite the pluralism of ethical perspectives that exist around the planet, all are united in the pursuit of a common goal: to discover the "good" that will most likely lead humankind down the path toward creating the best society imaginable. While terms like "most" and "best" are illusive and difficult to define with precision, nonetheless they point us toward imagining ways to enhance the lot of humankind. They inspire utopian visions of the type that have existed since Plato's *Republic* or Thomas More's *Utopia*. They are the stuff of much modern science fiction.

Christian Ethics is a specific form of Ethics in general and defines the nature of the good from the perspective of Christian Faith. In its simplest sense it translates the theological convictions of the Faith into moral visions and norms that guide the development of community life in both the Church and society. Even though Christians through past centuries have varied and continue to vary in their interpretations of the Faith, Christianity's main ethical image is the Kingdom or Reign of God toward which Christians believe all creation is moving. This means that at its core Christian Ethics is a Transformation Ethics because Christians possess a vision of goodness and endeavor to change themselves and the world in light of it. This book describes the major elements of this transforming impulse, how they developed, and how their strengths can be combined and applied to critical moral dilemmas confronting the twenty-first century.

The moral imagination sits at the center of the transformation process. In short, transformation presupposes the existence of a vision that will guide it. When we speak of the imagination, we refer to the ability of the human mind to create mental pictures of various types such as ideas, impressions, or descriptive and colorful visions. The imagination can combine previous experiences and anticipate the possibility of new ones. It can draw from memory and invent alternative ways of perceiving the future. It can take old ideas or impressions, break them down into smaller parts, and reassemble them into new patterns that have never before existed.

In Christian Ethics, the imagination is the wellspring of moral envisioning and reasoning. It uses mental frameworks for filtering experience, and it gives coherence to the myriad sights, smells, sounds, and sensations that continuously bombard us from all directions. In the late eighteenth century, Immanuel Kant described how the mind actively organizes our disparate impressions of reality into meaningful patterns.[1] Since then, other writers have set forth their own understanding of how the human imagination constructs its internal images. The late nineteenth-early twentieth century sociologist Max Weber coined the phrase "ideal type" to describe how Protestants and Catholics understand differently what God expects of them.[2] More recently in 1970, the philosopher Thomas Kuhn popularized the word "paradigm" to illustrate how scientists impose mental models onto the world in their search for empirical truth.[3]

By whatever name we call them, all of our mental images serve one purpose. In the words of William James, they help us create meaning out of the "buzzin-bloomin confusion" that surrounds us.[4] Christians bring their own moral imagination to the world in order to help transform it in the direction they believe God is taking it. In this book we will focus on the major frameworks of moral reasoning through which Christians perceive the transformation process.

While words such as paradigm, ideal-type, root metaphor, or other, would serve us well, we have chosen to use "framework" because it provides maximum mental flexibility for describing the most fundamental images that comprise the Christian moral imagination. When we speak the word framework, we conjure up visions of pictures or colorful paintings. We can envision portraits or photographs that are framed by borders. The images that we see in films and videos consist of thousands of rapidly moving individual frames. Frameworks can remain stable like the windows of a train even though the images we see through them change as we travel through the countryside. One of the goals of this book is to define the major window-like frameworks of the Christian moral imagination and how the moving images within them have changed over time.

Christian visions of the good society, that is, the Kingdom or Reign of God, emerge in the moral imagination of those who form their personal and social identity out of an experience of Christian Faith. Once formed, the moral imagination guides the process of transformation toward the ethical goals embedded in the Kingdom vision. The good that Christians seek is always God's goodness as Christ revealed it. Another way to say this is that Christians become motivated to transform both the Church and the world according to their moral frameworks through which they envision how God's goodness is manifesting itself in the world. Once we have described these frameworks and their relationship to each other in the Chapters that follow, we will apply them to three specific ethical problems.

Our approach to describing Christianity's ethical frameworks is an integrative one. This means that we will examine how the moral imagination combines both motivation and consequences. Many disputes exist in the field of Ethics, both religious and philosophical, over whether motives or outcomes should take priority. The deontological thought of Immanuel Kant, who emphasizes motives, and the utilitarian ideas of John Steward Mill,[5] who stresses outcomes, embody these two perspectives. Each has its strengths. The position of this book is that both are essential to the process of moral reasoning. Transformation Ethics combines the internal dimensions of the Christian moral imagination with the behavioral consequences that flow from them.

In addition, writers are often divided in their perceptions of whether the individual or society takes priority as the basis for ethical analysis. Friedrich Nietzsche championed the strong individual and Karl Marx spotlighted macro-economic processes. They represent the extremes of this debate.[6] Like motives and consequences, the distinction between the self and society is artificial. Individuals do not exist apart from their social groups and groups are comprised of persons. The key is to connect them in order to gain insight into how society influences its members and how they as individuals contribute to the development of society. In our description of the moral imagination, we will focus on Christian Faith as a foundation for tying the two together.

Our integrative method also combines past, present, and future. It goes without saying that the present did not emerge out of a vacuum but rather through the events and ideas that preceded it. After we have described the major Christian ethical frameworks, we will trace their origin over time starting with the Old Testament and continuing into the Modern world. This will serve as a platform for integrating the strengths of all the frameworks and for stretching the Christian moral imagination into the future. This means that we will unite description with prescription. We will combine historical analysis with normative recommendations for resolving some of today's thorniest ethical problems.

The book consists of three Sections and ten Chapters. There are two Chapters in the first Section. Chapter 1 lays out the major frameworks of Christian moral reasoning and Chapter 2 describes the important theological origins of the frameworks. It also summarizes the sources of authority that are being used to develop the frameworks and the Transformation viewpoint. Section II includes the next four Chapters. Chapters 3 through 6 elaborate in detail the four ethical frameworks that are summarized briefly in the first Chapter. Each Chapter from 3 through 6 focuses on only one framework at a time and traces its historic development. Section III incorporates the final four Chapters, 7 through 10. Chapter 7 combines the strengths of the four frameworks into an integrated Transformation perspective that is applied in Chapters 8 through 10 to three ethical problems, capital punishment, genetic modification, and homosexuality.

Finally, before we turn to Section I and begin the first Chapter, we want to identify the book's intended reading audience. Perhaps we should say—audiences. The book is suitable as a reading source for colleges, universities, or schools of Theology that offer courses in Christian Ethics. In addition, it would be useful for a broad range of Christian discussion groups whose members are driven to explore important ethical issues of our time. This does not mean that it is limited to Christians only.

Persons from other religious traditions of the world might find it to be a helpful source for understanding the inner dynamics of the Christian moral imagination and examine how Christians can transform their Faith into action amidst the challenging moral dilemmas of the new millennium.

Notes

1. See especially three of Immanuel Kant's most influential writings, *The Critique of Pure Reason,* translated by F. Max Muller, New York: Anchor Books, 1966; *The Critique of Practical Reason,* translated by Lewis White Beck, New York: The Bobbs-Merrill Company, 1956; and *Groundwork of the Metaphysic of Morals,* translated by H. J. Paton, New York: Harper Torchbooks, 1964.

2. Max Weber, *The Protestant Ethic and the Spirit of Capitalism,* translated by Talcott Parsons, London: George Allen & Unwin, Ltd., 1930.

3. Thomas Kuhn, *The Structure of Scientific Revolutions,* second edition, enlarged, Chicago: University of Chicago Press, 1970. Also see Kenneth E. Boulding, *The Image,* Ann Arbor, Mich.: University of Michigan Press, 1966.

4. See William James, *The Varieties of Religious Experience,* New York: Simon & Schuster, Inc., 1997.

5. John Stewart Mill, *Utilitarianism,* Indianapolis: Hackett Publishing Company, Inc., 1979. Also see John Stewart Mill, *On Liberty,* Indianaoplis: Hackett Publishing Company, Inc., 1978.

6. See Friedrich Nietzsche, *Beyond Good and Evil,* translated by Marianne Cowan, Chicago: Henry Regnery Company, 1955; Karl Marx and Frederich Engels, *Manifesto of the Communist Party,* New York: International Publishers, 1948.

Section I

Foundations of Transformation Ethics

Section I consists of the first two Chapters. While it is shorter than the other two Sections, it is no less significant. It sets the background and lays out the important issues that the rest of the book addresses in detail. In Chapter 1 our primary emphasis will be on identifying the major frameworks of moral reasoning in Christian Ethics. We will summarize them briefly and then compare and contrast their strengths and weaknesses. We will not rank order them but instead assume that they are all equally important to developing the Christian moral imagination. For nearly two millennia Christians have used all of them repeatedly to address moral dilemmas of their times.

Chapter 2 discusses the sources of authority that we recognize as essential to articulating the four frameworks and the Transformation perspective that combines their strengths. We will examine the theological origins of the Christian moral imagination and discuss the major historical settings within which Christians developed the four frameworks. When we have finished the second Chapter, we will be ready to turn to a deeper discussion of where the frameworks fit into the Christian moral imagination and how Christians used them over time.

Chapter 1

Transformation and Frameworks of Moral Reasoning

Christian Ethics begins with one question. What should Christians believe and how should they act in the world? The answer to this question is that Christians ought to live the highest moral life possible according to the purposes of Christ, who has revealed the nature of God. At one level, this answer seems simple. At another level, however, many hidden complexities lie below the surface of this apparent simplicity. The purpose of this book is to uncover and explain these complexities as clearly as possible in order to clarify how Christians make moral judgments and act on them.

The fundamental premise of this book is that Christian Ethics is an ethics of Transformation, which rests on the supposition that people who are Christians will become transformed in their thinking and acting in ways that reflect their allegiance to Christ. Once again, this sounds simple; but it is not. The linkages between being a Christian and becoming a moral person within the traditions of Christianity are complex, and at times can be confusing.

Anyone who has read Christian writers from Abelard to Zwingli or examined Christian positions on issues spanning from abortion to war will discover quickly the wide range of opinions that exist among Christian thinkers. There is no simple one-to-one correlation between beliefs and actions, or all Christians who share similar theological convictions would hold similar positions on ethical issues. Instead, this is not the case. Christian Ethics is characterized as much by its diversity as by its unanimity. Christians are "all over the map" on their points of view on virtually every ethical concern.

This does not mean that some Christians are necessarily "less Christian" than others in their intentions. Christians of good will can and do genuinely disagree on matters of mutual importance. On the other hand, we do not assume that all the different moral positions that Christian people take on any variety of issues are equal. Rather, we hold that some positions are morally superior to others. Thus, one of our goals is to identify the criteria and procedures for determining how to make the best possible moral response in any specific set of circumstances, while recognizing that disagreements have existed, still exist, and will continue to exist among Christian people of good will.

The transformational point of view explains the nature and origins of Christian moral disagreements and how to go beyond them. It is an integrated approach to ethical reasoning that pulls together many diverse points of view, so that the sum total of all the parts, that is, the overall perspective, is greater than any one part by itself or less than a comprehensive combination of all the parts.

Transformation Ethics does not polarize moral thinking around the concepts of "I am completely right" and "You are completely wrong." It is not dualistic. Instead, we recognize that solutions to moral problems can range along a continuum with some leading to better moral outcomes than others. Nor is Transformation Ethics relativistic. Our goal is to develop a way of thinking that leads to the best possible ethical outcome in any give situation among many possible outcomes, all of which might contain relative amounts of goodness. Christians of good will might disagree on moral questions, but we assume that the ethical position that leads to the greatest amount of goodness is ethically superior to those that result in lesser amounts of goodness.

Transformation Ethics also acknowledges that evil is real and is more than just a lesser good. Doing harm to others is a concrete reality that can come in many forms, such as lying, betraying, stealing, and murder. The terrorist attack on the World Trade Center and preparation for it is a case in point. The moral imagination can envision a continuum of possible ethical alternatives in any given situation. At one extreme is the best possible moral outcome, and at the other is the worst. Transformation Ethics always aspires to arrive at the best possible moral outcome and to avoid lesser ones. At a minimum, it seeks to avoid doing harm. At a maximum, it endeavors to create the greatest amount of goodness. An integrated approach serves this purpose best, one that combines the most significant elements found among the diverse ways of ethical reasoning that Christians have developed historically for arriving at ethical judgments and for acting in the world.

Transformation Ethics holds that there exist four major frameworks of ethical reasoning within Christianity and that the divergent viewpoints that appear among Christian writers stem from these differences. These four major approaches started to emerge at the time of Abraham and continue to the present day. This assertion might appear to be an over-simplification in light of the diverse points of view that have been articulated over many centuries. However, it is the contention of this book that when all is said and done, there are only four major "voices" through which Christian moral reasoning has been and continues to be expressed, although some of them received greater emphasis than others during different historical periods.

The four frameworks are Faith-Love Ethics, Moral Law Ethics, Character Ethics, and Justice-Liberation Ethics.[1] Two of these frameworks incorporate hyphenated pairs because the moral categories expressed in them are closely connected. Faith and Love are frequently coupled in the Christian moral imagination, as are Justice and Liberation. Transformation Ethics combines aspects of all four frameworks into a larger conceptual perspective for understanding how Christians can arrive at the best moral judgment within a range of alternative possibilities.

Within the past several decades there has emerged a lively debate among Christian writers over the primacy of one type of ethical reasoning over others. Writers who emphasize Faith or Love point to how rapid social change and the complexities of modern life transcend the easy application of traditional moral rules. Moral Law ethicists insist that principles and rules take priority over all else. Advocates of Character development emphasize the limitations of both Faith-Love and Moral Law approaches as a basis for arriving at moral judgments. Instead, they advocate the development of Character traits as the only reliable internal moral "gyroscope" for deciding how to act. The proponents of a Justice or Liberation point of view maintain that all three of these other frameworks fail to take account of the structural patterns of social oppression.[2]

Each of these four ways of moral reasoning contains essential but limited insights. Transformation Ethics integrates all of them into a larger framework and maintains that a comprehensive approach to Christian Ethics has to make room for all of them. The goal is not to argue one of them up" to a position of superiority and the others "down" to the status of inferiority. Instead, the goal is to develop a Christian *moral imagination* that includes the best aspects of all four of them.

Before demonstrating this integrative approach, it is first necessary to define the common elements of all four of the frameworks and then delineate the major emphases of each one of them.

Common Elements

All four of the major frameworks of Christian Ethics possess two common elements.

First, the proponents of the four perspectives tie their presumptions about the nature of Christian morality to the will of God. Christian Ethics extends directly from this primary assumption, and moral thinking does not stand by itself as the result of human reason alone. Rather, human reason becomes the vehicle through which God's will finds expression. The only issue then becomes understanding how morality is an extension of the divine will within the context of Christian faith. For Faith-Love Ethics, the best means of disclosing the divine will in human communities is through faithful and/or loving actions. For Moral Law Ethics, God's will is best expressed in principles, laws, and rules. Character Ethics focuses on living virtuously as the way to imitate God's righteousness in the world. Justice-Liberation Ethics advocates the just treatment of all persons as the ultimate expression of God's liberating presence in history.

The second common element extends directly from the first. For all four ethical frameworks, Jesus is the exemplar who reveals the will of God. For Faith and Love writers, while Jesus walked on earth, he possessed perfect Faith and acted from the motive of perfect Love. His life epitomized this perspective. For Moral Law ethicists, Jesus is the image of the perfect "law giver." His Sermon on the Mount in Chapters 5-7 in the Gospel of Matthew embodies fully this point of view. For Character ethicists, Jesus was the ideal person of virtue. While alive he manifested perfectly all the internal character traits necessary for living the ideal moral life. For the fourth framework, Jesus was the exemplar of Justice. He set the captives free; and by liberating the oppressed he revealed completely the true nature of God's righteousness.

Thus, all of the four ethical points of view anchor their ethical ideals in an image of Christ who reveals the nature of God's will. This means that writers from all the frameworks pursue a mutually shared goal. They hold in common the belief that the ethical life is about doing the will of God as revealed in Jesus Christ.

From this common point of departure, writers from the four ethical frameworks proceed in different directions in their perceptions of the most effective means for making moral judgments and for doing Christ's work in the world.

Faith-Love Ethics

As stated above, the Faith-Love framework of moral reasoning begins with the supposition that it is the obligation of Christians to act in the world according to the will of God as revealed in Jesus Christ. Authors who write from this perspective start with either Faith or Love. For these ethicists whose ideas we will examine in detail in Chapter 3, Christians obey the will of God by living in Faith and/or by acting from the motive of Love.

Whether they emphasize the primacy of Faith or Love or some combination of both, writers who fall within the Faith-Love framework share a common viewpoint. Actions are morally justifiable if they serve as expressions of Faith and/or Love. Both the Faith and the Love perspectives perceive human life as subject to continuous modification with very few, if any, permanent cultural patterns or social structures. Christian persons must endeavor to do the will of God in the midst of constant change, where new social forms come and go rapidly and with a high degree of unpredictability. Both positions value flexibility and adaptability as essential tools for coping with the constantly changing conditions of social life.

Even though they share this similarity, writers within this tradition differ on how Christians can be committed witnesses to God's will. For those who focus on *Faith*, doing God's will means living faithfully in the midst of life's transitions from one condition to another. For persons who anchor their ethics in this position, it is common to *feel* the presence of God as a companion in the midst of their daily activities. They understand themselves, and in some cases even mentally envision themselves, literally to be walking through life with Christ at their side. Their relationship with God is highly personal and immediate. Christ is not an abstract idea but a living presence. Christ dwells within them and guides them into and out of all of the circumstances of their lives.

Christ gives their life meaning at the deepest center of their being, and their sense of personal destiny is often conceived in predetermined ways. For example, for many Christians holding this position, some typical comments are: "God called me to do this," "God intends for me to do that," or "God has a purpose for all of us. We just need to find out what it is and do it." There is no uncertainty here or ambiguity to confuse the mind. For the Faith-oriented Christian, God as understood in Christ is leading the way and providing the inner strength and moral direction in every moment. Everything that happens does so for a reason, even though we might not comprehend the divine intent because we are finite human beings.

Thus, moral actions flow from Faith. The question of what it means to do the will of God in the world is answered by following where Faith leads. What is the role of rules? Rules are important, as we will discuss in the next section on Moral Law, but not ultimately important. Instead, what is ultimately important is doing God's will faithfully. If the life of Faith requires following rules, then the Christian person will follow them. If not, then he or she won't. What really matters in the final analysis is not simply following rules but living according to what God requires in every second of every situation as discerned through a personal Faith relationship with Christ.

Following the demands of God through faithful living does not ensure a life of comfort or happiness. It could lead to sacrifice and pain, even death, after the example of Christ who was mocked and crucified because the religious and political powers that dominated Palestine during the period of Roman occupation perceived him as a threat. For Christians who live by Faith alone, God confronts humanity with different moral challenges, and the task of each Christian person is to respond to them as faithfully as possible no matter where they might lead.

Within this ethical framework, writers who regard *Love* as their supreme value follow a different path of ethical reasoning. They strive to carry out the will of God by doing what is most loving in any given situation. Their method of moral reasoning parallels that of Faith-oriented believers in many ways. However, rather than focus on Faith, they accentuate the priority of Love as the basis for determining the most fitting response. They seek to carry out the will of God by applying the norm of Love in all their encounters with other people.

Rules are relevant only in so far as they remain consistent with Love's demands. It is not enough just to apply rules or respond in Faith to complex moral situations, if the outcome from these two ways of acting would be less loving than some alternative that would result in a greater expression of Love. Love is the acid test, and acting in the most loving manner is always the moral mandate that is most consistent with God's will. Anything else falls short of the mark.

For Love-oriented Christians, Jesus is the moral exemplar of divine love. In every situation that he encountered during his earthly life, he sought to express God's love for all people. He did not allow rules to keep him from healing or helping others, even if it meant that he had to break Israel's commandment to set aside the Sabbath as a time for worship and not work. His principle concern was to express God's loving will wherever the occasion called for it, even though it got him into trouble with the local religious and political authorities and gatekeepers of the sacred commandments. Then in one final expression of perfect Love, he sacrificed his life on the cross as the supreme act of God's redemptive love for all humankind. Christians who base their moral reasoning primarily on Love seek to imitate Christ's loving example in all the diverse contexts of their lives, thereby complying with utmost effort to the will of God.

Throughout the long history of the Church's ethical teachings, Faith and Love have been closely connected. The Pauline phrase, "faith working through love," (Galatians 5:6; all subsequent Biblical quotations will be taken from the New Revised Standard Version.) is a core moral image that has recurred throughout the generations. It has deep grounding in the Biblical heritage as well contemporary relevance. It can be traced to Jesus' relationship to God, which led to his compassion for people. His Love was an extension of his Faith, and those who follow in his footstep have long sought to imitate his example. As one of the four major frameworks of Christian Ethics, Faith and Love are closely connected.

Moral Law Ethics

The Moral Law framework within Christian Ethics, which we will discuss in detail in Chapter 4, can be subdivided into two ways of understanding how to arrive at a moral judgment. The first way is prescriptive, and the second way is procedural.

The prescriptive method incorporates the specific "dos" and "don'ts" of moral behavior. Its aim is to prescribe and proscribe certain beliefs and behaviors, such as "think this way" and "don't think that way," or "do this," and "don't do that." The procedural approach, on the other hand, articulates a set of rules to follow for arriving at a moral judgment, but it does not specify in advance what that specific judgment would be. Rather, it assumes that if a person follows a particular way of thinking about how to arrive at a moral decision, then the right moral decision would most likely be made.

Christians who use the *prescriptive* approach usually envision a continuum of ethical norms that range from abstract to specific. They define moral principles as the most general concepts and rules as the most specific. Laws fall somewhere in between these two outer boundaries. The specific cut off points between the most general principles, the lesser comprehensive laws, and the detailed rules are arbitrary, and no clear line can finally be drawn to demonstrate conclusively where one leaves off and the other begin.

Writers within the Moral Law framework always begin with the assumption that God has revealed the principles, laws, and rules by which human beings are expected to live. In Chapter 2, we will describe the sources of authority through which these Christian authors believe God has revealed the Moral Law. Their starting supposition is that humanity has not been left alone without divine guidance. God has made known the Moral Law that is necessary for righteous living. This means that there is no mystery to the ethical life. Follow God's Moral Laws and you will be doing God's will. Obey them and you will be rewarded. Disobey them and you will be punished, if not in this life then in the next life after death. God created the universe to operate by natural laws and made humanity to live by Moral Laws. Both are inherent within the structure of the universe and exist by God's design.

Following these assumptions, two other issues are of critical importance for the writers who take the prescriptive approach. The first is coherency. The relationship that extends from the most general principles to the most specific rules must be logically coherent, that is, there must be "internal consistency." The Moral Laws exist as circles within circles, with the outer one being the most universal and the inner one being the most particular. They must be logically related, and their connections must appear to be reasonable.

For example, the Ninth Commandment of the Ten Commandments instructs that a person "shall not bear false witness" against a neighbor. (Exodus 20:16) This general principle is defined more specifically in the

Holiness Code of Leviticus. When someone is on trial for life, one should speak out if his or her testimony will help. "You shall not render an unjust judgment; you shall not be partial to the poor or defer to the great." (Leviticus 19:15) The general principle of not bearing false witness translates consistently into a specific injunction related to how to give testimony during a trial. The particular rule of behavior is coherently connected to the universal moral principle.

Another critical issue within the Moral Law perspective is how to deal with the problem of social change. This dilemma usually applies more to specific rules that to general principles. As historical circumstances change, rules that were appropriate in one historical era might not be applicable in another, whereas general principles would remain relevant across a wide range of historical settings.

For example, the sixth of the Ten Commandments prohibits killing, or murder, depending on how the text is translated (Exodus 20:13) Virtually all societies, whatever their time period or location, proscribe the intentional taking of human life through malice of forethought. While there are some contexts within which killing might be morally justified, such as to defend the life of innocent people, premeditated murder of one's neighbor is not one of them. The general principle has universal application; and it never changes or is never discarded and replaced by an alternative principle. It abides over time and space and is embraced by human communities everywhere on earth.

However, there are many rules that once might have applied to a specific historical context but no longer do because that context has changed. The question then arises regarding what to do with obsolete rules. Should they be discarded, modified in some way, or retained? If modified, then they might continue to have some application to the new circumstances. However, if obsolete rules are discarded, they might be replaced by new rules that would apply to the new situation. At the same time, the new rules must also remain consistent with the most general principles that transcend changing circumstances.

For example, the Old Testament specifies codes of conduct that for many persons seem unnecessary in today's world. "You shall not sow your field with two kinds of seed; nor shall you put on a garment made of two different materials." (Leviticus 19:19) Or, "You shall not wear cloth made of wool and linen woven together. You shall make tassels on the four corners of the cloak with which you cover yourself." (Deuteronomy 22:11-12) Compared to a general moral principle that

prohibits premeditated murder, specific rules regulating clothing preferences seem ephemeral and non-binding. In today's world, clothing styles
come and go, especially in those countries where individuals are free to
choose how they want to dress.

Thus, in an ever changing world, one of the chief challenges for
Christians who adopt the prescriptive Moral Law method as their major
means of moral reasoning is to decide which rules to keep and which
ones to reject. This task is made even more complex because of the rapid
changes inherent within the modern technological society. The faster the
world changes the more difficult it is to keep revising the "dos" and
"don'ts" list of prescriptive moral injunctions.

Another challenge inherent in the Moral Laws approach is how to
decide to act in novel situations where no existing rules apply. For example, now that cloning technology exists, is it ethical to clone human
beings? Is it ethical to patent new life forms created in the laboratory or
specific knowledge of some aspect of the human genome? Is it ethical to
enhance specific human traits, such as intelligence or physical size and
appearance, through germ-line genetic modification? Should we manipu-
late the DNA structure to slow down or stop altogether the process of
human aging? At this point in time, there do not exist specific rules to
direct moral judgments in these areas. They have to be invented. By what
means they will be created and how they will relate to general principles
and/or existing specific moral rules will be major challenges within the
prescriptive Moral Law tradition of Christian Ethics in the years ahead.

The approach to moral decision making for Christians who use the
procedural Moral Law framework is different. As we will discuss in
Chapter 4, rather than starting with codes that define the divine Moral
Law God structured into the universe, these ethicists follow a procedure
for thinking about an ethical dilemma and arriving at a conclusion. This
method is similar to what pilots do before they fly their airplanes. They
go over a checklist of operations that must be reviewed in order to guarantee the safety of their aircraft and forthcoming flight.

The stages of the thinking process are carefully delineated in order
to cover all the considerations that have to be made before making a final
determination. For the procedural thinker, it is critical to always follow
the steps systematically, such as, "First consider this, second this, third
this, and so on," until a decision is reached. In this way, all the important questions that bear on the judgment are included. Nothing important
is excluded from consideration, because, like the airplane pilot, the check-

list directs the thinking process from beginning to end; and in the end an informed moral judgement can be made.

Character Ethics

The third framework used for arriving at an ethical judgment emphasizes the *Character* of the self as a moral agent who must make a variety of decisions in many different types of situations. We will describe this point of view in greater detail in Chapter 5. The concept of the virtuous self is central to this approach, which assumes that a person's mental and intellectual framework and character traits are the most important factors in analyzing any situation and making the best moral judgment. The focus is not on rules or on changing contexts and how to respond to them. Rather, it is on the inner dispositions that serve as a moral compass and that guide the Christian person to go in the right moral direction no matter what the circumstances.

Character Ethics stresses the importance of internalizing the kinds of virtues that it is desirable for a person to have. It assumes that the virtuous person will know automatically how to act: virtuous people act in one way only—virtuously. Actions that are moral spring from people who are moral. They do not have to think about how to act, because their goodness is spontaneous. Acting virtuously becomes a habit. They do not refer to written rules to guide them, and they are not particularly perplexed because of changing circumstances. They act morally because they are moral persons whose goodness flows spontaneously from them.

The challenge for this third approach to ethics is to develop within all Christian persons a virtuous character, so that they will become the kind of moral agents that Christ intends for them to be. This process starts early and continues through the entire length of a person's life. It does not happen all at once. Virtuous traits cannot be inserted into a person's character like a new program can be added to a computer. There is no "complete character software" that can be loaded into a newborn baby.

Rather, virtue must be learned and practiced repeatedly over an entire lifetime until acting like a virtuous person becomes habitual, even though no one ever arrives at the point of being perfectly virtuous. Each Christian person is always in the process of becoming more virtuous. The more one practices at being a virtuous person, the better one gets at performing virtuous acts. There is no mystery to the virtuous life. It must be willed and reinforced over and over again until living virtuously is automatic. It becomes the manner in which the Character of each Christian person, as a moral agent, is expressed.

The Biblical roots of Character Ethics have existed from the time of Abraham. Emphasis on the importance of Character development is especially pronounced in the Wisdom tradition of the Old Testament. In addition, the ancient Israelites understood well the importance of virtues as dispositions for action. They knew that unless the Law of the Covenant was internalized into the character of each Jewish person it would exist in word only. The written Law had to become the lived Law, as Jeremiah said, written on the heart. Only then would it serve to direct the entire Jewish community to become the people God intended them to be. They could only live the Law by becoming the Law in their "inner parts."

In the New Testament, Jesus uses the metaphor of the heart as the means of motivation for moral actions. In the Gospel of Matthew, Jesus points to the heart as the source of evil ideas that lead to murder, adultery, theft, lying, slander, and a host of other immoral actions. (See Matthew 15:10-20) For Jesus, being ethical had little to do with ritual purification, but rather with the moral dispositions that motivated behaviors in the world and to the ways in which people of his time, and all times, related to each other. For Jesus, virtuous actions emanate from an individual's Character—from the inside out. Thus, from the perspective of Character Ethics, doing God's will for the Christian person means living the virtuous life by imitating the example set by Christ.

Justice-Liberation Ethics

The final framework for Christian Ethics focuses on *Justice and Liberation*. Writers in this tradition, which we will discuss more thoroughly in Chapter 6, do not concentrate on Faith, Love, Moral Law, or Character development or other internal traits. These areas might receive some attention but only secondarily. The primary emphasis for Justice-oriented thinkers is on wealth and power and how they are distributed throughout the whole of society. This form of moral reasoning stresses the centrality of groups over individuals and aims its criticism at abusive relationships that place some individuals in positions of privilege at the expense of others.

For writers within this framework, it is not possible to achieve Justice in society without the exercise of political, economic, and other forms of social power. The starting point for examining the distribution of such power usually centers on structures rather than individuals, although persons can act in unjust ways, and sometimes egregiously so. Without Justice, the other forms of moral expression cannot realize their far-reaching possibilities. While individuals might desire to be faithful, act in loving ways, live by divine laws, or become virtuous, they will be restricted in their moral potential. If the social order is constructed so that some groups or individuals benefit at the expense of others, then the structures of society need to be changed so that the social arrangements can benefit everyone and not just some. Thus, Justice-oriented writers focus on the "big picture," that is, on the total social framework within which Faith, Love, Moral Law, and Character find expression.

By focusing on how evil can exist in economic, political, and other structures, Justice-centered Christians analyze the distribution of the burdens and benefits of any give social arrangement in order to determine which groups or individuals gain from them and which ones do not. They are especially critical of structures that lead some to prosper while others lag far behind, or where some move ahead by harming others.

Where injustices exist, the will of God is not being done irrespective of whether individuals live by Faith, Love, rules, or virtue. All these must be combined and become mutually reinforcing as society moves in the direction of creating more inclusive patterns of social justice. Otherwise, they fall short. In order to achieve Justice, groups and individuals must be empowered to exert their will in the social order, so that they can receive their fair share of the collective goods and absorb the burdens in a manner that is consistent with the sacrifices expected of others. If they do not exert their will, they will be subordinated to the power interests of others. When this happens, injustices emerge.

Christians who write from this framework connect their analyses of Justice with the ethical theme of *Liberation*. Under the conditions of oppression, exploited groups or person must become liberated in order to receive their just due. They must be freed from the shackles of subjugation. Liberation takes many forms. It can include the transformation of the mind from negative to positive self-perceptions. It can lead to altering the material conditions of life from poverty and deprivation to greater material security and access to social opportunities. In some situations, it might mean being enfranchised to vote or modifying buildings so that they become accessible to persons challenged by physical disabilities.

To be liberated means freedom from arbitrary treatment, especially when restrictions are imposed by social arrangements that hamper access to the same life chances that privileged members of society take for granted. In its most extreme form, receiving Justice through Liberation means being freed from slavery or from cultural or structural oppression. It is not inequality *per se* that constitutes injustice. Rather, it is inequality that excludes some groups or persons and not others based on factors that have nothing to do with their potential as human beings. From a Christian perspective, for Justice to exist throughout the social order, oppressed groups and persons must be liberated from exploitation, mistreatment, and/or dispossession.

For writers who perceive the social order through this lens of Christian Ethics, seeking Liberation on behalf of oppressed peoples is equivalent to doing the will of God. They possess a vision of Justice that has deep Biblical roots in both the Jewish and Christian heritages. Moses is the Old Testament's image of the ideal liberator. Under his leadership, the ancient Israelites were freed from their oppressive conditions of slavery in Egypt. This experience left a permanent impression in the Jewish memory and became the model for interpreting all subsequent experiences of Liberation throughout the entire history of the ancient Israelites.

In the New Testament, Jesus gave special attention to those persons who were excluded from the unjust social arrangements that benefited the privileged groups of his time. He proclaimed the coming of the Kingdom of God and announced that everyone who participated in God's reign would be freed from bondage. His presence threatened the dominant religious and political powers of his time, and he was summarily executed because of his message. For the writers of the New Testament, Jesus' resurrection liberated him from death. It also served as the foundation for freeing Christian believers from their sinful past and for assuring their eternal life after death. For writers such as the apostle Paul, God's Justice was served through the merciful act of redemptive Liberation for all eternity, based on the resurrection received in faith through God's grace.

Thus, the eternal Justice of God becomes the basis for earthly Justice. The theme of Justice provides a theological starting point for interpreting how God intervenes in the events of history. An inclusive vision of Justice serves to reorder personal perceptions. It also fosters the participation of all groups in the creation of social arrangements that promote the fair sharing of all social goods for everyone.

Strengths and Limitations

As described in the above analysis of the four major frameworks, the chief difference among the writers lies not in their perception of the goal of Christian Ethics. There is mutual agreement at this level. Christian Ethics is about doing God's will in the image of Jesus Christ. However, they disagree in understanding how best to achieve this end. Each of the four perspectives emphasizes an essential, but different, dimension of the overall process of moral reasoning. Each can lay claim to a fundamental insight. Each ethical framework has its strength, but it is a one-sided strength that overlooks the significant contributions of the other three.

For example, Faith-Love Ethics identifies the dynamic and ever changing contexts within which ambiguous or novel moral choices have to be made. With a central focus on Faith and/or Love, this first framework excels at flexible and imaginative moral reasoning. This is its strength. However, the Faith-Love framework is limited and weaker in those areas where the other types of moral reasoning are stronger. The Faith-Love perspective undervalues the role that principles, laws, or rules play in making moral judgments. In its most extreme form, it runs the risk of negating altogether the importance of these as moral safeguards in an imperfect world. Faith-Love Ethics may take little notice of the need for the long-term nurture of consistently virtuous behavior. It runs the risk of moral contradictions as Faith or Love is expressed in the swirl of constantly changing circumstances. It may devolve into an ethic driven mainly by the emotions, and it may lack discipline. With its strong emphasis on acting faithfully or lovingly amidst changing situations, it increases the possibility of overlooking the persistent hierarchical injustices embedded in rigid social structures or cultural norms.

The strength of the Moral Law approach is its emphasis on the principles and rules that direct moral behavior or on the procedures for arriving at a moral judgment. However, like the Faith-Love perspective it is limited in other areas, such as under-appreciating the impact that chang-

ing circumstances have on diminishing the continuing relevance of traditional moral injunctions. In Moral Law Ethics, ethical decision runs the
risk of being reduced to the mere application of unchanging rules to
changing moral dilemmas. With its strong emphasis on strict obedience
to a "do this and don't do that" way of reasoning, it minimizes the role
that creativity plays in the moral imagination based on Faith, Love,
Justice, or Liberation. It excludes thinking about how the virtuous Character contributes to ethical living or how social structures cause the unjust oppression of certain social groups.

Character Ethics focuses on the nature of the person as a moral
agent, on developing the right virtues, and on habituated Character traits
that it is desirable to have. This is it strength. However, this framework
is limited in giving due emphasis to the importance of external Moral
Law, the dynamic world of social change, and collective injustices. More
than writers from the other three perspectives, Character Ethics authors
possess a more optimistic view of human nature. They assume that good
motives are the spring waters from which virtuous actions flow and will
guide behavior spontaneously in the most moral direction.

However, the best intentions do not always guarantee the best moral
consequences, because external circumstances might undercut a desired
outcome. For example, acting kindly in unjust social structures could
reinforce hierarchical injustices in a patronizing manner when the real
goal ought to be to eliminate the structural arrangements that cause the
injustices in the first place. Giving money to a panhandler on the street is
an act of personal kindness that might contribute to the perpetuation of a
pattern of alcoholism or destructive drug dependency.

This does not mean that persons should stop acting kindly toward
each other. It means only that an expression of kindness always occurs
within specific social circumstances and that the motive of kindness should
be connected to behavioral consequences in a way that maximizes the
total amount of moral goodness. Character Ethics alone does not assure
this desired outcome.

The strength of Justice-Liberation Ethics, the last of the four frameworks of moral reasoning, lies in its emphasis on examining the larger
structural patterns within which the benefits and burdens of a society are
distributed. It challenges the other three perspectives to direct Moral
Law, Faith, Love, and Character development in the direction of reordering society toward greater expression of Justice and Liberation. It
pulls the other "micro" views toward the "macro" end of moral reason-

ing, that is, toward thinking comprehensively about the whole from the perspective of who gets what and why in any social arrangement that distributes political and economic rewards to some groups and not to others.

In the process, it hazards discounting altogether the importance of motives or loses sight of the importance of each person as a child of God. In its enthusiasm for reordering "the whole," ethicists with a strong Justice orientation may run the risk of losing sight of the whole by pitting the parts against each other in a zero-sum game of "they win—we lose" versus "we win—they lose." If the impetus for Justice moves in this direction, then injustice is not eliminated. It is merely inverted. Unjust patterns continue because the once oppressed groups become the oppressors of the groups that once oppressed them. Ultimately, Justice and Liberation for all do not get served.

This is not to suggest that protests against any particular pattern of historical injustices are not morally legitimate. It means merely that from a narrow perspective, Justice-Liberation Ethics is vulnerable to sliding into a limited vision of itself. It then becomes encapsulated within a specific pattern of historical injustice. Justice writers can lose sight of the whole because of a preoccupation, and a legitimate one, with the liberation of only one part of the whole, namely, theirs.

How might Christians transcend this impasse of disagreements about the best ethical means for doing God's will in the world in the name of Jesus Christ? Must we say, "Basically, only four frameworks exist in Christian Ethics; choose one." Are we stuck at this level? The answer is "no"; another alternative exists. The way around the impasse is to go beyond it by combining the strengths of all four frameworks into a broader perspective. As a result of integrating the positive aspects of all four of them, the total amount of moral goodness in the world should be greater than by emphasizing the positive aspects of only one of them or a less than comprehensive combination of all of them. This is the goal of Transformation Ethics.

In the next Chapter, we will direct our thinking toward the theological and historical origins of the four ethical frameworks of Christianity. This will set the stage for an in-depth discussion of the reappearance of the four frameworks throughout various eras, for combining their strengths, and finally for applying the Transformation perspective to three of the most important moral issues confronting the contemporary Church and society.

Notes

1. Throughout the remainder of the book, we will continue using capital letters whenever reference is made to any of the four frameworks.

2. The four frameworks will be elaborated in Chapters 3 through 6.

Chapter 2

Theological Origins and Historical Settings of the Four Frameworks

The preceding Chapter describes the four major frameworks of Christian Ethics along with the key concepts and strengths that the Transformation perspective of this book will integrate into a comprehensive approach to moral reasoning. In this Chapter, we will examine their theological origins and outline the historical settings within which Christian authors have used them repeatedly. We will model our method of analysis after John Wesley's "quadrilateral," which combines the Bible, experience, reason, and tradition as the foundation for theological and ethical reflection. Other authors have followed Wesley's example in their own writings.[1] We will also employ it here because it allows for breadth and depth of analysis.

The Bible and the Four Frameworks

The Biblical heritage is the most important of the four components of the quadrilateral, because the theological convictions that underpin the four ethical frameworks sprang from the history of ancient Israel and the early Church. As a result, the Bible is the primary source of all the frameworks. Christian Ethics of any kind cannot exist apart from the Bible because the core Christian convictions about how God works in the world are contained in both the Old and New Testaments. By the end of the New Testament era, the Faith-Love, Moral Law, Character, and Justice-Liberation perspectives had crystallized into the Christianity's primary frameworks of moral reasoning.

As stated in Chapter 1, the desire to do the will of God as revealed in Christ is the spiritual impulse that fuels the Christian moral imagination and produces the four ethical frameworks. The Bible provides the language and images that shape the Christian understanding of reality and God's relationship to it. Both the Old and New Testaments contribute to this understanding. The Bible is like a house with two floors. The Old Testament is the first floor, and the New Testament is the second story that completes the construction of the building.

We cannot understand the Christ of the New Testament apart from knowing the Old Testament. For the New Testament writers, the blessing and promise that God gave to Abraham (Genesis 12:1-3) culminated in the Christ event. The New Testament grew out of the core conviction of Jesus' early followers that God's purposes were progressively revealed in the Old Testament and became fully disclosed in Jesus' life, death, and resurrection. Before the New Testament took the form of a separate sacred text, the Old Testament, or Hebrew Bible, served as the Scripture for the early Church.

Only gradually did the New Testament emerge from the collection of early letters, gospels and other writings that declared Jesus as Christ the Redeemer. All of the New Testament writers quoted extensively from the Old Testament to demonstrate that the entire sweep of Hebrew history served only one purpose—as preparation for the long awaited Messiah whom they identified as Jesus. When the emerging Christian Scripture was finally canonized at the end of the fourth century C.E., the Church joined together both the Old and New Testaments to form one sacred text—the Bible.

For all intents and purposes, this means that the Christian moral imagination, which emerges in the New Testament writings, had its theological origins in the historical setting of the ancient Israelites as described in the Old Testament. Even though the Jesus movement split from Judaism over whether Jesus was the long-awaited Messiah, the embryonic Church could not have developed its own ethical perspectives apart from its Jewish background. The Faith-Love, Moral Law, Character, and Justice-Liberation frameworks solidified around the moral visions of the ancient Israelites and functioned like an ethical template for early Christians as they began to construct their own moral imagination out of deep seated images of Jesus' divine calling and his mission as the world's savior.

All the Biblical writers view God as the most powerful transforming force in the universe and that the creation of goodness is central to God's being and doing. Both the Old and New Testaments are written from this perspective. Above all else, the Bible is a book about *transformations*. In the Old Testament, God transforms the chaos of pre-creation into an ordered universe. (Genesis, Chapters 1 and 2). After the spiritual and moral deterioration that follows in the wake of Adam and Eve's expulsion from Eden, as symbolized by God's anger in the story of the forty day flood and the human construction of the Tower of Babel (Genesis, Chapters 3-11), God covenants with Abraham to start the process of transforming wandering Semitic tribes into a righteous nation for all the world to see and imitate. At Mount Sinai, God gives Moses the Ten Commandments and other codes of conduct that serve as guidelines for the transformation. (Exodus 19:20-24:3)

The transformation story continues in the account of Israel's rise and fall as a regional political power. (See Joshua through 2 Kings) As the Israelites and their kings follow a steady and irreversible course of rebellion that leads to their ultimate demise, God sends a string of prophets like Amos, Hosea, Isaiah, Jeremiah, Ezekiel, and others, in an effort to re-transform them back to patterns of faithfulness. However, their disobedience leads to national destruction and deportation to a far away country. After decades of exile in Babylon, God brings them back to Jerusalem and under Ezra and Nehemiah transforms them once again through an enduring vision of Judaic holiness. After the post-exilic Jewish reconstruction, Alexander the Great and his Grecian army sweep across Asia Minor and eventually conquer Jerusalem. When the Greek rulers set out to eradicate Jewish culture and import their polytheistic deities for worship in the Jerusalem Temple, Judas Maccabee and his zealous followers rise up and drive them from Palestine. A renewed and once again transformed Judaism is at long last free from outside control. However, their political autonomy is short-lived. After barely one hundred years, foreign domination returns to Jerusalem when the Romans impose their power over the whole of the Mediterranean region.[2]

Through the ups and downs of ancient Israelite history, the Covenant and the Law stand as a constant reminder to the Jews that their special mission is to be a holy people in both being and doing as God had called them through Abraham. Over and over again, God sent the prophets and powerful leaders to show them the pathway to the future. The four ways of moral reasoning emerged out of their centuries of struggle to become transformed into a community of sustained goodness in the world. They created the Faith-Love, Moral Law, Character, and Justice-Liberation frameworks as means to achieve this end and employed them repeatedly in their moral reasoning down through the centuries that comprise the chapters of their incredible story.

In Section II, we will describe how the New Testament writers took these four frameworks for granted and reinterpreted them in light of the Christ event. Building on their Old Testament heritage, all of the early Church authors told the story of Jesus from the perspective of God's ongoing transformation of the world. They were convinced that Jesus fulfilled the promise God gave to Abraham and that he was the Messiah foretold by the Old Testament prophets. In faith they proclaimed that the Old Covenant God made with Moses culminated in the New Covenant that God created through the death and resurrection of Jesus.

They believed that Jesus' resurrection signaled the beginning of a new age that would eventually replace the old one that was passing away. For all of the New Testament writers, the Christ event was the definitive eschatological moment when God broke into history to begin the final transformation of all creation. Jesus had proclaimed that the Kingdom of God was at hand (See Mt 4:17 and Mark 1:15), and they took him at his literal word. God's historic involvement with Israel through the Mosaic Covenant served as an essential steppingstone to prepare for God's ultimate intervention through the creation of the coming Kingdom that Christ announced.

From the time Albert Schweitzer wrote *The Quest for the Historical Jesus* in 1906,[3] New Testament scholars have focused much of their research on what Jesus meant by proclaiming that the Kingdom of God was near. Some of them believe that he expected the immediate restoration of Israel through divine intervention and that the old epoch would end upon his dramatic return. Others scholars believe that for Jesus the Kingdom referred to a purely reformed historical Israel. They perceive that through the Gospel writers the Church created the expectation of Jesus' apocalyptic Second Coming and integrated it into the remembered events and proclamations of his life.[4]

We will probably never know for sure which of these views is the more historically accurate. Nor will we review them here. However, from the perspective of the New Testament writings, it is clear that Jesus' earliest followers, including Paul who never encountered him in the flesh, believed that Jesus would return before the eyewitness generation died, as he indicated in his first letter to the Thessalonians (4:13-17), which is possibly the oldest extant New Testament writing. For the New Testament authors, Jesus' Kingdom declarations planted the seeds of their belief in his imminent return. They stimulated the early Church's sense of hope and enthusiasm and contributed in major ways to its emerging moral imagination. Little doubt exists that Jesus dramatically transformed his loyal followers by the extraordinary power of his presence and words. Through his parables, expressive poetic-religious imagery, and moral teachings he imbued them with a sense of urgency about creating the kind of ethical community that he envisioned.

As the New Testament record shows, the leaders who arose after Jesus' death believed that the dynamic community that he created before his crucifixion was a new Kingdom breaking into the old order. His followers were convinced that they were living in an Interim between his ascension into heaven (as recorded in Mark 16:19, Luke 24:51, and Acts 1:9-10) and his Second Coming, as envisioned in writings such as the twenty-fifth Chapter of Matthew or The Revelation to John. Jesus' early followers were convinced they were living in an Interim prior to the apocalyptic moment when he would arrive back on earth to complete the transformation he began prior to his execution.[5] Their goal was to transform as completely as possible their "earthly kingdom" according to Jesus' vision of the "heavenly Kingdom" that he announced while alive.

Edwin D. Freed defines New Testament Christianity as a millenarian movement,[6] which helps explain why it burst forth upon the world with such transforming force. Jesus' charismatic presence convinced his followers that he was Israel's long-awaited Messiah, who promised a new heaven on earth—soon—and a dramatic change in the existing social order. This energized his supporters and released a tremendous outpouring of emotion and activity. Because they believed that the world as they knew it was ending, they raced to be ready for Jesus' apocalyptic return through vigorous self and group transformation inspired by his Kingdom visions.

Jesus instilled in his followers an intense evangelical impulse that motivated them to proselytize in his name. All of his closest disciples recruited others on his behalf, especially his inner circle led by Peter; but more than any one else, it was Apostle Paul who, after his dramatic conversion on the Damascus road (See Acts 9:1-6), proclaimed throughout Asia Minor the message of salvation through Faith in Christ the Risen Lord. As a result of relentless travel and tireless preaching, he started a string of transformed congregations that lived and worshipped according to the Faith that he announced and often had to defend, even under the threat of death. The Church's distinctive identity and the theological starting point for the evolution of its moral imagination rest on a foundation of professed Faith.

Out of the energy that this Faith created and the sense of urgency that anticipation over the pending *parousia* provided, the number of newly transformed followers grew as the Church's early missionary activities penetrated ever more deeply into the Gentile territories of the Greco-Roman world. Concern over ethical issues emerged early in the incipient congregations as they struggled to develop beliefs and behaviors consistent with becoming converted Christians who were living in an Interim between the old age that was passing away and the new age of transformation that would soon break forth upon them.

Of course, we know that the Second Coming of Jesus did not occur during the time the eyewitness generation encountered him in the flesh. Nor has it since, despite the reoccurrence of the many millenarian movements that have arisen in practically every generation since his death, including those that appeared at the end of the twentieth century in anticipation of the third millennium. All Christian millenarian movements that expect the world to end or for Jesus to return to earth in their time confront a life-threatening crisis at the level of their most basic beliefs when life continues unchanged beyond the point of their cataclysmic anticipations. If they are not able to readjust to this challenge, then in time their impact will fade or disappear altogether.[7]

From the very start, one of the defining characteristics of Christianity has been not only the success of the first generation to survive the crisis that Jesus' non-return created for them but for the Church to keep growing in every subsequent generation after the early enthusiasm for his Second Coming waned. Christianity has shown itself to be highly portable. The message of Christ the Redeemer has been like a seed sown widely throughout the world. For centuries, Christianity has flourished because it has been a flexible Faith that can adjust to changing circumstances without losing the core theological convictions that emerged at the time of its historical origins.

From its earliest beginnings, Christianity gave evidence of its adaptability, which can be traced through the writings of the New Testament. When Jesus' Second Coming did not occur during the first generation, as Paul and other early leaders expected it would, the Church settled in for the long haul. According to New Testament scholars like C.H. Dodd, this triggered a transformation in the Church's eschatological expectations, which changed from "expectant" to "realized."[8] With the postponing of Christ's dramatic re-entry, New Testament writers came to re-envision the Church as his Kingdom already beginning to surface in their midst, although imperfectly. They saw themselves as entrusted with the task of preaching the Kingdom message of redemption until the appointed hour of his return, when the Kingdom would be perfectly established.

The later writings of the New Testament reveal the acceptance of this deferred expectation while at the same time their authors counseled Church members not to become lax in their preparation for his return. For example, the Gospel of Matthew, which along with the other Gospels was written decades after Jesus' death, addresses the concern over the delay through the parable of the wise and foolish bridesmaids (25:1-13). Using the colorful mental images typical of Jesus' parables, Matthew instructs Church members to keep their lamps full of oil and well lit so that when the bridegroom arrives they will be able to see their way through the door that opens onto the wedding banquet that he will give his faithful followers. As Jesus supporters became impatient over the postponed *parousia*, Church leaders buoyed their sagging spirits with words and images of encouragement—out of the mouth of the Savior Messiah himself.

In essence, the expectation of a short-term Interim became transformed into a vision of an indefinite Interim whose terminal date only the Lord knew. As the bridesmaid parable suggests, the gradual acceptance of this perceptual shift can be seen in the later writings of the New Testament authors. This is especially evident in their ethical teachings, because the longer Jesus deferred his Second Coming the more the growing Church had to address an expanding range of moral issues. As the Christianity grew and encountered an increasingly open-ended future, the number of ethical issues that the early Church writers encountered also grew with it, as is evident in the New Testament's collection of letters and in the Gospel reconstructions of Jesus' life.

This can be illustrated in the case of the Apostle Paul who converted scores of followers to Christianity during his many missionary journeys throughout Greco-Roman territories. From Paul's theological viewpoint, the resurrected Christ was calling his loyal followers to become transformed into a new creation. They were to be a new community dedicated to following the way of the cross and demonstrating commitment to their risen savior through faithful and ethical living—until he should come again.

As the expected brief Interim stretched into an indeterminate Interim, several of Paul's newly found congregations started feuding because of internal disagreements. His letters to the Galatians, Corinthians, and other startup Christian communities reveal many of the early disputes that tore at the fragile fabric of their communal life. These include but are not limited to clashes over the need for circumcision, how to identify false prophets, what to eat, what to wear to worship, how to celebrate the Lord's Supper, how to understand the relationship of faith to works, whether to remain single or marry, whether or when to speak in tongues, how to distribute community possessions among believers, and so on. In the midst of Paul's recommendations for resolving many of these early conflicts, his letters contain some of the most profound and enduring insights ever written about how Faith serves as the transforming seedbed for Christian morality.

All of the four canonized Gospels contain Jesus' ethical pronouncements. Examples include the Sermon on the Mount in Matthew (Chapters 5-7), the parables of the Good Samaritan and the Prodigal Son in Luke (10:25-37 and 15:11-32), and the love commandment that Jesus gave his followers in John's Gospel (13:34-35) and that John reiterated in his letters (1 John 2:7-11, 4:7-21; 2 John verses 4-6). The Gospels incorporate Jesus' ethical sayings and portray him first and foremost as a person of deep moral sensitivities, as someone who is more committed to alleviating the sufferings of those in need than in adhering to many of the religious practices of his day.

All of the diverse New Testament ethical teachings contributed to the Church's emerging moral imagination. The moral prescriptions and proscriptions that appear in Paul's letters, the Gospels, and in the other New Testament writings exist for one primary purpose: to show transformed Christians how to live faithfully and ethically during an Interim time period in preparation for the return of the risen Christ, even though they did not know how long it would last or when he would come again.

Like the Old Testament, the ethical teachings of the New Testament can be organized under the Faith-Love, Moral Law, Character, and Justice-Liberation frameworks, as we will demonstrate in Section II of this book. Together these two Testaments serve as the foundation for any and all forms of Christian moral reasoning.

Experience, Reason, Tradition and the Four Frameworks in Different Historical Settings

In this section we will explain how the other three components of Wesley's quadrilateral, that is, experience, reason, and tradition, tie to the four ethical frameworks that originated in the Bible. In light of the above discussion, we can infer that these three components were already present when Christianity blossomed from the soil of Judaism. The writers of the New Testament employed them repeatedly whether or not they were aware of it when they asserted that Jesus was the Messiah or when they explained the relationship between Faith and works in the drama of God's plan for salvation.

Whenever they met opposition to their views, they employed their judicious powers of reason to make their case by slicing through every argument they encountered. This applies especially to the rabbinic-trained Apostle Paul. Based on their direct encounters with the living Jesus or the resurrected Christ, they created new traditions out of the ancient traditions of Israel. Another way to state this is that the New Testament came into existence because its many authors used their reason to reflect on and reinterpret their Old Testament traditions in light of their new experiences. As Wesley well understood, the Bible, experience, reason, and tradition are always inseparably entwined in any process of Christian theological or moral reflection.

Long before the New Testament was canonized near the end of the fourth century C.E. and became, along with the Old Testament, the foundation for all forms of Christian moral reflection, Church writers had been drawing on experience, reason, and tradition for centuries to create new theological and ethical insights. This process began early and has continued uninterrupted to this day. In large measure, from the start the Church's historical adaptability has derived from this fourfold combination as Christians have reflected repeatedly on how God's presence has continued to manifest itself in the changing world. Through the prism of the Bible and tradition, Christian writers have concluded time and again in the midst of social transformations that new occasions do indeed teach new duties.

This can be seen as early as the New Testament era when Jesus' movement began spreading among the Gentile population. The novel situations encountered by the early Church summoned its leaders to be creative in adapting their Jewish heritage and message of Christ the Re-

deemer to changing conditions. More than anyone else among the early
followers of Jesus, the Apostle Paul defined himself as Christ's emissary
to the Gentiles—the uncircumcised, (See Galatians 2:7) and his letters
are filled with the steady stream of suggestions for resolving disruptions
between Jewish and Gentile converts. In addition, the Book of the Acts
of the Apostles records how Peter and the "circumcised believers" were
astounded that the "Holy Spirit had been poured out even on the Gentiles" (Acts 10:45), as depicted in the story of the conversion of Cornelius,
the Italian centurion.

In a word, the Church's early success rested on its leaders' capacity
to draw imaginatively from their Jewish traditions, transform them in
light of the Christ event, and make creative adaptations to non-Jewish
settings. As depicted in the New Testament, Paul's early missionary
activities and Peter's recognition that God's Holy Spirit embraced the
Gentiles as well as the Jews signaled how important new experiences
beyond the Jewish homeland would figure into Christianity's unfolding
future. The conversion of Cornelius, along with the profound shift in
perception that this entailed, set the pattern for all subsequent expan-
sions among diverse populations and changing circumstances.

The process of combining new experiences with reason to create
new traditions and ethical insights is especially pronounced after the
time period covered by the New Testament writings. When the Church
began expanding into Asia Minor centuries before the New Testament
was canonized, a standardized and sacred Christian Scripture did not
exist. However, this did not stop Church writers from continuing to
promote and defend the Faith against pagan beliefs as Christianity com-
peted for the hearts and minds of men and women throughout the ancient
world. Christian authors struggled either to demonstrate the superiority
of Christianity over other religions or to combine Christian insights with
the prevailing philosophies of the Greco-Roman world.

Christianity has been a syncretistic religion from the beginning even
as it has held firm to its central assurance that Jesus is the resurrected
redeemer of the world. In each new historical setting, Christian authors
have interpreted the changing trends and events of their time by looking
through the lens of both their Faith and four ethical frameworks. New
experiences have been and continue to be the raw materials for each
generation's theological and moral reflections. History shows that the
Church's moral imagination generates maximum creativity when it op-

erates at the intersection of the Bible, new experiences, reason, and tradition.

Writers have identified the different historical settings within which critical shifts have occurred in the evolution of Christian teachings. In general, they share the perception that significant new transformations arose during six major time periods. Denise Lardner Carmody and John Tully Carmody identify these six as the Old Testament, New Testament, Patristic, Medieval, Reformation, and Modern Eras.[9] J. Philip Wogaman follows a similar format by classifying major developments in Christian Ethics according to the Biblical Legacy (both Old and New Testaments), Early Christianity, Medieval Christianity, the Reformation, and influences since the Enlightenment.[10]

The critical transitions usually turned on major events or trends that took Western society in new directions and that served as bookends, so to speak, between different eras. Before Christianity became the dominant religion of the Roman Empire, it was a minority movement that struggled to survive and expand after the New Testament period ended. Eventually the tide turned and Christianity moved to the political and cultural center. Scholars usually point to the conversion of Constantine and his military victory in 313 C.E. as watershed events because they gave Europe its first Christian King.

He ended persecution of Christians with his Edict of Milan, provided Christianity with official state recognition, and stimulated the Church's unprecedented expansion.

Prior to Constantine's conversion, Christianity had grown steadily but slowly throughout the Western world. Rodney Stark estimates that in 312 C.E. Christians accounted for only about six percent of the total population of the Roman Empire, or about six-and-a-half million people. During the next four decades, Church growth accelerated rapidly. By 350 C.E., less than forty years after Constantine became King, membership had mushroomed to almost 34 million or about 57% of the population.[11]

Under Constantine's protective hand, Christianity moved from outsider to insider status. During the next several decades, the Church created its first creeds, standardized liturgical practices, and canonized the New Testament. The small Jesus movement that began in Israel centuries earlier had finally arrived at the center of European power and influence. Then, barely one hundred years after Constantine's rise to power, Europe underwent yet another major transformation when the Goths

sacked Rome in 410 C.E. and ended the centuries-old reign of the Roman Empire. Between the time the Empire got its first Christian King in
313 and the conquest of Rome by the barbarian tribes ninety-seven years
later, Christianity became deeply embedded in the core of a rapidly changing Western civilization.

Thus, the Patristic or Early Christian era that started at the end of
the New Testament period had given way to another emerging historical
setting, Medieval Christianity, which continued for more than a thousand years until it too underwent yet another milestone transformation.
When Martin Luther nailed his 95 Theses on the castle door at Wittenburg,
Germany in 1517 C.E., he launched the Reformation.[12] By integrating
his carefully reasoned reflections on the Bible with new experiences, he
and his generation of Reformers created radically different traditions
from those that the Church had developed during the first fifteen centuries of its existence. After Luther, the once united Western Christendom
found itself irreversibly severed into competing camps of Protestants
and Catholics.

This was not the first time that Christianity experienced internal
division, but with the Reformation, it was all encompassing. In 1054
C.E., the Church split into Eastern and Western factions mainly over
issues of liturgical practice and questions of leadership location and administrative control. Despite this rift, Western and Eastern Christianity
shared similar theological views. The Reformation was different because
it challenged the Church's self-understanding at its most basic level.

The central issue that divided Protestants from Catholics was Luther's
insistence that the Bible was the primary source of authority for Christians (*Sola Scriptura*) and not the institutional Church, even though the
Church created the Bible at the end of the fourth century. In lieu of the
Church's seven sacraments and authoritative synthesis, Luther substi-
tuted the doctrine of justification by Faith alone. He removed from the
priests the power to control the keys to the Kingdom. Through the doctrine of the priesthood of all believers, he placed the key to eternal salvation in the faithful heart of each person.

During the next one hundred years after Luther launched his protest,
the Reformation spread like wildfire through central and northern Europe. As other protests proliferated, Protestants found themselves vying
not only with Catholics but with each other as well. By the end of the
sixteenth century, the explosion of doctrinal disputes that the Reformation ignited left deep fissures in the map of European Christendom. From

the seed of "individual conscience" that Luther planted in the soil of the Reformation, many different flowers bloomed even though they were not always a happy blend of colors.

Like the Old Testament, New Testament, Early Christian, and Medieval historical epochs that preceded it, the Reformation epitomized how fresh ways of reflecting on the Bible could be combined with changing experiences to create new traditions out of old ones. The parallels between the New Testament and Protestant eras are especially striking. Just as the emerging Church used the Old Testament to create its new traditions in light of the Christ event, Luther and the other Reformers used the New Testament to create innovative Protestant traditions in light of the Church's canonized interpretations of that very same event.

One final major historical transformation remains. In the midst of the Reformation and the dramatic changes that it produced, an even more powerful force was beginning to take shape, one that would transform human history and even the Church itself like nothing before it. We are referring to the rise of modern science. The precise point in time when this new phenomenon surfaced in Western society cannot be pin pointed with complete certainty because doing science is more a process than an event. No doubt even as early as twelfth and thirteenth centuries C.E., the European Renaissance played an essential role by emphasizing the importance of the individual. This helped lay the foundation for the Enlightenment that further fostered development of the scientific mode of inquiry.

Like any other historical transformation, modern science appeared gradually out of the collective experiences of many individuals over many decades. Nonetheless, one event signaled the arrival of this entirely new way of understanding the universe. In 1609 C.E. Galileo looked to the heavens through his new technological invention called the telescope and observed empirically for the first time that the earth revolves around the sun and not vice versa. The significance of this event cannot be overstated. It symbolized a turning point in human history like none other before it because it foreshadowed the coming of modernity. During the four centuries that followed Galileo's discovery, a series of massive transformations shook European civilization and eventually the entire planet to the core and thrust the Church into the midst of a volcano of exploding moral dilemmas.

Modern science's rational-empirical method of inquiry into the nature of truth clashed dramatically with the Christianity's traditional approach that rested on the Bible and Greco-Roman philosophy. The Church's understanding of creation and of humanity's place within it depended on the centuries-old synthesis between pre-scientific Biblical cosmology and ancient Aristotelian metaphysics. Prior to the rise of modern science, in virtually every historical setting, Christianity adapted so successfully because it imaginatively harmonized the Scriptural view of creation and humankind's place in it with the different forms of Greco-Roman rationalism.

Even as early as the New Testament era, the Apostle Paul's writings contained connections to Roman Stoicism, as recent scholars have noted.[13] By the third century C.E., the Church's first great theologian, Origen of Alexandria, Egypt (182-251 C.E.) combined Stoic, Hebraic, and Christian ideas to demonstrate Christianity's superiority over all Greco-Roman religions. More than one hundred years later, the prolific Augustine of Hippo (354-430) incorporated Manichaean and Neo-Platonic concepts in a Christian synthesis that transcended both of them. As the Church's dominance over Europe reached its apex in the thirteenth century, Aquinas borrowed Aristotle's philosophical framework to build his massive Christian theological and moral system.[14]

With the rise of modern science and the ascendancy of the empirical approach to investigating and discovering the laws of nature, commitment to the ancient Jewish-Christian-Greek-Roman synthesis declined. As the new form of empirical rationalism gained momentum and ushered in the modern world, the old method of revelation and philosophical rationalism, along with the cosmology that sustained Christianity for centuries, lost ground. The modern empirical approach to knowledge confronted Christianity like no other movement before it. While the Reformation used the Bible to challenge the Catholic Church's authority to determine the nature of Christian Faith, modern science penetrated even more deeply into the heart of Christendom by using the methods of empirical rationalism to challenge the Bible's view of the very nature of truth itself.

The new experimental forms of scientific inquiry led to revolutionary changes in perceptions of the origins of the universe and the evolution of the earth's life forms. The accumulated weight of scientific evidence that showed the solar system was billions of years in the making ate away at the Genesis account of the six-day creation. In 1859, Charles Darwin published *The Origins of Species* in which he proposed that all the species of the earth, including humankind, evolved over millions of years through the process of natural selection and superior adaptation over inferior and/or extinct progenitors. Darwin's ideas struck at the heart of the Biblical view that God created humanity as the crown of creation through divine command

The worldview revolution that science spawned sent shock waves through Christendom. The Church recoiled out of deep fear and reacted defensively to safeguard its ancient beliefs. In the early seventeenth century, Catholic leaders condemned Galileo and forced him to recant under threat of death. In the nineteenth century, Darwin's evolutionary theory pushed the impulse for self-preservation to an even higher level. Conservative Protestants like Charles Hodge,[15] fearing that the new science might cause the demise of Christianity altogether, founded modern fundamentalism on the principle of Biblical infallibility. Just as the Reformation divided Catholics from Protestants and created a fragmented Christendom, modern science caused even more splintering by pitting liberals against conservatives and fundamentalists.

In addition, modern science and the technological innovations that it generated swept away an ancient feudal order and ushered in a completely novel urban industrial capitalist society. Virtually all aspects of community life changed from where people lived, how they interacted, how they arranged their social class and political systems, how they organized their economic structures, how they defined the origins and destiny of the universe and humanity's place within it, and so on. The major changes of previous historical settings occurred within an agrarian social system that had lasted for centuries. The power of modern science and the all-embracing transformation it created resided in science's ability to abolish this ancient agriculture-based system altogether and replace it with a radically different factory-based urban alternative.

The mighty transformations that emerged in the modern world produced an explosion of moral dilemmas that Christian authors of all previous epochs combined could not even begin to imagine. The new structures of market place capitalism gave rise to great concentrations of corporate power. They created unspeakable conditions of labor exploitation and ugly urban slums. Western nations with huge concentration of industrial wealth colonized non-Western countries at will and divided the world according to their wishes.

The new world order witnessed the rise of deadly disputes between capitalists who followed the *laissez faire* views of Adam Smith and supporters of various forms of socialism or Marxism. The acrimonious discord that erupted between the adherents of these two worldviews, along with the rise of fascism during the twentieth century, triggered two world wars that caused millions of deaths. As the planet drifted toward Cold War polarization, two great ideological camps confronted each other with insane strategies of Mutually Assured Destruction (appropriately called MAD) and threats of nuclear annihilation.

The world industrial system that modern science helped spawn has not remained stagnant. By its very nature, internal forces have propelled it toward constant self-transformation. During the past four hundred years industrialism has progressed toward unprecedented levels of sophistication and intricate complexity. Just as the old agrarian order gave way to industrialism, over the past fifty years industrialism has evolved into the advanced stage of post-industrialism where information processing has replaced factory production as society's primary economic engine. Unlike the settled agrarian structures that nurtured Christianity for centuries, the instabilities of industrial and post-industrial society have guaranteed constant transformation.[16]

Throughout all four of the main post-Biblical historical settings of Early and Medieval Christianity, the Reformation, and Modernity, the Church has consistently filtered the major ethical challenges of each era through the four frameworks that emerged during the Old and New Testament periods. While the authors of each era accentuated some frameworks more than others, Christians have remained constant in their search for ways to express their Faith and Love in each and every epoch. They have struggled to identify how the Moral Law might contribute to promoting Justice or to the Liberation of society's disadvantaged members. They have sought to imbue the faithful with a Christian Character and the virtues necessary to participate as ethical beings within any social context. Whatever the form, the Church's constant moral purpose has been to transform persons and communities according to God's purposes as revealed in Jesus Christ and thereby to increase the total amount of goodness in the world.

In sum, little doubt exists that the new experiences of each historical setting served up new challenges that called for reflective re-interpretations of Bible-based beliefs and existing traditions. As the Church evolved out of the Old Testament era and took shape during the New Testament time period, it laid the groundwork for adapting to social transformations that led to Early and Medieval Christianity, the Reformation, and the Modern world. It used the four ethical frameworks to express its deep religious and moral convictions about how to be Christ's witness to the world. As transitions occurred in the surrounding society, the Church employed its moral imagination to identify God's transforming footprint in the midst of them. By reflecting on the divine presence at work in the changing circumstances of their lives, Christian leaders and writers of each historical setting responded anew to what God called them to do amidst the challenges of changing circumstances.

Reason and Revelation

Before turning to Section II, we need to examine one more issue—the relationship between reason and revelation. From the moment that Tertullian, a well-known writer from the Patristic era, wondered whether Athens had anything at all in common with Jerusalem, many Christians have contrasted reason and revelation as incompatible sources of authority in Christian Ethics. Modern disagreements on this issue surfaced when scientific knowledge about the nature of our sun-centered solar system began challenging the earth-centered Biblical view revealed in the book of Genesis. The Catholic Church's initial defensiveness in condemning Galileo and the Fundamentalists' later doctrine of the scientific inerrancy of Scripture pitted revelation against reason, especially empirical rationalism, as the Church's primary method for determining the nature of truth, religious or otherwise.

The position of this book is that we ought not see reason as antithetical to revelation because reason does not operate outside of a set of assumptions, including those based on revelation. Reason does not stand by itself within human consciousness. Nor does revelation. Rather, reason is a tool that the mind uses to arrange experiences, including those resting on professed revelations, into knowledge in order to create a credible perception of reality. Reason is merely the means of articulating coherency among the various experiential, imagistic, and cognitive pieces that comprise perception, mental comprehension, and the moral imagination. All of the mind's perceptual and moral images depend on accepted assumptions about how the world works. The goal of reason is to construct a cogent vision of reality based on those assumptions.

Within the Transformation perspective, we accept reason as a necessary tool for ethical reflection because it enables us to connect Biblical revelation with new experiences and Church traditions. It is an essential tool for developing the Christian moral imagination. It is crucial for analyzing ethical dilemmas and establishing standards. It is also essential for articulating alternative moral positions and for determining which ones create the greatest amount of goodness in the world. While the Biblical heritage serves as foundation for the formation of Christianity's four frameworks of moral reasoning, it would be impossible for the Church to continue creating new ethical teachings without rational reflections on fresh experiences and former traditions. Reason and revelation are not opposites. Rather, they are complementary, interdependent, and mutually supportive.

In sum, developing the moral imagination in Christian Ethics is a creative endeavor of the highest order; and there is no doubt that the Bible sits at the center of this enterprise. At the same time, developing such an imagination requires the careful use of reason to interpret new experiences, expand old perspectives, and connect the Church to vital issues confronting the world. The Church is an extension of its Biblical heritage, which is also the source of the four ethical frameworks of Faith-Love, Moral Law, Character, and Justice-Liberation that Christians have used repeatedly to articulate new ethical teachings throughout the centuries that encompass the six historical settings. It is to these four frameworks and how they have been used throughout the six historical settings that we now turn.

Notes

1. See Albert C. Outler, "The Wesleyan Quadrilateral—In John Wesley," in *Doctrine and Theology in the United Methodist Church,* edited by Thomas A. Lanford, Nashville: Abingdon Press, 1991, pp. 75-81. Also see James B. Nelson, "Sources for Body Theology: Homosexuality As a Test Case," in *Moral Issues and Christian Response,* edited by Paul T. Jersild, and others, sixth edition, New York: Harcoutrt Brace College Publishers, 1998, pp. 160-169.

2. See Barry Banstra, *Reading the Old Testament,* Second Edition, Belmont, Cal.: Wadsworth, 1999.

3. Albert Schweitzer, *The Quest for the Historical Jesus,* (1906), translated by W. Montgomery, New York: Macmillan, 1968.

4. For an excellent overview of this debate, see Mark Allan Powell, *Jesus As a Figure In History: How Modern Historians View the Man from Galilee,* Louisville, Kentucky: Westminster John Know Press, 1998.

5. See Richard B. Hays, *The Moral Vision of the New Testament: A Contemporary Introduction to New Testament Ethics,* New York: HarperSanFrancisco, 1996, Parts One and Two for an extensive analysis of the various New Testament writer's interpretations of this early Church belief.

6. Edwin D. Freed, *The New Testament: A Critical Introduction,* second edition, Belmont, Cal.: Wadsworth Publishing Company, 1991, pp. 192-193. Also see John and Kathleen Court, *The New Testament World,* Englewood Cliffs, N.J.: Prentice-Hall, 1990, pp. 268-273.

7. See Michael St. Clair, *Millenarian Movements in Historical Context,* New York: Garland Publishers, 1992.

8. C.H. Dodd, *The Apostolic Preaching and Its Developments,* London: Hodder and Stoughton, 1936.

9. Denise Lardner Carmody and John Tully Carmody, *Christian Ethics: An Introduction through History & Current Issues,* Englewood Cliffs, N.J.: Prentice Hall, 1993.

10. J.Philip Wogaman, *Christian Ethics: A Historical Introduction,* Louisville, Kentucky: Westminster/John Knox Press, 1993.

11. Rodney Stark, *The Rise of Christianity,* New York: HarperCollins, 1997, page 7.

12. It should be noted that many of the changes that became permanent under Protestantism had been intiated unsuccessfully earlier by John Wycliff (1325-1384) in England and John Hus (1372-1415) in Bohemia.

13. See Troels Engberg-Pedersen, *Paul and the Stoics,* Edinburgh: T&T Clark, 2000; and J. N. Sevenster, *Paul and Seneca,* Leiden: E.J. Brill, 1961.

14. See Wogaman, *Christian Ethics,* pp. 38-43, 51-60, 82-95.

15. See James C. Livingston, *Modern Christian Thought, Volume I, The Enlightenment and the Nineteenth Century,* second edition, Upper Saddle River, N.J.: Prentice Hall, 1997, pp. 304-315.

16. See Wendell Bell, *The Foundation of Futures Studies: Human Science for a New Era,* 2 Volumes, New Brunswick: Transaction Publishers, 1997. Also see Alvin Toffler, *The Third Wave,* New York: Bantam Edition, 1981.

Section II

Moral Imagination and the Four Frameworks

In this Section, we will demonstrate how the four ethical frameworks emerged from the experiences of ancient Israel, shaped the Christian Church's moral imagination, appeared repeatedly through two millennia, and inspired multiple moral visions in the Modern world. In each of the next four Chapters we will examine only one framework per Chapter and follow it across time.

This will set the stage for Section III in which we will describe how many of Christianity's most influential authors used multiple frameworks in their writings. We will also integrate the strengths of the four frameworks into a broader Transformation perspective. Finally, we will apply this perspective to three major moral issues confronting the contemporary Church and society for the purpose of determining which moral choices within each of these areas might bring the greatest amount of goodness into the world.

Chapter 3

Faith and Love

Even though the Christian moral imagination incorporates four major ethical frameworks, we might be inclined to make the case that the Faith-Love perspective occupies the center and the other three are to a greater or lesser degree an extension of it or hold a secondary position. No doubt this perception is due to the realization that a pervasive emphasis on Faith and Love leaps off the pages of Scripture. Even the most cursory reading of the Bible, as expressed in both the Old and New Testaments, will lead us to recognize how frequently these two words appear. Our goal is not to argue for the priority of one framework over the others, but to acknowledge that all of them work in partnership to form the Christian moral imagination. Within this fourfold mix, the Faith and Love approach to Christian moral reasoning provides us with a fruitful point of departure.

The religious experiences of the ancient Hebrews supply us with the Biblical context for the emergence of this framework as well as the remaining three. As stated in Section I, the transformation theme runs like an unbroken thread through the turbulent history of ancient Israel. The Old Testament records how God transformed a disparate assembly of nomadic tribes into a coherent nation with a common identity. The first Chapter of Genesis begins with God's creation of the earth and all its inhabitants and the eleventh Chapter ends with humanity's downward spiral into spiritual deterioration as symbolized in the erection of the Tower of Babel.

According to the Genesis account, the generations that followed Adam and Eve were the first to backslide into disobedience and as a consequence encountered the full fury of divine judgment. Except for the righteous Noah, his family, and an ark full of animals, God destroyed them all in the forty-day flood (6:9-8:19). However, God's love was greater than God's wrath. Through Noah's offspring, God gave the people of the earth a second chance to prove their worthiness as the crown of creation. God covenanted with Noah to never again visit such destruction on the earth. To the lament of the Hebrew storytellers, the heirs of Noah turned out to be as bad as the offspring of Adam and Eve. Like the earlier generations, they too gave great display to their rebellious arrogance. The Tower of Babel signaled their desire to be like God rather than to be obedient to God. In the Genesis narrative, this event marked a crucial turning point in God's relationship to humanity.

Because of the covenant with Noah, God embarked on a different course of action. Starting with the twelfth Chapter of Genesis, God called the devoted servant Abraham to begin a long journey of Faith that would culminate in the creation of a great people. "Go from your country and your kindred and your father's house to the land that I will show you. I will make of you a great nation." (12:1-2) Rather than re-destroying the world a second time, God created a special people and through Abraham imbued them with a vision of a transformed future.

For every generation of Israelites, the Biblical account of God's call of Abraham served as their defining image and inspired their moral imagination. This story implanted in them the dream of a divine destiny. Even though it took centuries for the dream to fully unfold and then to disintegrate into their worst nightmare, the Jewish journey of Faith began with a promise based on God's Love. It convinced them that they were a chosen people who would inspire humanity's devotion through the example of their righteous living. From the very beginning, Faith and Love shaped Israel's collective identity.

From Abraham to David, the belief in God's abiding Love guided the Israelites on their centuries-long journey of Faith (See Genesis through 2 Kings), as told from the Deuteronomic perspective.[1] From the early patriarchal and matriarchal wanderings to the establishment of the Monarchy, their vision of entering the promise land pulled them forward through many twists and turns and seemingly insurmountable pitfalls that blocked their way, especially their Egyptian enslavement and struggles to conquer Canaan. However, through it all, they prevailed; and as monarchial control passed from Saul to David and then to David's son Solomon, Israel climbed at the apex of power.

As seen through the eyes of Faith, this was positive proof that they were special to God and that God's Love had remained steadfast and true. For the authors of the Old Testament books, God's blessings guided the formation of the Jewish nation from the start of Abraham's journey to the culmination of Solomon's glory. God had delivered on the promise to make Israel a great nation.

Alas, it did not last. In time, the wayward Jewish kings and their followers tumbled into rebellion just like the earlier generations that followed Adam and Eve and Noah. In the end God punished them by taking away the very homeland that had been promised to Abraham when he began the long trek of Faith. After Solomon's death in 922 B.C.E, the nation took a turn for the worst when it split into two Kingdoms. Two hundred years later in 722, the Assyrians sacked the Northern Kingdom of Israel. In 587, the Babylonians destroyed the Southern Kingdom of Judah, leveled the Temple in Jerusalem, and drove the Jewish people into exile. As interpreted through the rewards and punishments formula of the Deuteronomists, the Israelites caused their own ruin through self-initiated disobedience. The Almighty Lord who formed them into a triumphant nation and took them to the peak of power under Solomon brought them down nearly three hundred and fifty years after the great King's death.

For the ancient Jews, it was their bleakest hour because destruction threatened their Faith in God as well as their perception of God's special Love for them. Through it all, however, God's Love proved to be greater than God's judgment. It was in the worst of times that God sent prophets to the Israelites to restore their Faith by giving reassurance that they had not been abandoned even as their prophetic voices warned of their pending demise. The great literary prophetic traditions of ancient Israel covered the monarchial time period when the pronouncements of God's abiding Love of the Israelites were interspersed with proclamations of forthcoming catastrophe.

For example, in the middle of the eighth century B.C.E., the prophet Hosea warned the Northern Kingdom of God's approaching punishment at the hands of the Assyrians. In a dramatic gesture, he married the prostitute Gomer to demonstrate that God was bound to a prostitute people and gave his three children names signifying God's rejection of them. Even though Gomer abandoned him for her former life of prostitution, Hosea remarried her to illustrate God's enduring Love of the wayward Israelites. He was the first to declare that out of the ashes of their punishment, God would preserve a faithful remnant and guide them through divine Love into an unknown future. (See Hosea Chapters 1-3, 11)

Following Hosea, in the sixth century B.C.E. the prophet Jeremiah announced forthcoming disaster to the inhabitants of the Southern Kingdom of Judah. Amidst the chaos, he foretold how God's Love would continue to embrace them beyond their political demise. (Jeremiah 16:14-15; 23:1-8; 30:1-11; 31:31-40) Under the confining conditions of the Babylonian exile, the visionary prophet, Ezekiel, reassured the Israelites that God would bring their "dry bones" back to life after a time of spiritual cleansing. (Ezekiel 11:14-25; 37:1-14) The greatest of all the exilic prophets, Second Isaiah, conveyed words of mercy and hope in the midst of the despair of captivity. Despite their punishment, God would remain faithful and never abandon them. God would send a Messiah, a suffering servant, to lead them toward a restored and redeemed future. (Isaiah Chapters 40-66)

In sum, ancient Israel's perception of being special was rooted in an all-encompassing conviction that God's Love guided their fate. When they lacked the fortitude to remain faithful to their righteous mission and relapsed into repeated cycles of defiance, God reacted to their wickedness with harsh punishment. When events propelled them toward national calamity, their greatest prophetic leaders spoke out of the ancestral Faith that God's Love would abide no matter what tragedy might befall them. From Abraham to Second Isaiah, the Old Testament writers reiterated a common message: God's Love endures forever. God chose the Jews to show humanity the pathway to goodness not because they deserved it but because God loved them. This belief and the Faith that fused with it fueled their moral imagination and anchored every stage of their astonishing story of transformation.

During the New Testament era, Jesus and his followers stood as the heirs of this extraordinary legacy of Faith and Love. On one occasion a lawyer of Jesus' day asked him to identify the greatest of the commandments. Jesus responded by quoting Deuteronomy 6:4-5, "Hear, O Israel: The Lord is our God, the Lord alone. You shall love the Lord with all your heart, and with all your soul, and with all your might" and Leviticus 19:18, "you shall love your neighbor as yourself." (See Matthew 22:37-39, Mark 12:29-31, and Luke 10:27) When the circumstances warranted it, Jesus quoted directly from the Old Testament to share with others his conviction that the Love of God and neighbor stood at the center of Jewish Faith.

The followers of Jesus carried this Faith one step farther. For them, he was Israel's long-awaited Messiah in whom God's Love was perfectly revealed. In their eyes, he was the Christ who came to save the world through the drama of his death, resurrection, and imminent return. As we discussed in the last Chapter, when Jesus announced the coming Reign of God, his devoted disciples believed that were living on the front edge of history's final transformation. As the old order seemed to be passing away, they accepted that Jesus' vision of the new order would erupt all around them through his soon-to-be Second Coming.

For Jesus' early devotees, the resurrection signaled a turning point event in God's relationship to humanity. By raising Jesus from the dead, God took the initiative in the drama of redemption. For Apostles like Paul, the entire history of the Jewish people was but preparation for God's supreme act of Love—the coming of Christ the redeemer to all who would accept this magnificent gift of divine grace. "The righteousness of God has been disclosed . . . through faith in Jesus Christ for all who believe. For there is no distinction, since all have sinned and fall short of the glory of God; they are now justified by his grace as a gift, through the redemption that is in Christ Jesus, whom God put forward as a sacrifice of atonement by his blood, effective through faith." (Romans 3:21-35)

Paul's letters reiterated his conviction that humanity lacked the capacity to become reconciled back to God through human achievement alone. For redemption to occur, God had to take the initiative. This was the meaning of the Christ event at its most profound level. All of the New Testament writers shared this perception. For example, Ephesians 2:8-9 states that "By grace you have been saved through faith, and this is not your own doing; it is a gift from God—not the result of works, so that no one may boast." John's Gospel in 3:16 proclaims, "God so loved the world that he gave his only Son, so that everyone who believes in him may not perish but may have eternal life."

Just as Faith in God's Love bound together the ancient Israelites as recorded in the Old Testament, so also a transformed understanding of Faith and Love in light of the Christ event united the early Church as witnessed in the writings of the New Testament. The continuity between the two Testaments on the centrality of both Faith and Love remains uninterrupted despite Jesus' followers' reinterpretation that the Old Testament presaged his Messianic calling. The early Church authors' reinterpretations of Israel's Faith and Love traditions in light of their new experiences involving Jesus as the Christ could have appeared only against the backdrop of the Old Testament.

Many New Testament writers explicitly integrate Old Testament passages into their new Christ-centered reinterpretations of Israel's Faith-Love emphasis. Jesus' loyal supporters defined his death and resurrection as God's ultimate demonstration of the kind of Love they should imitate. For example, 1 John reminds his readers,

> God's love was revealed among us in this way: God sent his only Son into the world so that we might live through him. In this is love, not that we loved God but that he loved us and sent his Son to be the atoning sacrifice for our sins. Beloved, since God loved us so much, we also ought to love one another. (4:9-11)

In the following passage, Paul construes Israel's Ten Commandments as expressions of Love.

> Owe no one anything, except to love one another; for the one who loves another has fulfilled the law. The commandments, 'You shall not commit adultery; you shall not murder; you shall not steal; you shall not covet'; and any other commandment, are summed up in this word, 'Love your neighbor as yourself.' Love does no wrong to a neighbor; therefore, love is the fulfilling of the law. (Romans 13:8-10)

In addition to the pervasiveness of Love passages in the New Testament letters, the Gospels also view Jesus as the personification of God's caring nature. Three aspects of his earthly mission impressed them the most: his concern for the downtrodden, his emphasis on mercy, and his call to serve others. All the Gospel writers agree that he moved among the outcasts of his society as he proclaimed the coming Reign of God. Maltreatment of the poor was for him a profound violation of the lofty moral mandates of his Jewish traditions.

He accused many of the Jewish leaders of his time of regressing into an arid formalism that placed greater emphasis on outward conformity than on the inner motive of compassion. When he healed on the Sabbath, he placed himself in direct conflict with the religious gatekeepers. On one occasion, as recorded in all three of the Synoptic Gospels, the teachers of the law challenged him for healing a man with a withered hand at synagogue worship. He replied, "Suppose one of you has only one sheep and it falls into a pit on the sabbath; will you not lay hold of it and lift it out? How much more valuable is a human being than a sheep! So it is lawful to do good on the Sabbath." (Mt 12:9-14; also see Mark 3:1-6;

Luke 6:6-11) For Jesus, showing concern for the well being of the less fortunate at any time revealed God's Love far more than mere conformity to religious conventions.

Stories of Jesus' healing powers permeate the New Testament. His empathy for the down and out became one of the dominant images of his legacy. All the Gospel writers portray him as a compassionate healer who brought hearing to the deaf, speaking to the dumb, sight to the blind, and walking to the lame. John's Gospel extends Jesus' miraculous healing powers to unparalleled heights in the story of Jesus raising Lazarus from the dead. (John 11:38-44) In John's moral imagination, Love is the defining characteristic of Jesus' ethic. Jesus tells his disciples, "I give you a new commandment, that you love one another. Just as I have loved you, you also should love one another. By this everyone will know that you are my disciples, if you have love for one another." (John 13:34-35)

Jesus' call for compassion coincides with his accent on mercy. In the Gospel of Matthew, Jesus counsels his followers to forgive each other not just seven times but seventy-seven times. (Mt 18:21-22) In the parable of the unforgiving servant, the king castigates his forgiven servant for failure to forgive his own servant. (Mt 18:23-35) Luke praises the Good Samaritan for being merciful to the victim of highway robbery. (Luke 10:25-37) The father shows mercy toward his profligate prodigal son. (Luke 15:11-32) Jesus was renowned for his parable of searching for the one lost sheep that went astray and not the ninety-nine that did not. (Mt 18:12-13; Luke 15:1-7)

Jesus coupled his compassion and mercy with a vision that being a servant to others pleased God more than dominating them through political power. When Jesus' followers declared that he was Israel's long-awaited Messiah, they did not imply that he was a David-like political leader who would restore Israel to its former national glory. Like Jesus, they did not equate greatness with world supremacy but rather with serving others. "The greatest among you will be your servants. All who exalt themselves will be humbled, and all who humble themselves will be exalted." (Mt 23:11-12) In the Sermon on the Mount, Jesus blesses the humble of heart as special in the sight of God. In God's coming new Reign, those meek, faithful, and loving servants whom earthly rulers perceive as the least important according to the ways of the world will be the first to triumph. (See Mt 5:1-8)

By the end of the New Testament era, the Church's revisionist interpretation of the Old Testament coalesced around the conviction that Jesus was God incarnate, Israel's Messiah who came to save the world from its sins. Accepting the New Testament's views of Faith and Love did not involve rejecting the Old Testament but rather reinterpreting it through the mental filter of Jesus' life, death, resurrection, and Second Coming. To the Gospel and letter writers, Jesus fulfilled the Hebrew promises and prophecies. In every subsequent historical setting after the end of the New Testament time period, Christians emphasized the importance of both Faith and Love as the indispensable cornerstones of their spiritual and moral convictions.

When he was alive, Jesus' preaching about the coming Reign of God invoked images of a peaceable Kingdom governed by Love and void of violence. As the Church evolved during the Early Christian or Patristic period that followed the New Testament generation, Christians pursued Jesus' vision of peace. They took to heart his appeal to avoid vengeance, forgive wrongdoers, love enemies, and not to return evil for evil. When the Roman leaders called upon Christians to join them in military campaigns and to defend the Empire with brutality and bloodshed if necessary, they professed their non-violence and refused to participate.

This occasioned criticism by Roman officials who alleged that refusal to engage in armed protection of the Empire would render it defenseless in times of attack by barbarian invaders. Christians responded by pointing to Jesus' teachings and example of self-sacrificing, nonviolent Love. Early Christian writers like Justin defended the Church's pacifism by claiming that Christians would rather die confessing Christ than to make war against each other or an alleged enemy.[2] Their real tests occurred during periods of persecution when many chose a martyr's death rather than pick up the sword. Prior to 170 C.E., no evidence exists that Christians served in the Imperial forces.[3] As new converts began to take their place as citizens of the Roman Empire after the New Testament era ended, they eschewed violence and lived peacefully with their neighbors no doubt motivated by their profound Faith in Christ the Redeemer and his Love for them and their Love for one another.

As Christianity expanded throughout the Roman Empire during the three centuries after Christ's death, the resistance against military involvement faded over time. By the third century more and more Christians began entering the ranks of the Roman legions. By 313, when Constantine conquered his enemies in the name the cross and gave Christianity official recognition and protection within the Empire, the transition from pacifism to military participation was complete. It was during the post-Constantine period that Church writers first began to develop the theory of the Just War, which we will discuss in the next Chapter on the Moral Law framework. However, even as more Christians joined the Imperial army in support of the Empire many still refused to commit to acts of violence.

During the next one hundred years following Constantine's conversion, the northern Germanic tribes launched a steady stream of invasions against the Empire until the Gothic leader Alaric successfully sacked Rome in 410. More than any other, this event signaled the end of the Patristic period and ushered in the transition to Medieval Christianity. By then many Church members participated in the deadly military battles that the Empire waged against the barbarian invaders. Despite the involvement of Christians in the Emperor's armed forces, diehard pagan defenders of the once mighty but dying empire blamed Rome's collapse on Christianity's peace loving nature.

In response to this allegation, Augustine of Hippo (354 – 430), one of the Church's greatest theologians, turned the finger of blame back on Rome itself. In his monumental book, *The City of God,* he used the Faith-Love framework of moral reasoning to articulate his defense of Christianity against the pagan accusers. Despite the book's considerable length, Augustine's thesis is simple: The world is comprised of two intermingled cities. The first is the heavenly city; and the second is the earthly city. He writes that the "two cities have been formed by two loves; the earthly love of self, even to the contempt of God; the heavenly by the love of God, even to the contempt of self."4

Rome represented the earthy city and the Church the heavenly city. "The former, in a word, glorifies in itself, the latter in the Lord. For the one seeks glory from men; but the greatest glory is God, the witness of conscience. The one lifts up its head to its own glory; the other says to God, 'Thou art my glory.'"5 Augustine traced his dualism of the two cities back to the New Testament distinction between the fruits of the Spirit and of the flesh as it appears in Paul's letter to the Galatians, Chapter 5:16-26. For Augustine, Rome fell because of its own inner corruption and had only itself to blame for its demise. It embraced the fruits of the flesh and not of the Spirit.

These two great cities coexist in history; but ultimately the earthly city, which revels in itself, will fail and the heavenly city, which delights in the Lord, will succeed. Until history ceases, the two cities will remain co-mingled. At the end of time, Christ will return in his Second Coming, reward eternal life to the faithful, and punish the wicked. Until this occurs, Augustine cautioned against judging who holds membership in which city, because only God knows for sure.

He acknowledged that Church membership does not automatically guarantee entrance into the heavenly city because deceitful appearances can mask the motive of selfishness, even among Church leaders. Nor does absence of membership ensure exclusion because outsiders can live according to God's will. Only at the end of history will Christ separate the faithful from the false followers. In the meantime, each Christian's primary task is to glorify God by committing to a life of Faith in Christ and Love of neighbor.

Until Thomas Aquinas (1225-1274) composed his multi-volume *Summa Theologica* in the thirteenth century,[6] Augustine set the standards of theological discourse during most of Medieval Christianity. The Faith and Love images that permeated his writings have continued to ignite the moral imaginations of numerous Christian ethicists through the ages, including Luther and other writers of the Reformation as well as during the Modern era, which we will describe later in this Chapter.

In addition to Augustine, no discussion of Medieval Christianity and the importance of the Faith-Love framework during this time period would be complete without brief reference to Francis of Assisi (1182-1226), who died one year after Aquinas was born. Prior to Francis, the monasteries of Medieval Europe were organized as self-contained communities. While they practiced hospitality to everyone who passed through their doors, in general they sealed themselves off from society. Francis transformed this practice by taking the monks out of the monasteries and placing them in the world among the poor.

Following the New Testament example of Jesus, Francis and the devoted members of his movement lived simply in their efforts to serve the disadvantaged souls of the world. Out of their deep Faith, they believed that God's Love would provide for all their needs, including food and shelter. Like the devoted supporters who gathered around Jesus during his earthly life, they lived kindly with each other and engaged in acts of charity, no matter where their journey through life took them. The spiritual legacy of Saint Francis stands steadfastly as one of Medieval Christianity's most enduring and morally imaginative expressions of the Faith-Love framework.[7]

This framework was also deeply embedded in the thinking of Martin Luther and served as the point of departure for the Reformation that he initiated. Luther's writings epitomize how the Bible serves as the inspiration for this framework. For Luther, the Bible alone, *sola Scriptura,* gives Christians the key for opening the door to eternal life because it contains God's revelations on how to achieve it. The cornerstone vision that anchored the imagination of all the Protestant Reformers is that salvation comes through Faith alone; and the Bible is the primary source for understanding its true nature.

Luther believed that eternal life is guaranteed to every believer who has Faith in the New Testament's claim that Christ died to redeem the sins of the world. With this assertion, Luther joined the company of Augustine and Paul whose letter to the Romans transformed his thinking more than any other Scriptural writing. Luther stressed repeatedly throughout his prodigious works that it was not through any kind of work, whether secular or sacred, but by Faith alone that a person was justified and therefore saved.[8]

Luther's emphasis on salvation by Faith alone struck at the heart of the Medieval Church's entire range of meritorious behaviors that prepared the faithful for eternal life. These included participation in the sacramental system, the practice of priestly confession and penance, obedience to monastic rules, and so on. Luther found especially untenable from both a theological and ethical point of view the Pope's scheme to sell forgiveness (indulgences) in amounts proportionate to any person's ability to pay. By substituting the simple act of Faith as described in the Bible for the entirety of the Catholic Church's works options, Luther dismantled many of the sacred beliefs and institutional structures that Roman Christianity took centuries to create.

Luther's Faith perspective permeated every aspect of his moral imagination. Quoting Romans 14:23, he wrote in *Treatise on Good Works,* "Whatever is not done of faith or in faith is sin." Apart from Faith, nothing pleases God because "faith alone makes all other works good, acceptable, and worthy because it trusts God and never doubts that everything a man does in faith is done well in God's sight." Only one supreme work exists. "Faith must be the master-workman and captain of all works, or they are nothing."[9] In short, for Luther, Faith was the great equalizer not only because it guaranteed eternal salvation for anyone who had it, but because it abolished the belief that God gave preferential treatment to some persons over others based on their greater accomplishments, whether in the world or in the Church.

Luther embraced the Pauline imagery of salvation by Faith alone with such exuberance that at times his thinking seemed to blot out all other forms of moral reasoning. "If every man had faith we would need no more laws. Everyone would of himself do good works all the time, as his faith shows him."[10] H. Richard Niebuhr, in his seminal work, *Christ and Culture,* described Luther's writings as paradoxical.[11] On the one end, Luther could wax eloquently about the power of Faith to transform completely from the inside out the life of devout Christians. Under Faith's guidance, they could soar to the heights of loving behavior. J. Philip Wogaman captures well this side of Luther's paradoxical approach when he writes, "One receives the gift of salvation and the capacity to love from the heart and not as external conformity to law."[12]

On the other end of Luther's paradox sits the dark side of the human spirit held in bondage by the persistent grip of sin. Like Paul and Augustine before him, Luther marveled at Faith's capacity to inspire believers to express God's Love through the many dimensions of their lives. At the same time, he also shared with his predecessors a deep distrust in humankind. As with Paul and Augustine, Luther was no optimist bout human nature. As stated, in his letter to the Galatians, Paul expressed this dichotomy through the image of the Fruits of the flesh verses those of the Spirit; and Augustine, in *The City of God,* envisioned an intermingling of the heavenly and earthly cities until the end of history. Luther paralleled these two earlier authors with his doctrine of the Two Kingdoms.

One way of summarizing Luther's paradoxical position is to say that what he gave with the right hand he took away with the left. While Faith inspires Love, which serves as the basis for governing Christ's Kingdom, Luther believed it was naïve to think that the world could be governed by Love. The reason: "Few believe and still fewer live a Christian life." As a result, God has created "a different government outside the Christian estate and God's kingdom."[13] Because of sin, human evil floods over the world. In response, God has constituted civil government and laws as a restraining dyke against wickedness. Once again, Luther turned to the Apostle Paul to justify his position. "Let every person be subject to the governing authorities; for there is no authority except from God, and those authorities that exist have been instituted by God." (Romans 13:1)

One of the ironies that lies at the heart of the Faith-Love framework is that those who use it vary considerably in their perception of the extent to which human sin limits Love's transforming power. Those who are inclined to pessimism about human nature like Paul, Augustine, and

Luther can extol Christian Love on the one hand and then box it in with sin on the other. Reformers like Jesus or Saint Francis can wander the wider world among the downtrodden and spread the good news of God's Love despite the chaotic social or political conditions that surround them. Through preaching Faith they bring more joy and hope amidst despair; and with acts of charity they seek to transform the world to the highest possible levels of goodness. Despite their differences, optimists and pessimists alike share a common vision of the Christian life. It proceeds from Faith, which leads to Love. Faith and Love link inseparably as the cornerstones of the Christian moral imagination.

Employing the Faith-Love framework did not end with the Reformation. It has been used continuously throughout the Modern period as well. As we discussed in Chapter 2, by the middle of the seventeenth century all of the forces that had been building since the Renaissance crystallized into a new type of scientific-urban-industrial-market place oriented society that differed in just about every respect from the agrarian one it was replacing. The Modern Era is perhaps best symbolized by the presence of complex machines and organizations that transformed patterns of human interaction and created an entire array of new moral dilemmas that previous Eras could not even begin to imagine.

As the industrial system expanded across Europe, the peasant populations who were driven from the countryside migrated to the growing cities in search of work. Many of them ended up in conditions that can only be described as wretched. They became a source of cheap labor for ruthless entrepreneurs. Men, women and children were forced to work long hours at minimal pay in dangerous and dirty sweatshops. The old inequalities of feudalism gave way to the new inequalities of an early industrial capitalism

Many Christian leaders struggled to understand how God's transforming spirit was remaking the world through these new dynamic changes. During the eighteenth century, John Wesley (1703-1791), the founder modern Methodism, emerged as one of Christianity's most important interpreters in the Modern period. Wesley was ordained and remained an Anglican priest his entire life and was active during the early stage of capitalism in Britain. He experienced first hand the dreadful conditions under which the English working class was forced to live and focused his compassion on their plight.

Wesley embraced several of the central convictions of the Reformation but drew upon the teachings of Catholicism as well through his

Anglican high Church background. Wesley's approach to ministering among the impoverished laborers came to represent one of the Modern world's most significant Faith-Love strategies for confronting the problems caused by the new industrial order. His emphasis lay mainly, although not exclusively, on the transformation of individuals rather than social structures. As we will discuss under the Justice-Liberation framework in Chapter 6, other movements such as the Social Gospel took the opposite stance and aimed their theological and ethical critique at unjust structures, not individuals.

Wesley is best known for coupling the concept of spiritual justification with moral sanctification. He shared with all other Protestants the belief that inner justification came through Faith as a gift of divine grace, especially when combined with a genuine sense of humility. By his own words, he affirmed that the personal experience of Faith left his heart "strangely warmed" by which he meant God's grace gripped his spirit at the deepest level. For Wesley, experiencing grace through Faith meant being unconditionally received into God's eternal Love as a justified sinner who could stand in God's presence without condemnation. For more than fifty years, like so many Protestant Reformers who preceded him, the central message of his oft-repeated sermons was justification by Faith.[14]

For Wesley the gift of justification carries the corresponding expectation of sanctification, which means to become perfected in Love. Love follows from Faith. Over the course of an entire lifetime, Wesley believed that continuous living in Faith under the guidance of God's grace would improve each person's ability to express Love more fully and thereby bring more goodness into the world.

Wesley did not share Luther's pessimistic view of human nature, even though other key Reformers like John Calvin did. Wesley differed from them in his perception of the ability of Faith to transform an individual's capacity to express Love in both the Church and the world. At the same time he was not a naïve optimist. He remained acutely aware that even forgiven sinners must continue to combat immoral temptations. Being saved by Faith in God's grace as revealed in Christ does not eliminate the justified self's inner struggles to become progressively more loving. While Faith does not abolish the sinful side of human nature, nonetheless when sanctification follows justification, Love can transform the world and reduce evil.

Wesley advocated the need for rigorous moral discipline, which he believed nurtures the justified self and supports its movement toward sanctification. He methodically instilled in his many small religious societies (hence, Methodism) the necessity for constant self-examination. He always connected Faith to charitable actions among the poor. He counseled his working class followers to avoid vices such as alcohol abuse or greed and to show kindness and compassion to persons in need. Because of Wesley's influence, the tight interweaving of being in Faith and doing in disciplined Love gave Methodism its enduring Christian character in the Modern Era.

This combination revealed itself most noticeably in the social causes that Wesley and his followers supported. Their charitable activities helped many working class families escape the harsh conditions of poverty and transformed them in positive ways. Wesley was a fierce opponent of slavery, but he did not embrace the kind of pacifism that the developing Church adopted during the Early Christian era. He was a conservative loyalist who distrusted democracy and supported the British monarchy against the colonies during the American Revolution. At the same time, he abhorred war, which he considered the epitome or original sin and contrary to the very essence of Love. Above all else, Wesley possessed a lively moral imagination that combined Faith, Love and the need for moral discipline in all areas of personal and social life. His life work exemplifies one important way in which the Faith-Love framework has found expression during of the Modern era.

Another modern advocate of this approach is the Lutheran pastor Dietrich Bonhoeffer (1906-1945), who lived nearly two hundred years after Wesley and under very different social circumstances, the heinous crimes of Nazi Germany. The account of Bonhoeffer's failed attempt to assassinate Hitler and his subsequent death by hanging shortly before the end of the Second World War in 1945 is one of the most dramatic examples of Christian self-sacrifice during the twentieth century. On the surface, this most unloving of actions appears to disqualify him from the ranks of Faith and Love oriented Christians. However, on further examination, we discover that this is not so. Instead, the very opposite is true. He is one of the twentieth century's foremost ethicists of the Faith-Love tradition. To understand why this once pacifist Lutheran pastor engaged in a conspiracy to murder Hitler, we have to grasp how his vision of radical Faith in Christ transformed his moral imagination.

Bonhoeffer understood that inquiry into the nature of good and evil defined all ethical reflection. However, unlike other types of ethical reasoning, according to Bonhoeffer, the first task of Christian ethics is to invalidate this knowledge. In launching his attack on the underlying assumptions of all other ethics, he wrote, "Christian ethics stands so completely alone that it becomes questionable whether there is any purpose in speaking of Christian ethics at all."[15] For Bonhoeffer, the word ethics refers to human knowledge of good and evil, which under Nazism revealed so tragically how wide the gap that separated humanity from God had grown. When humans claim for themselves the authority to define good and evil, then like Noah's heirs who built the Tower of Babel, they seek to become like God rather than dependent on God. The Christian alternative to reliance on human codes of right and wrong is to trust in God through Faith in Christ who revealed the will of God to the world by his suffering and redemptive Love.

Bonhoeffer remained acutely aware that this was easier said than done, because given the brutalities of Nazism, following the pulse of Faith involved great personal risk. He aimed his harshest criticism at Christians who disconnected Faith from the selflessness that the times required and who slid into complacency under a cover of Faith. The Nazi era demanded enormous sacrifices of the German Christians, and Bonhoeffer was appalled at what he labeled their cheap grace. "Cheap grace is the deadly enemy of our Church. We are fighting today for costly grace."[16]

Like Wesley and all the proponents of the Faith-Love framework, he recognized that God calls upon Christians to make hard moral choices, even in times of relative social peace and tranquility. However, when society degenerates into extraordinary evils like those of Nazism, then Faith demands extraordinary actions. For Bonhoeffer, confronting the Nazi monster called for nothing less than life threatening moral choices. The legacy of Bonhoeffer is that Christian discipleship, as expressed through Faith and Love, is not cheap.

In addition to the concept of costly grace, Bonhoeffer's decision to join the unsuccessful conspiracy to kill Hitler grew out of another aspect of his thinking. He divided the world into two spheres, the ultimate and the penultimate. In his words, "Justification by grace and faith alone remains in every respect the final word . . . the ultimate. . . . It is for the sake of the ultimate that we must now speak of the penultimate."[17] The penultimate prepares the way to the ultimate and consists of "everything that precedes the ultimate, everything that precedes the justification of the sinner by grace alone."[18] The ultimate validates the penultimate as a morally acceptable means to the ultimate, and the penultimate either contributes to or obstructs progress toward the ultimate.

This means that all social structures and codes of ethics, including the proscription against murder, belong to the category of the penultimate.

> There is, therefore, no penultimate in itself; as though a thing could justify itself in itself as being a thing before the last thing; a thing becomes penultimate only through the ultimate, . . . The penultimate, then, does not determine the ultimate; it is the ultimate which determines the penultimate.[19]

Furthermore, when human life is deprived of opportunities to achieve justification, then the conditions that prohibit them must be changed.

From Bonhoeffer's perspective, the Nazi movement represented *in extremis* the deprivation of all positive penultimate possibilities for achieving justification. Thus, out of his own radical Faith, he tried to destroy Hitler through violence as a paradoxical act of Love. It was his way of participating in the suffering Love of Christ as an expression of costly grace under the horrors of Nazism. In Bonhoeffer's moral imagination, we see Faith and Love drawn together in radical combination.

This leads us to one final example of the Faith-Love method of doing Christian Ethics, the writings of Joseph Fletcher (1905-1991). Like Wesley and Bonhoeffer, Fletcher employed this approach extensively in his writings. In the mid-1960's he became a major proponent of the school called Situation Ethics, which is perhaps the most recent modern adaptation of this framework. He wrote, "*Christian* situation ethics has only one norm or principle or law (call it what you will) that is binding and unexceptional, always good and right regardless of the circumstances. That is 'love'—the *agape* of the summary commandment to love God and the neighbor."[20] Fletcher identified Bonhoeffer and other modern writers such as Emil Brunner, H. Richard Niebuhr, Paul Tillich, among others, as Christians who shared his viewpoint.

The situational approach generated widespread controversy within Christian Ethics because it relegated traditional moral laws to conditional status. Only Love is absolute. Everything else is relative. "All laws and rules, and principles and ideals and norms, are only *contingent*, only valid *if they happen* to serve love in any situation."[21] Fletcher's position rests on the perception that modern anthropology has demonstrated through its discovery of diverse cultural patterns that there are no universal moral laws. "Perhaps the most pervasive cultural trait of the scientific era . . . is the relativism with which everything is seen and understood." For the field of Ethics, this means, "We have become fully and irreversibly 'contingent,' not only about our particular ideas, but about the very idea of ideas themselves (cognitive value) and about goodness itself (moral value)."[22]

Modern Social Science research pushes us to rethink the fundamental principles of Christian Ethics. According to Fletcher, we can combine cultural relativism with the norm of Love because it is the most universally adaptable moral standard. Wherever Love finds expression through the patterns of diversity that exist around the world, Christians should accept them. When these patterns fall short, Christians should endeavor to remove or modify them or create new ones more consistent with Love's demands. For Fletcher, the theological justification for the Love norm is Faith. "Christian ethics 'posits' faith in God and *reasons* out what obedience to his commandment of love requires in any situation."[23] For Fletcher Love can unite people across a wide spectrum of diverse worldviews, structures and cultural variations.

Fletcher applied his Situation Ethics to a broad range of novel issues to demonstrate the creativity of Love. Just as Wesley confronted the moral dilemmas of early industrial capitalism and Bonhoeffer challenged the evils of Nazism, Fletcher related his situational perspective to the rapidly changing field of modern medicine in a time of post-industrialism. He was one of the first Christian ethicists to do so in his 1954 book, *Morals and Medicine*,[24] and again in 1967 with *Moral Responsibility: Situation Ethics at Work*.[25]

By the mid-1950s, rapid technological advances in biomedicine created an entirely new ethical environment that called for creative responses to unprecedented moral dilemmas. Fletcher was one of the first Christian ethicist to enter this arena and through the use of his Faith-Love framework of Situation Ethics he became a pioneer in the field of Bioethics. His flexible approach enabled him to search for the most loving solutions to new problems involving reproductive control, respirator removal, organ transplants, the right to die, and many more.

We are now ready to summarize this Chapter. The primary ethical images that form the Faith-Love framework are found in the Bible. The experiences of ancient Israel as recorded in the Old Testament provided the New Testament writers with a theological template for making sense of Jesus' life, death, and resurrection. The New Testament vision of Jesus as God's Messiah Savior of the world could not have come into existence apart from the religious traditions of the Old Testament. Both Testaments employ Faith and Love as core images for defining God's relationship to humankind and vice versa. At the same time, even as these two Testaments unite in their embrace of Faith and Love, they divide because the New Testament writer's transformed the Old Testament images in light of their vision of the Christ event.

After the New Testament era ended, Church writers used the Biblical Faith-Love framework to articulate their own views. During the Early Christian or Patristic period, Jesus' faithful followers justified their pacifism by pointing to the example of his peace filled Love and their Faith in his redemptive sacrifice on their behalf. In the Medieval epoch Augustine made Love of either the heavenly or earthly city the spiritual dividing line between Christ's loyal supporters or Rome's deluded sinners. St. Francis was the ideal embodiment of Faith and Love during this era. Based on the writings of the New Testament, Luther made Faith the foundation of the Reformation and defined Love as the fullest fruit of its harvest even though he remained a pessimist about human nature like Paul and Augustine.

Wesley, Bonhoeffer, and Fletcher continued the Faith and Love tradition in the Modern world as industrial, Nazi, and post-industrial biomedical challenges called forth their most profound ethical insights. Wesley approached the problems of the new urban order by envisioning the loving transformation of the human spirit in combination with the sanctified and disciplined life. Bonhoeffer joined with opponents of Hitler in a failed effort at violent assassination because of his radical Faith commitments. Fletcher addressed the emerging biomedical ethical dilemmas of post-industrialism by applying a broad standard of loving God in the neighbor.

All in all, despite the constantly changing circumstances and widely disparate ethical dilemmas that delineated the different epochs, the reappearance over time of the Faith-Love framework among Christian writers is remarkable. Equally amazing is the extent to which the other three frameworks also appeared repeatedly. In the next Chapter, we will turn our attention to the Moral Law framework.

Notes

1. According to Barry L. Bandstra, *Reading the Old Testament: An Introduction to the Hebrew Bible,* second edition, Belmont, Cal.: Wadsworth Publishing Company, 1999, p. 198, the history of ancient Israel is told from the "Deuteronomistic" perspective. "The writer of Joshua through Kings is called the Deuteronomistic historian (Drr) because he derived his basic theology from Deuteronomy." Through this lens he tells "the story of the nation from the theological perspective that Israel prospered or suffered in relation to how obedient or disobedient they were to the covenant." In short, God blessed them when they were faithful and punished them when they were not.

2. See, "First Apology of Justin," in *Early Church Fathers,* edited by Cyril C. Richardson, New York: Macmillan, 1970, p. 39.

3. See J. Philip Wogaman, *Christian Ethics: A Historical Introduction,* Louisville, Kentucky: Westminster/John Knox Press, 1993, p. 33.

4. As quoted in Wogaman, *Christian Ethics,* p. 54.

5. Wogaman, *Christian Ethics,* p. 54.

6. See Thomas Aquinas, *Summa Theologica,* in *Basic Writings of Saint Thomas Aquinas,* edited by Anton C. Pegis, New York: Random House, 1945.

7. See C. H. Lawrence, *Medieval Monasticism,* second edition, New York: Longman Publishers, 1989.

8. See Martin Luther, *Concerning Christian Liberty,* translated by R. S. Grignon, in Harvard Classics, volume 36, New York: P.F. Collier & Son, 1938.

9. Martin Luther, *Treatise on Good Works,* in *A Textbook on Christian Ethics,* edited by Robin Gill, Edinburgh: T. & T. Clark Limited, 1985, see pages 93 and 97.

10. Luther, *Treatise on Good Works,* in Gill, *A Textbook on Christian Ethics,* p. 97.

11. H. Richard Niebuhr, *Christ and Culture,* New York: Harper & Row, 1951, pp. 170-189.

12. Wogaman, *Christian Ethics,* p. 112.

13. Martin Luther, *Secular Authority: To What Extent It Should Be Obeyed,* in *Works of Martin Luther,* Volume III, Philadelphia: A. J. Holman Co. and The Castle Press, 1930, pp. 236-237.

14. John Wesley, *Plain Account of Christian Perfection,* Boston: McDonald, Gill & Co., Publishers, no date; also see John Wesley, *Sermons on Several Occasions,* two volumes, London: Hayman Brothers and Lilly.

15. Dietrich Bonhoeffer, *Ethics,* edited by Eberhard Bethge, New York: The Macmillan Co., 1964, p. 142.

16. Dietrich Bonhoeffer, *The Cost of Discipleship,* New York: The Macmillan Co., 1964, p. 35.

17. Bonhoeffer, *Ethics,* p. 84.

18. Bonhoeffer, *Ethics,* p. 91.

19. Bonhoeffer, *Ethics,* pp. 91-92.

20. Josephy Fletcher, *Situation Ethics,* Philadelphia: The Westminster Press, 1966, p. 30.

21. Fletcher, *Situation Ethics,* p. 30.

22. Fletcher, *Situation Ethics,* p. 43.

23. Fletcher, *Situation Ethics,* p. 47.

24. Joseph Fletcher, *Morals and Medicine,* Princeton, N.J.: Princeton University Press, 1954.

25. Joseph Fletcher, *Moral Responsibility: Situation Ethics at Work,* Philadelphia: The Westminster Press, 1967.

Chapter 4

Moral Law

The Moral Law framework of Christian Ethics begins where the Faith and Love tradition ends. Once again, the Hebrew Scripture is the starting point. As we described in the last Chapter, ancient Israel formed its self-definition as a chosen people on a theological foundation of belief in God's Love. Inevitably, sooner or later they would need a more precise definition of what God expected of them. God's call of Abraham took the form of a promise that launched the patriarchal and matriarchal journeys but it did not tell them what to do. As they traveled in Faith, they had no idea that the road into the future would lead them into over four hundred years of slavery under the harsh lash of the Egyptians. (Exodus 1:8-14)

As the book of Exodus records, even in the depths of suffering God never abandoned them. Instead, just as God chose Abraham to begin the long sojourn of Faith, God called forth the greatest of their leaders, Moses, to lead them out of Egyptian enslavement. (Exodus Chapters 2-14) As they wandered in the desert and slowly drifted back toward the promise land of Canaan, they lacked spiritual direction. After centuries of slavery, they lost their sense of divine destiny until Moses restored it to them by delivering at Mount Sinai the Law of the Covenant. (Exodus 20) The Mosaic Covenant rekindled their Faith; and the Law articulated the normative expectations that God required of them as a chosen people. After Moses, the Faith and Love framework incorporated the Moral Law.

When God added the Sinai stipulations through Moses, Israel's special mission as a chosen people became clearer. Through upright living,

God expected them to become a light unto the world—a beacon to guide earth's wayfaring travelers back to God. In Abraham's name, God chose Israel to serve as an exemplar of righteousness by obeying the Mosaic Law of the Covenant. If they remained faithful in showing their Love of God by following the Moral Law, God would bless them with abundance beyond their wildest belief by making them a great nation as promised to Abraham.

Over time, the structure of the Moral Law that Moses initiated at Sinai expanded through the steady accumulation of both general moral principles and rules of conduct, including many that covered the minutia of daily life from dress codes to food preparation. In between the two ends of this normative continuum, Israel created laws that were more specific than the general principles but not as narrow as the rules. Although it is difficult to determine where the Israelites drew the boundaries between general principles and less encompassing laws and between laws and highly detailed rules, or whether it even entered their mind to make such distinctions, we can identify many lines of delineation.

Ancient Israel's entire legal framework is embedded in the Torah, or the first five Books of the Hebrew Scripture, Genesis through Deuteronomy. Even though the writers of the Torah set the development of their moral injunctions, along with liturgical and cultic regulations, within the span of Moses' lifetime, in reality the Codes of conduct emerged over many centuries in many different social and political settings through a complicated process of writing and revision. As a result, there are three sets of Codes in the Torah reflecting changes that occurred in Israelite history.[1]

The first, and most important, is the Covenant Code that appears in Exodus 20:1 through 23:33 and that dates from the time of Moses. This Code sets the pattern for all subsequent moral Codes. It contains the Ten Commandments, which are the most general and best-known moral principles found in the Torah. The first three relate to Israel's Covenant with God and mandate faithfulness, the non-worship of idols, and non-defamation of the sacred name. The fourth Commandment sets aside the Sabbath as a day of rest for worship activities. The remaining six Commandments address behaviors that are essential to maintain communal harmony. They require respect for parents and proscriptions against murder, adultery, theft, lying, and envy. (Exodus 20:1-17) The most general principle of retributive justice, or *lex talionis*, is also located in the Covenant Code: "life for life, eye for eye, tooth for tooth, hand for hand, foot for foot, burn for burn, wound for wound, stripe for stripe." (21:23-24)

At the other extreme, the Covenant Code also includes numerous rules that detail precise moral expectations involving the treatment of slaves, punishment for violent acts, and laws of repayment and punishment. "If you buy a male Hebrew slave, he shall serve six years, but in the seventh he shall go out a free person, without debt." (Exodus 21:2) "When someone borrows an animal from another and it is injured or dies, the owner not being present, full restitution shall be made. If the owner was present, there shall be no restitution; if it was hired, only the hiring fee is due."(22:14-15)

In between the most general and specific injunctions, the Covenant Code includes numerous laws. They counsel acting justly in relationship to specific classes of people or situations. "You shall not pervert the justice due to your poor in their lawsuits. Keep far from a false charge, and do not kill the innocent and those in the right, for I will not acquit the guilty."(23:6-7) And with direct reference to the Egyptian enslavement, "You shall not oppress a resident alien; you know the heart of an alien, for you were aliens in the land of Egypt."(23:9)

The Torah also contains the post-exilic Holiness Code in Leviticus Chapters 17-26. It reiterates much of the Covenant Code and incorporates rules related to priestly ritual practices and specific moral mandates. It defines for the Israelites what it means to be a holy people. Leviticus 19:2 states the Code's purpose. "You shall be holy, for I the Lord your God am holy." Like the original Covenant Code of Moses, the priestly Holiness Code assumes that if the Israelites live according to its stipulated conditions, then their holiness will fulfill their mission as a chosen people. In effect, they will mirror God's holiness.

When they returned from the Babylonian exile, the Israelites struggled to establish their own identity apart from the surrounding Canaanite cultures, whose worship of Baal and impure moral practices offended them. The Holiness Code identifies both the acceptable and unacceptable standards by which they believed God judged them. It contains numerous proscriptions, such as forbidden sexual activities, rules for the conduct of religious festivals, and priestly rituals necessary for worship purity. Specific rules covered the details of daily dress and domestic duties. "You shall not round off the hair on your temples or mar the edges of your beard. You shall not make any gashes in your flesh for the dead or tattoo any marks upon you." (19:27-28) "You shall not let your animals breed with a different kind; you shall not sow your field with two kinds of seed; nor shall you put on a garment made of two different materials." (19:19)

The Holiness Code incorporates many of the same Justice sentiments that appear in the Covenant Code. "You shall not defraud your neighbor; you shall not steal; and you shall not keep for yourself the wages of a laborer until morning; you shall not revile the deaf or put a stumbling block before the blind." (19:13-14) "You shall not render an unjust judgment; you shall not be partial to the poor or defer to the great; with justice you shall judge your neighbor. You shall not go around as a slanderer among the people." (19:15-16)

The Deuteronomic Code, which inspired Josiah's reforms in 629 B.C.E. long before the priestly Holiness Code was written during the post-exilic Judaic reconstruction, is the third legal Code woven into the narrative of Moses' life. As its name suggests, it is found in Chapters 12-26 in Deuteronomy, the fifth and last book of the Torah. Deuteronomy summarizes the major events of the first four books along with many of the ritual and moral commands of the Covenant and Holiness Codes. The Deuteronomic Code restates the Ten Commandments and the mandate that the Israelites act justly in their relationships with each other as well as with foreigners. New rules are also added. "When you build a new house, be shall make a parapet for your roof; otherwise you might have bloodguilt on your house, if anyone should fall from it." (22:8) "You shall not wear clothes made of wool and linen woven together. You shall make tassels on the four corners of the cloak with which you cover yourself."(22:11-12)

Taken together, the guidelines that appear in the Covenant, Holiness, and Deteronomic Codes comprise Israel's Moral Law framework. They defined the nation's moral obligations and were applied across a wide range of historical circumstances. No matter where or when the Israelites lived, the Codes instructed the nation. The success of Israel's transformation into a special people whom God had chosen out of Love depended on how faithfully they followed the Moral Law.

The Jewish writers of New Testament took the Torah and the demands of the Moral Law for granted but reinterpreted them in light of the Christ event. The New Covenant community that Jesus established believed that God redeemed the world through his cross and resurrection. They perceived themselves to be the rightful heirs of the Old Cov-

enant and its image of righteousness. However, they radically transformed it. The Old Covenant community coupled righteousness with the
Law, whereas the New Covenant Church tied it to Faith.

One of the major theological disputes of the New Testament centers
on the relationship between New Covenant Faith and Old Covenant Law
and their degree of compatibility. Two writers in particular, Paul and
Matthew, entered this debate with the full force of their moral imaginations. At stake was the issue of whether Faith abolished the Law or
whether the two might be harmonized with each other. The response of
Paul and Matthew to this dilemma was straightforward. Jesus did not
come to eliminate the Law. Paul expected Christ's followers to uphold
the Law. For Matthew Jesus fulfilled the Law.

In Paul's view, each new convert dies to past sins by being resurrected with Christ into a new state of spiritual righteousness based on
God's grace received in Faith. Living in Faith does not nullify the importance of the Torah. Even though Paul rejects salvation through obedience to the laws of the Torah, he holds the Torah in high regard. He
views it as both a gift and a curse. On the one hand, it defines God's high
moral expectations. On the other hand, humans cannot satisfy its extraordinary demands because of their sinful limitations. In Paul's eyes,
all fall short of the glory of God.

By joining Christ's community, each person undergoes an inner transformation. "So if anyone is in Christ, there is a new creation: everything
old has passed away; see, everything has become new! All this is from
God, who reconciled us to himself through Christ." (2 Corinthians 5:17-
18) Becoming a new creation in Christ does not warrant either boasting
or removing the mandate to uphold the Torah law. "Then what becomes
of boasting? It is excluded. By what law? By that of works? No, but by
the law of faith. For we hold that a person is justified by faith apart from
works prescribed by the law." (Romans 3:27-28) "Do we then over-
throw the law by this faith? By no means! On the contrary, we uphold
the law." (Romans 3:31)

Being freed by Faith from the power of sin and death does not mean
being free of the law. Instead, becoming a new creation in Christ leads
to the recognition that obedience to the law is a gift from God and to the
inward motivation to obey it. In Paul's imagination, New Covenant transformation does not eliminate the Moral Law requirements of the Old
Covenant. The New Covenant shifts the source of salvation from Moral
Law to Faith, but it also carries a continuing obligation to live under

God's gift of the Law. Living in Christ's eschatological community while awaiting his return is not a new license to engage in the sinful practices that the Moral Law prohibits. The New Covenant guarantees eternal life to all believers, and it also requires them to settle for nothing less than living by the high ethical standards of the Old Covenant.[2]

Like Paul, Matthew holds fast to the perception that Jesus did not come to eliminate the Law. Rather, he came to satisfy it completely. Many New Testament scholars consider Matthew's Gospel to be the most Jewish of the four canonized Gospels because it gives evidence of numerous parallels to the Old Testament.[3] In Matthew's Gospel, Jesus proclaims, "Do not think that I have come to abolish the law or the prophets: I have come not to abolish but to fulfill. For truly I tell you, until heaven and earth pass away, not one letter, not one stroke of the letter, will pass from the law until all is accomplished." (Mt 5:17-18)

As we indicated above, the Torah contains the Moral Law by which the Israelites understood their obligations under the Old Covenant. For Matthew, Jesus is the Messiah teacher whose life perfectly reflects the Law's highest ideals because he embodies the motive behind the Torah. He reveals the intent behind the text. He speaks to the deep spirit of the Torah and not just its narrow letter. He is the cornerstone of the New Covenant not merely because he satisfies the Moral Law but because he exposes its purpose and surpasses it at the same time. In the Sermon on the Mount (Matthew Chapters 5-7), Jesus repeatedly says to his audience, "You have heard it said (in reference to some aspect of the Torah or Ten Commandments), but I say to you," to demonstrate his authority to interpret God's real intention behind the Law.

Matthew's Gospel incorporates other Old and New Covenant comparisons as well. Just as Moses receives the Decalogue on Mount Sinai, Jesus gives his Sermon on the Mount. In the Old Testament, God calls the Israelites to light up the darkness. In the New Testament, Jesus also calls his followers to go forth and shine. "You are the light of the world. . . . let your light shine before others, so that they may see your good works and give glory to your Father in heaven." (Mt 5:14, 16) For Matthew, Jesus' ethical recitations in the Sermon on the Mount both incorporate and transcend Moses' edicts from Mount Sinai. For Matthew, this means that God sent Jesus to fulfill the Moral Law, which thereby qualifies him as God's Messianic replacement for the prophet Moses who until Jesus' time was considered Israel's greatest leader.

In effect, Matthew provided the early Church with a clear set of ethical guidelines for living during the eschatological interim in preparation for Jesus' Second Coming. Like the parable of the Ten Bridesmaids, Matthew counsels the faithful to follow the example of the risen Messiah and prepare for his eventual return. When Christ comes again, not everyone will be found worthy. He "will separate people from one another as a shepherd separates the sheep from the goats," (Mt 25:32) according to their good works in the world. Only the faithful who show compassion for the downtrodden by feeding the hungry, giving water to the thirsty, welcoming the stranger, clothing the naked, and caring for the sick (Mt 25:34-46) will inherit the Kingdom. For Matthew, Faith, Love, and Moral Law are inseparable as exemplified in Jesus' life, death, and resurrection.

In sum, during the New Testament period it is clear that both Paul and Matthew retained their deep commitment to the Moral Law framework. For Paul, the inner transformation that occurs by becoming a new creation in Christ involves ongoing adherence to the Law while exceeding it in the name of Faith and Love. For Matthew, Jesus is the new Moses who fulfills the Moral Law by incarnating in his person God's goodness, which stands as the motivating power behind the Law. Both Paul and Matthew preserve the Moral Law framework of the Old Testament but transform it through their images of Christ and his call to all believers that they live faithfully as members of the eschatological community he created—until he should come again.

As Christianity transitioned from New Testament times to the Patristic period, the Moral Law tradition traveled with it because of the need for the Church to instruct new converts into the ethical expectations of the Faith. When Christianity emerged as a new movement in the Greco-Roman world, no precedents existed for distinguishing the Church's moral expectations from the pagan practices of the Empire's polytheistic religions. Church leaders responded quickly to fill the void with verbal advice and lists of guidelines.

During the early second century, one of the most exemplary morality tracts of the Early Christian era appeared. Allegedly written by Jesus' twelve disciples, it is called the *Didache*.[4] It combines sayings from both Jesus and the Old Testament and includes many prescriptions and proscriptions of Christian morality. Above all, it provides counsel to Christ's faithful followers to make the correct choices amidst the conflicting ethical practices of other religions. The *Didache* contrasts the

Way of Life against the Way of Death in parallel to Paul's comparison between the fruits of the Spirit and the fruits of the flesh in his letter to the Galatians. The Way of Life begins with Love of God and neighbor. Like Jesus' Sermon on the Mount in Matthew's Gospel, it advocates praying for enemies and fasting for persecutors, among others.

The Way of Death defines the behaviors that Christians should avoid such as staying away from evil people and controlling anger. The *Didache* is full of rules that instruct Church members to refrain from many types of destructive behaviors, including anger, fanaticism, quarrelling, hot-temperedness, homicide, lust, fornication, unclean talk, the roving eye, adultery, omen obsession, idolatry, witchcraft, astrology, magic, lying, theft, and anxiety over wealth.

Writings like the *Didache* served a valuable purpose during the era of Early Christianity, because they staked out the Church's ethical terrain and gave clear direction to its emerging moral imagination during the first three centuries when it was still a struggling minority movement in the Greco-Roman world. The Church consistently counseled its members to follow the example of Christ by seeking ethical purity. An unbroken ethical chain connected Jesus' sayings and Paul's perceptions about upholding the Law with the *Didache's* inventory of acceptable and unacceptable behaviors. The dichotomy between the Ways of Life and Death provided converts with clear images of the "do's and don'ts" that were expected of them as the traveled over a pagan religious landscape that invited many precarious wrong turns.

Other writers of the Early Christian Era followed the *Didache's* lead in stressing the importance of moral purity. Because their writings do not appear in the New Testament, their names are largely unknown to most modern day Christians. However, their contributions were indispensable to reinforcing the Moral Law framework in the young Church. During the second century, Christian leaders circulated letters throughout the growing number of congregations of Asia Minor and advocated strict adherence to rules of behavior. The letters of Bishop Ignatius of Antioch, who was martyred in 107, along with those of Barnabas and Clement, who became Peter's successor in the church at Rome, incorporated the *Didache's* image of the two Ways or carried highly moralistic messages.

The Patristic writers paved the way for the Medieval Age, when the Moral Law tradition hit its high water mark. We would not be far from the truth to say that Moral Law was to Medieval Christendom what Faith was to the Reformation. Between Constantine's conversion in the early fourth century and the Goth's victory over Rome in the early fifth century, the Medieval Church moved from the periphery of the Empire to the political center where it remained for more than a thousand years. Augustine and Aquinas were the intellectual bookends, so to speak, of the era, the former having lived near the start and the latter near the end. In between, the Church created the sacramental system, numerous penitential texts, the *Rule of Benedict* and other manuals for governing the monastic orders, and the Just War doctrine. Aquinas capped off the Moral Law momentum by creating a theological system based on layered levels of law.

More than any other writer, Augustine's paradoxical thinking set the moral tone for most of the Medieval time period. Like Paul before him, his optimistic attraction to Faith and Love is matched only by his pessimistic attitude toward the human will, which he believed is so corrupted by sin that humanity is incapable of even a modicum of moral goodness apart from God's grace. Augustine's theological legacy left a deep impression on Church leaders, who took special care to turn the faithful away from the world's wickedness. By the fifth century, the Church saw itself as the repository of God's grace, which it dispensed through its sacramental system of rules and procedures. By administering baptism, confirmation, confession, communion, and the last rites, the priestly hierarchy possessed the power to loosen and to bind. If effect, they became the gatekeepers to eternal life. No one could get into heaven without passing through the Church and receiving its blessings.

Auricular confession stood at the heart of this sacramental system, which gave the priests direct access to the moral conscience of all believers. The Church stressed to the faithful the necessity of staying in God's grace by periodically cleansing their souls of the sinful stains that they accumulated during their passages through life's imperfections. When they confessed their moral shortcomings, the priests prescribed penance proportionate to the severity of their sin. In order to guarantee the proper balance between sin and penance, the Church developed several penitential manuals to standardize the priests' judgments.

It would not be an overstatement to say that obeying the penitential books is the Moral Law equivalent to climbing Mount Everest. They represent a form of moral legalism *in extremis*. By the ninth century, they reached the summit. The manuals index every possible sin for every imaginable group under any conceivable circumstance. The French

Bishop Halitgar gets credit for preparing the most elaborate list of sins and their corresponding standardized penance responses. His writing stands in the tradition of the *Didache* but surpasses it by several orders of magnitude by grouping human failings under myriad categories such as homicide, fornication, theft, perjury, magic, ritual sacrilege, drunkenness, incest, idolatry, adultery, bestiality, self-mutilation, abortion, usury, burning down a house, anger, physical violence, and so on. Each violation includes the penance that the priest prescribes for the confessing sinner.[5]

Although the priests were excessive, at times even humorous, in trying to corral every human wrongdoing so that they would know how much punishment to administer during auricular confession, the penitential manuals helped shape the moral imagination of Medieval Christianity. They helped the Church regularize the ethical expectations for both the lifelong members and recently transformed converts who never completely abandoned their pagan practices. For ordinary and mostly illiterate laypersons, the Moral Law penitential manuals helped the clergy give moral guidance during the difficult and frequently confusing demands of daily life.

The Medieval Church's desire to normalize every aspect of Christian Faith through Moral Law oriented penitential manuals did not stop with the laity. It extended to the monasteries as well. The Medieval monastic system evolved out of the Patristic period when many of the post-New Testament followers of Jesus found that the only way they could aspire to a life of moral purity was to form enclosed communities and withdraw from the temptations of the outside world. By the sixth century, the monasteries they created spread across Europe, but they had become inwardly chaotic and badly in need of restructuring.

Benedict of Nursia (480-543) responded to this necessity by creating the *Rule of Benedict*. His *Rule* set the standard for the future of monastic organization and to this day remains one of the Medieval Church's examples *par excellence* of the Moral Law framework of moral reasoning. When monastic discipline declined in the tenth, twelfth, and thirteenth centuries, reform movements like the Cluniacs, Cistercians, and Dominicans turned to the Benedictine *Rule* as their model of renewal.

At the heart of the *Rule* is the twelve-step ladder of humility, which counseled the monks to be obedient to their superiors, walk with downcast eyes, denounce themselves "as inferior to all and more worthless," and "to keep silence and not speak till questioned."[6] The *Rule* regulated every detail of monastic existence from sunrise to sunset—when to pray, eat, work, recreate, and sleep. Like the penitential manuals that guided the moral life of the laity, the *Rule* provided the monastic religious with the discipline necessary to follow the path of moral purity free of worldly distractions. From commoners to clergy and from merchants to monks, the Moral Law framework embraced everyone.

As the Church moved from its original status as a struggling outsider during the Patristic period to its position as the dominant insider during Medieval Christianity, it underwent a dramatic transformation in its view of military participation. Consistent with the Moral Law tradition of the penitential books and the *Rule of Benedict,* the Church created the Just War doctrine. By the fifth century, the deep seeded Faith-Love pacifism of Early Christianity, as described in the preceding Chapter, gave way to a perception that participation in war could be justified under certain circumstances. Augustine led the way. He witnessed the barbarity that the invading Germanic tribes inflicted on Europe as Alaric and his warriors marched toward Rome. After observing their displays of heinous slaughter, he concluded that he could not be a pacifist.

This does not mean that he embraced war with the enthusiasm of a world-conquering crusader. Rather, he reasoned that going to war should always remain a moral exception and a decision of last resort, one that should not be made lightly. Engaging in the evils of killing through bloody armed conflict could be defended only if its purpose would be to negate a greater evil. Augustine laid out the specific rules of behavior that justified military intervention. These became the basis for the Just War doctrine that subsequent writers, including Aquinas, elaborated in greater detail. In the end, using the Moral Law framework, the Medieval Church condensed its stance on Just War involvement to seven basic principles:

1. The cause must be just.
2. The war must be declared and waged by a lawful authority.
3. War must be a last resort.
4. War must be the only possible means of securing justice.
5. War must be conducted by the right means: respect for noncombatants.
6. There must be a reasonable chance of victory.
7. The good to be achieved must be greater than the evil effects of war.[7]

No doubt, the Church's changing social position influenced the transformation from pacifism to Just War. During Augustine's lifetime, the
Church occupied a different position than it had during New Testament
times, when it existed as a fledgling movement on the perimeter of Greco-
Roman society. By the time of Augustine, an expanding Christianity
already existed as the Empire's official religion. More than eight hundred years later, during the time of Aquinas in the thirteenth century, it
had grown to dominate Europe. The Church routinely participated in the
affairs of State and viewed itself as the defender of the Faith. If called up
to do so, it engaged in military intervention to preserve the very civilization it helped create, and it used the Just War doctrine as its moral
justification.

The temperament and methods of St. Thomas meshed perfectly with
Medieval Christendom's Moral Law approach. For centuries after his
death in 1274, his theological system dominated Catholic thinking. In
1879 Pope Leo XIII gave his multi-volume *Summa Theologica* a privileged position among all of the Church's other religious writings.[8]
Aquinas integrated both Augustine and Aristotle's ideas into his massive
moral writings. Following Aristotle, he held that every aspect of creation aims toward its true end, or *telos*, which is nothing other than its
potential to fulfill itself. The human *telos* is happiness.

Although not a naïve optimist, Aquinas was far less pessimistic about
human nature than the oft-brooding Augustine. Aquinas presupposed
that humans being have a dual destiny. One is natural or temporal, and
the other supernatural or spiritual. Achieving happiness applies to both
the natural and supernatural ends. A dynamic tension exists between the
two sides of human nature. Human beings can achieve a high degree of
earthly happiness, which their supernatural side can enhance. However,
humanity's ultimate end or *telos* is spiritual happiness, which cannot be
achieved in this temporal life.

Aquinas uses the concepts of the Moral Law and the Divine Law to
connect the two sides of human nature. The Moral Law applies to the
natural side and consists of three seamlessly integrated levels. The Divine Law pertains to the supernatural side and has only one level.[9] The
three levels in the Moral Law are eternal law, natural law, and human
law. The eternal law is based on divine reason and exists only in the
mind of God. Because human beings have the capacity for reason, they
have access to God's eternal law in the form of a rational natural law,
which embodies the eternal law and is embedded in humanity's natural

side. Both the eternal and natural laws are permanent and unchangeable. Aquinas points to the Ten Commandments to illustrate how God's eternal law is linked to the innate natural law.

Human law, the third level of the Moral Law, flows from the natural law; but unlike the natural law, it is not permanent. It can change depending on the historical circumstances but with one provision. The changing human law must not conflict with the unchanging natural law. Aquinas recognized that societies display a great deal of diversity in their customs and legal practices. As society changes, certain human laws might need to be altered or eliminated and new ones created. However, this does not negate either the existence or necessity of the natural law. Changing human laws can continue to reflect unchanging moral standards on which previous but no longer relevant human laws were based. Proscriptions against murder, stealing, envy, lying, and so on, exist universally and permanently irrespective of changing historical contexts.

The fourth level is Divine law, which differs from the eternal, natural, and human laws in one major way. Whereas the latter three types of law apply universally to all humans through reason on their natural side, the Divine law refers to God's supernatural salvation in Christ on their spiritual side. Aquinas recognized that Divine law is unique to Christianity. Only those who receive in faith that God redeemed the world through Christ live under Divine law. At this point the spiritual side of humanity influences the temporal side. The Divine law lifts human law to a higher moral level. By living according to the Divine law, humans can achieve a higher level of happiness on earth than through natural reason and human law alone.

By the end of the fifteenth century just prior to the start of the Reformation, the Church's Moral Law framework enveloped virtually every aspect of Medieval Europe. The penitential books and the *Rule of Benedict* covered the practical side and Aquinas' four levels of law encompassed the conceptual. Just as Augustine's Just War ideas helped mold the Moral Law tradition at the onset of Medieval Christendom, Aquinas consummated it with a theological and moral vision based on four levels of law. More than any other contributors, together they shaped the Moral Law framework that span several centuries. They also helped set the stage for the Reformation, which despite its overarching emphasis on the centrality of Faith, never abandoned the Church's deeply embedded embrace of the Moral Law.

As we discussed in the last Chapter, the Reformers' writings were rife with paradoxes, and Luther embodied them more than anyone else. While he extolled Love as the quintessential moral ideal of the Christian Faith, he locked it up in human sin, as discussed in the last Chapter. The world was an appalling place wherein the forces of evil lurked in every corner. For Luther, only unquestioned obedience to the external law and its enforcement by the State could contain the destructive excesses of human sin. In 1525, when Thomas Muntzer stirred up the peasants in a desperate but failed attempt to seize land from the nobility, Luther seethed with anger. He called for swift and severe retaliation and for the political authorities to "smite, slay, and stab" them as one must "kill a mad dog."[10]

Luther shared the apostle Paul's conviction that God instituted government to keep the social peace. Like Augustine, Luther also believed that God might call Christians to engage in violence and if necessary kill in order to protect the innocent or prevent terrible evils form occurring. Through his doctrine of the two Kingdoms, he counseled the faithful not to oppose secular authorities no matter what, even when the officials perpetuated wrongdoing. God would contend with them in due time. The Royalty reign supreme over matters of State and Christ presides over the life of the spirit. Each belongs in its separate sphere; and each should refrain from interfering with the other's duties.[11]

John Calvin (1509-1564), the best-known Reformer after Luther, shared many of Luther's views, although he added his own theological twist. Like Luther, Calvin saw the Moral Law, especially as found in Scripture, as a constraint against evil; but he also held it in a more positive light. Moral Law serves to guide the development of human goodness. At the same time, its perfectionist standards reveal the enormous gap that exists between God's majesty and humanity's limitations. Following in the footsteps of Paul, Augustine, and Luther, Calvin recognized that all fall short of the glory of God. Despite God's unapproachable grandeur, Christians need not despair because God is also loving and quick to forgive human failings for those of humble heart. Through grace God turns the blemished human will away from evil and toward expressions of moral goodness.

Like Luther, Calvin was no optimist. He was convinced that apart from grace, humanity remains totally depraved and self-centered. Only God can transform the human will. Calvin embraced the doctrine of predestination as his theological cornerstone and believed that from the moment of creation God had already separated the saved from the damned. Moral Law exists to glorify God and not to honor humanity. When faithful Christians adhere to this Law, they acknowledge God's sovereignty and pre-selection, and they provide proof of being among the chosen.

Because of his perspective on human nature, Calvin shared Luther's view of government. Civil authority exists to protect society from the excesses of human sin. God calls magistrates to uphold civil law. Like Luther, he forbade citizens from violent rebellion against unjust rulers and even viewed the tyranny of governing officials as a form of divine punishment for evil. He also agreed with Luther that God would decide how to deal with despots, but unlike Luther he perceived that God might use lower magistrates for this purpose. He accepted resistance but only under very limited conditions and only if lesser officials within government circles initiated it. First and foremost, Calvin counseled Christians to remain in compliance with the Moral Law and civil statutes and to regard them as a gift to humanity, which God's sovereignty, selectivity, and salvation do not dissolve.[12]

The Catholic Church reacted to the Reformation with a Counter-Reformation. From 1545-1563 it convened the Council of Trent to clean up clergy corruption and review recent Protestant challenges to long held Catholic positions. After much debate, by Council's end Church leaders rejected the Reformation doctrine of salvation by Faith alone, defended the sacramental system, insisted that salvation required confession and penance, and reconfirmed the centrality of its Moral Law tradition.[13] Following Aquinas, the Council asserted that the eternal, natural, and human laws serve the life of Faith in positive ways. Laws, Biblical or civil, do not exist solely to prevent wickedness or to instruct the Church about God's sovereignty and humanity's depravity. By acting according to the Moral Law, Christians can bring God's Love into the world and move toward their end or *telos* of happiness. Through both the Moral Law and Divine Law of salvation, as Aquinas described them, Christ's faithful followers can increase their capacity for moral goodness.

As the Reformation and Counter-Reformation played out and the doors into the Modern world slowly opened, the debates that Luther initiated eventually hardened into permanent doctrinal differences between Catholics and Protestants. As we discussed in Chapter 2, modern science splintered this division even further into liberal, conservative, and fundamentalist factions. As in previous epochs, Christian writers continued to use the Moral Law framework in the midst of changing circumstances. For the remainder of this Chapter, we will examine three modern variations of this tradition. The first involves the Catholic encyclicals, the second the writings of Norman Geisler, and the third those of Walter Muelder.

After Trent, the Catholic embrace of Aquinas remained steadfast and sturdy despite the ongoing tumble of changes that modernity produced. The rise of democracy in Europe threatened to undermine the Church's traditional hierarchical structure and Darwin's publication of *The Origins of Species* further eroded its truth validating credibility, which started with Galileo's earlier observations. In light of both of these challenges, leaders moved to protect the Church's authority. In the second half of the nineteenth century, Pope Pius IX issued two major pronouncements. First, in 1864 he issued the *Syllabus of Errors,* which critiqued democracy and the political ideals of Europe's revolutions in England, the United States, France and elsewhere. Second, in 1871, under the auspices of the First Vatican Council, he declared the doctrine of papal infallibility.

Through these two initiatives, Pius IX endeavored to reassert a privileged position for Catholic authority, which started to slip away with the Reformation and eroded further as modern science developed. In effect, he steered Catholicism in a conservative direction by seeking to warrant truth and morality through papal proclamation rather than through scientific experimentation and democratic persuasion. It was not until 1962 that the winds of change began to blow in a more liberalizing and democratic direction when Pope John XXIII convened the Second Vatican Council. While not abandoning the Moral Law tradition, this 1960's Pope urged Church scholars to give greater attention to the Biblical heritage in their theological and ethical reflections and to democratize the decision making processes within the hierarchy and between the leaders and laity.

Despite the many liberal tendencies that Vatican II brought to the Catholic Church between 1962-65, Pope Pius IX cast his long and conservative nineteenth century shadow well into the twentieth. His conservatism meshed well with Catholicism's traditional Moral Law framework, which the Church applied consistently in its encounter with the emerging moral issues of the Modern world. As we will discuss in Chapter 6 on Justice and Liberation, this framework could be employed as a progressive force to support the cause of labor against the exploiting impulses of industrial capitalism. At the same time, it could take Catholicism in a conservative direction when it clashed with many of the major scientific and technological innovations of modernity. One area in particular stands out more than any other in revealing the dramatic nature of this confrontation, human sexuality.

During the first three decades of the twentieth century, advances in medicine led to the development of new and safe birth control techniques that gave women greater control over their biological reproduction. It took Margaret Sanger over twenty years of constant struggle to change the public's attitudes toward the use of these new devices. Finally, in 1937 the American Medical Association endorsed the principle that women have the right to use artificial contraceptives to prevent pregnancy and plan their families.[14] Since then, the practice of using artificial birth control has become common practice throughout much of the world.

The Catholic Church's response to this modern trend has remained resolute and unwavering. In 1930, Pope Pius XI, a successor to Pius IX, published his encyclical *Casti connubii,* in which he articulated the Catholic Church's opposition to the development and use of the artificial contraceptives that Sanger and others promoted. The Pope used a Moral Laws approach based on Aquinas' natural law views as the basis for his criticism. According to this encyclical, marriage exists for mutual love and procreation; and sexual intercourse is the natural means to this end or *telos.* Any artificial interference with this process is by definition, according to natural law, immoral. The encyclical sanctions only those birth control methods that incorporate women's monthly menstrual rhythms.

When the liberal Vatican II ended in 1965, there was high expectation that the Catholic Church would reverse its 1930 prohibition against artificial contraception by modifying its moral imagination and grant women more reproductive control through the medical innovations of modern science. However, this was not to be. In 1968, Pope Paul VI issued *Humanae vitae*, which reaffirmed the position that Pius XI expressed in *Casti connubii* in 1930. Like Pius XI, Paul VI asserted that any interruption with the possible transmission of life through artificial means is contrary to the natural and divine law.[15]

In 1987, this time under Pope John Paul II, the Vatican published a third encyclical, *Instruction of Respect for Human Life in Its Origin and on the Dignity of Procreation: Replies to Certain Questions of the Day (Donum vitae).* In this document, the Church took up the question of whether married couples could use Artificial Insemination by Husband (AIH) or *In Vitro* Fertilization-Embryo Transplant (IVF-ET) using the husband's sperm and the wife's egg in cases of natural infecundity. This third encyclical restates the Catholic Church's conservative position. The only legitimate method for conceiving a child is through natural human sexuality.[16]

In three encyclicals published in 1930, 1968, and 1987, under the authority of three different Popes, the Catholic Church has taken consistently a conservative Moral Law route. Not only has it reiterated its prohibition against the use of modern technologies (artificial contraceptives) to prevent pregnancy, it also has forbidden their use (AIH and IVF-ET) to enable it even among married couples. Sexual intercourse remains the only acceptable moral means of procreation. Thus, the Catholic Church's use of the Moral Laws framework in the area of transmitting human life has led to a conservative, even ultra-conservative, position given the impact that modern medical technology has exerted, and will continue to exert, on methods of conception prevention and reproductive control.

The writings of Norman Geisler provide a second example of ethical reasoning through a Moral Law perspective. Whereas the Catholic Church draws from the natural law of Aquinas, Geisler pulls from Evangelical and Fundamentalist Protestantism that views the Bible as a source of literal truth and divinely dictated commandments. Geisler calls his perspective "graded absolutism," which assumes that God has revealed to humanity a system of higher and lower moral laws.[17] When moral conflicts occur, they can be resolved by understanding which moral laws take precedence.

According to Geisler, the Bible is clear about how God rank orders the divine commandments. Lower commandments can be violated but only in order to serve higher ones. Under this condition, God does not hold the individual responsible for violating a sacred commandment because the higher commandment takes priority. "Therefore, in real, unavoidable moral conflicts, God does not hold a person guilty for not keeping a lower moral law so long as he keeps the higher. God exempts one from his duty to keep the lower law since he could not keep it without breaking a higher law."[18]

Geisler wisely avoids trying to prioritize the scores of moral laws that the Bible includes. Instead, he holds that the variety of God's commandments can be reduced to three overarching ones that incorporate the rest. The three absolute moral laws are: love for God over love for humanity, obedience to God over government, and mercy over truth. According the Geisler, if parents teach their children to hate God, the children should disobey them and follow God. If government commands the murder of innocent victims, citizens should resist. If telling the truth would harm innocent persons, then one should show mercy and lie to protect them.

Geisler notes that his Moral Law method is vulnerable to the criticism of subjectivism. He responds,

> in graded absolutism the Christian does not decide for himself what the ethical priorities are . . . they are no more subjective than is anything else revealed in Scripture. The priority of values is objective and determined by God; the only subjective factor is our understanding and acceptance of God's values.[19]

Through such a staunch declaration about the objective status of God's moral laws, Geisler intends to critique Fletcher's Love-oriented Situation Ethics. "Fletcher concludes something is right or wrong because the 'existential particularities' of the situation determine it. Graded absolutism, on the other hand, concludes something is right or wrong because God has declared it so."[20] Such comments reveal the deep schisms that modernity has left in its wake among contemporary liberal and fundamentalist Christians. It would appear that one way to deal with the subjective side of moral reasoning is simply to declare the objectivity of one's view of God's Moral Law and deny being inclined to any subjectivity at all.

Not all Christian writers who follow the Moral Law form of reasoning are Catholics or fundamentalists. Walter Muelder (b. 1907), who is a liberal Protestant, also employs it but in a decidedly different way. Consistent with the method first developed by E. S. Brightman and L. Harold DeWolf, Muelder does not set out to identify all of God's prescriptions or proscriptions of behavior but rather to create a sequence of procedural rules to be used for arriving at the best possible moral judgment in any given situation. For the moral imagination to operate best it must draw from three areas, science, philosophy, and theology; and it should strive for both coherence and comprehensiveness.[21] For Muelder, the ethical image that incorporates all these dimensions better than any other is that of the Responsible Society. The procedural steps that he advocates are designed to achieve it.

Muelder's method contains four groups of procedural moral laws: formal, axiological, personalistic, and communitarian.[22] Formal laws refer to consistency and non-contradiction in making moral decisions as well as autonomy in the choice of values. Axiological laws include the six outcomes that any person of good will should seek. They are internal harmony among values, consideration of short and long term consequences, selection of the best possible outcome, decisions relevant to the situation, realization of the widest possible range of values, and subordination of action to ethical ideals.

Personalistic moral laws cover each individual's moral capacity to maximize value in life, treat others as ends in themselves and never merely as means (the second version of Kant's Categorical Imperative), and to choose values that enhance the whole personality. Communitarian laws refer to community perfection through cooperation, subordination of personal to group ideas, and the selection of values that improve the whole community. In combination, the formal, axiological, personalistic, and communitarian moral laws will contribute to creating the Responsible Society.[23]

Unlike the normative aspects of Catholic encyclicals or Geisler's graded absolutism, Muelder's moral laws only provide persons with guidelines for moral reasoning. His procedural method does not tell Christians what to think but rather how to think. The moral laws do not contain specific ethical content. Their aim is to assist a person in arriving at the best possible moral position on any given ethical issue. Using his own method, Muelder became a pacifist after concluding that killing violates virtually all of the moral laws. Violence only leads to the destruction of persons and destroys community. He also embraced democratic socialism as an alternative to capitalism because it fosters cooperation and not market competition, which only subverts social responsibility by promoting narrow self-interest.

It is time to summarize Chapter 4. Like the Faith and Love emphasis of the prior Chapter, the Bible is also the principle source for the Moral Law tradition in Christian Ethics. The Old Testament Mosaic Covenant created the framework through which God expected Israel to remain faithful. The Torah contains the Covenant, Holiness, and Deuteronomic Codes that the ancient Jews created over the centuries to guide their transformation as a chosen people.

New Testament authors did not abandon their commitment to the Moral Codes of the Torah. Rather they transformed them in light of their Faith that Jesus was the loving Messiah whom God sent to earth to save the world from its sins. Two writers in particular addressed the issue of the relationship of Faith and Law. According to Paul, becoming a new creation in Christ through Faith does not nullify the Law. Rather, it leads to obeying the Law while transcending it in the name of Love. A simpler way to say this is that for Paul, Faith absorbs Law in Love. Matthew's Gospel portrays Jesus as the one who fulfills the Law by revealing God's purposes behind it. For Matthew, through the Sermon on the Mount Jesus replaces the prophet Moses as God's new Messianic Law Giver. Faith, Love, and Law coalesce in the person of Jesus.

Between the New Testament and Medieval eras, moral directives like those found in the *Didache* helped Christians navigate their way around the pagan practices of the Patristic period. During the time of Medieval Christendom, the Moral Law tradition reached its zenith through the sacramental system, the laity penitential books and monastic instructions like Benedict's *Rule,* the Just War doctrine, and the writings of Thomas Aquinas.

Like the New Testament, which did not use Faith to annul the Law, during the Reformation Luther and Calvin combined Faith with the need to obey Biblical and social laws to check humanity's sinful tendencies. In the Modern era, the Catholic encyclicals and the writings of Geisler and Muelder reflect continuing use of the Moral Law framework, even though they interpret it differently through the theological lenses of the natural law, fundamentalism, or liberalism.

In conclusion, from the Old Testament to modernity, our survey has shown how Christ's followers have endeavored to bring goodness into the world by using the Moral Law framework. Amidst the ambiguities of life, when it is not always clear what we ought to do, the Moral Law traditions of the Church often point toward the best ethical alternatives. From this perspective, God has not left us alone but has provided the Moral Law to guide us along the way, even as in Faith Christians strive to make the right choices. Next we examine Christianity's Character Ethics traditions.

Notes

1. For a more elaborate description of Israel's Codes see Bernard W. Anderson, *Understanding the Old Testament*, fourth edition, Englewood Cliffs, N.J.: Prentice-Hall, Inc., 1986, pp. 95-101, 375-376, and 452.

2. Paul allowed for an important exception to this position. He strenuously opposed the circumcision requirements of the Law for Gentile converts. When the churches in Galatia locked horns over this issue, he wrote, "For neither circumcision nor uncircumcision is anything; but a new creation is everything!" (Galatians 6:15)

3. See John and Kathleen Court, *The New Testament World,* Englewood Cliffs, N.J.: Prentice-Hall, Inc., 1990, pp. 187-237.

4. *Didache,* in *Early Church Fathers,* edited by Cyril C. Richardson, New York: The Macmillan Company, 1970.

5. For further details see Denise Lardner Carmody and John Tully Carmody, *Christian Ethics: And Introduction through History & Current Issues,* Englewood Cliffs, N.J.: Prentice-Hall, Inc., 1993, pp. 77-78; and J. Philip Wogaman, *Christian Ethics: A Historical Introduction,* Louisville: Westminster/John Knox Press, 1993, pp. 75-81.

6. "The Rule of Benedict," in *Christian Ethics: Sources of the Living Tradition,* edited by Waldo Beech, New York: The Ronald Press, 1955, pp. 156-157.

7. Paul T Jersild and Dale A. Johnson, editors, *Moral Issues and Christian Response,* fourth edition, New York: Holt, Rinehart and Winston, Inc., 1988, p. 255.

8. James Livingston, *Modern Christian Thought, Volume I: Enlightenment and the Nineteenth Century,* second edition, Upper Saddle River, N.J.: Prentice Hall, 1997, pp. 342-343.

9. See Thomas Aquinas, *Treatise on Law (Summa Theologica, Questions 90-97),* Gateway Edition, Chicago: Henry Regnery Company, no date.

10. Martin Luther, "Against the Robbing and Murdering Hordes of Peasants," in *Works of Martin Luther,* Volume IV, Philadelphia: A. J. Holman, 1931, p. 248.

11. Martin Luther, "Secular Authority: To What Extent It Should Be Obeyed," in *Works of Martin Luther,* Volume III, pp. 236-238.

12. John Calvin, *Institutes of the Christian Religion,* edited by John T. McNeill, Philadelphia: The Westminster Press, 1960, Book II, Chapters I-VIII.

13. See the Council of Trent's "Confession," in *The Teaching of the Catholic Church,* edited by Josef Neuner, and others, State Island, N.Y.: Alba House Publishers, 1967, pp. 314-318.

14. See David M. Kennedy, "Birth Control in America: The Career of Margaret Sanger," in *Technology and Society in Twentieth Century America,* edited by Randall Stross, Belmont, Cal.: Wadsworth Publishing Co., 1989, pp. 96-110

15. See Wogaman, *Christian Ethics,* pp. 214-216, 242-244.

16. See Lisa Cahill, "The New Reproductive Technologies: A Catholic Perspective, *Santa Clara Magazine,* Winter 1989, pp. 10-13.

17. Norman Geisler, *Christian Ethics,* Grand Rapids, Michigan: Baker Book House Company, 1989, pp. 116-119.

18. Geisler, *Christian Ethics,* p. 120.

19. Geisler, *Christian Ethics,* p. 124.

20. Geisler, *Christian Ethics,* p. 123.

21. Walter G. Muelder, *Moral Law in Christian Ethics,* Richmond, Virginia: John Knox Press, 1966, p. 153

22. Muelder, *Moral Law in Christian Ethics,* pp. 50-53.

23. Walter G. Muelder, *Foundations of the Responsible Society,* Nashville: Abingdon Press, 1959.

Chapter 5

Character

L ike the Faith and Love and Moral Law frameworks, we begin our
discussion of Character Ethics with the Bible. As we stated in Chapter
1, Character Ethics focuses on developing the virtues that it is desirable
for persons to have. It looks to the inner human dispositions that lie
behind actions and emphasizes the personal traits that are likely to lead
to specific behaviors across a broad spectrum of situations. Character
Ethics understands that human beings are self-determining moral agents
who shape their future through activities that emanate from inner motivations.

Throughout the history of ancient Israel, this method of moral reasoning appeared in the wisdom tradition, especially, although not exclusively, in books such as Proverbs, Job, and Ecclesiastes. From the perspective of their profound Faith that God's Love would direct their destiny,
they grasped the importance of internalizing the moral stipulations embedded in their Covenant. The wisdom books embody this awareness.
At the same time, many of the prophetic figures who chastised the nation
during the monarchial period found the Israelites and their Kings sorely
lacking in their ability to make wise choices about their future. Below
we will examine some of the most significant wisdom insights from
Proverbs and similar prophetic voices.

Other cultures like the Greeks, Mesopotamians, Babylonians, and
Egyptians possessed their own wisdom traditions and intercultural contact among them was not uncommon. After King David's death, his son
and heir to the throne Solomon entered into numerous political alliances
with surrounding nations, which gave him access to the region's rich

traditions. This enabled him to collect, record, and consolidate much of the wisdom literature of the ancient Middle East.[1] When Moses uttered the words in Deuteronomy 4:6, "Surely this nation is a wise and discerning people," little did he know that centuries later at the height of national power, King Solomon would enjoy the reputation of being Israel's wisest leader.

The Book of Proverbs provides an important point of entry into ancient Israel's connection to wisdom because it identifies the kinds of character traits that the Israelites believed God expected they would internalize. Becoming wise begins by revering God's holiness and standing before God with respectful awe. First, according to Proverbs 9:10, "The fear of the Lord is the beginning of wisdom, and the knowledge of the Holy One is insight." Furthermore, "Trust in the Lord with all your heart, and do not rely on your own insight. In all your ways, acknowledge him, and he will make straight your paths. Do not be wise in your own eyes; fear the Lord, and turn away from evil." (3:5-7) Finally, "The Lord by wisdom founded the earth; by understanding he established the heavens." (3:19)

Wisdom sits at the center of Israel's moral imagination and nurtures the community as one of its most precious gifts. "Keep sound wisdom and prudence, and they will be life for your soul and adornment for your neck. Then you will walk on your way securely and your foot will not stumble." (3:21-23) God "is a shield to those who walk blamelessly, guarding the paths of justice and preserving the way of his faithful ones. Then you will understand righteousness and justice and equity, every good path; for wisdom will come into your heart." (2:7-10) The Old Testament authors knew that Israel could become God's light unto the world only by following the pathway that leads to wisdom.

Like every other aspect of Israel's collective existence, Proverbs ties its wisdom images to both the blessings and curses of the Covenant. Becoming wise is not optional; it is mandatory. "Do not let loyalty and faithfulness forsake you; bind them around your neck, write them on the tablet of your heart. So you will find favor and good repute in the sight of God and of people." (3:3-4) "Therefore walk in the way of the good, and keep to the paths of the just. For the upright will abide in the land, and the innocent will remain in it; but the wicked will be cut off from the land, and the treacherous will be rooted out of it." (2:20-22)

After Solomon's reign, the nation splintered into two acrimonious factions whose moral deterioration eventually sealed their fate. First, God sent the Assyrians to the northern kingdom in 722 and then the

Babylonians to the southern kingdom in 587 to uproot them from the promise land. Out of Love God brought them into existence and through the Covenant guided them with the Moral Law. However, they never became a wise people: they never became permanently transformed from within. They failed to plant within themselves the deep seeds that would sustain them in the ways goodness—over time—generation after generation. They spiraled downward into unfaithfulness, injustice, and dishonesty. From the perspective of Character Ethics as envisioned in Proverbs, they lacked wisdom—the internalizing of the enduring virtues necessary to secure their future forever.

As the split kingdoms drifted toward demise, the great prophets warned them of their failure to grow in the ways of righteousness, especially Amos and Hosea in the north and Jeremiah in the south. Amos' pronouncements headed a long list of prophetic condemnations. During the eighth century, at the height of Israel's prosperity in the north, he traveled from Judah in the south to proclaim the word of pending doom to King Jeroboam II. In the following quotation we see evidence of both the Character and Justice frameworks. "For three transgressions of Israel, and for four, I will not revoke the punishment; because they sell the righteous for silver and the needy for a pair of sandals—they who trample the head of the poor into the dust of the earth and push the afflicted out of the way." (Amos 2:6-7)

Hosea's prophetic indictment against the northern kingdom was no less severe. In one overarching condemnation of the depth of Israel's moral deprivation, his words combine the Character, Faith-Love, and Moral Law traditions.

> The Lord has an indictment against the inhabitants of the land. There is no faithfulness or loyalty, and no knowledge of God in the land. Swearing, lying, and murder, and stealing and adultery break out; bloodshed follows bloodshed. Therefore the land mourns, and all who live in it languish. (Hosea 4:1-3)

In 722, under the onslaught of the Assyrians, the northern kingdom of Israel forever ceased to be.

Later prophets, especially Jeremiah, delivered a similar litany of denunciations in the southern kingdom. For the great prophet, Judah's lack of wisdom was all too obvious. In Chapter 9:23 he writes, "Thus says the Lord: Do not let the wise boast in their wisdom, do not let the mighty boast in their might, do not let the wealthy boast in their wealth."

He grieved for a faithless and apostate people devoid of wisdom. As he looked around the market places of Jerusalem, he was hard pressed to find anyone who sought the truth or desired to become the righteous people God called them to be. "O Lord, do your eyes not look for truth? You have struck them, but they felt not anguish; you have consumed them, but they refused to take correction. They have made their faces harder than rock; they have refused to turn back. (Jeremiah 5:3)

For Jeremiah, God's future handwriting jumped off the wall in bold letters. Judah faced catastrophe. "Therefore a lion from the forest shall kill them, a wolf from the desert shall destroy them. A leopard is watching against their cities; everyone who goes out of them shall be torn in pieces—because their transgressions are many, their apostasies are great." (5:6) Despite God's Love they became rebellious and disobedient. They turned their backs on the Moral Law that God conveyed through Moses. They shunned the virtues essential to their sustained transformation. As a consequence, God sent the invading army of Nebuchadnezzer to pull them from the promise land like plants from the ground and thrust them into exile.

Jeremiah's prophetic proclamations did not end with harsh judgments. Even as he delivered his declarations of doom, he brought consolation. As the armies of Babylon swept down on Judah and the distraught people confronted their destruction and expulsion, he reminded them of God's abiding Love. At some unknown future time, God would return them to their beloved homeland as a transformed people and remain true to the promise given to Abraham. God would restore them to their special status but with one major change. "This is the covenant that I will make with the house of Israel after those days, says the Lord: I will put my law within them, and I will write it on their hearts; and I will be their God, and they shall be my people." (Jeremiah 31:33)

No longer would the law be limited to words chiseled in stone. It would emanate from within each Jewish person and permeate the entire community. The Israelites would become God's people in their inner being. Jeremiah's image of the new covenant written on the heart embodies Old Testament Character Ethics *par excellence.*

In the New Testament, the heart also appears as one of the central Character Ethics images, especially in the Gospels of Matthew and Luke. Paul's letters also contain numerous references to the ideal Christian virtues. As we discussed in the last Chapter, Matthew's Gospel depicts Jesus as the new lawgiver, whose Sermon on the Mount fulfills the Mosaic Law and transcends it at the same time. Matthew also portrays Jesus as embodying the ideal person to perfection.

On one occasion when Jesus' disciples failed to wash their hands before eating, the religious authorities confronted him about violating the tradition of the elders. He responded to them and the disciples by saying, "Do you not see that whatever goes into the mouth enters the stomach, and goes out into the sewer? But what comes out of the mouth proceeds from the heart, and this is what defiles." (Matthew 15:17-18) Defilement can take many forms. "For out of the heart come evil intentions, murder, adultery, fornication, theft, false witness, slander. These are what defile a person, but to eat with unwashed hands does not defile." (Matthew 15:19-20) Immoral behavior emanates from an immoral Character.

Luke's perspective on the impact of inner motivation on the moral life parallels Matthew's. In the following quotation, Luke uses the metaphor of the tree and its fruits to capture the essence of the virtuous person. "No good tree bears bad fruit, nor again does a bad tree bear good fruit; . . . The good person out of good treasure of the heart produces good, and the evil person out of the evil treasure produces evil; for it is out of the abundance of the heart that the mouth speaks." (Luke 6:43-45)

The author of the Letter to the Hebrews also picks up on this central moral metaphor and locates the source of evil within the unfaithful heart of each person. Hebrews counsels Christians not to harden their "hearts as in the rebellion, as on the day of testing in the wilderness." (Hebrews 3:8) "Take care, brothers and sisters, that none of you may have an evil, unbelieving heart that turns away from the living God." (3:12)

Nowhere do the New Testament writers provide a complete inventory of all that virtues that comprise the Christian Character. Despite this lack, the Apostle Paul comes closer to achieving this than anyone else when he describes the virtues that emanate from the spiritual transformation that occurs by becoming a new creation in Christ. In Chapters 3 and 4, we placed Paul within the Faith-Love and Moral Law frameworks. He also belongs in the Character tradition of Christian Ethics.

For Paul, no person achieves righteousness through obedience to the Mosaic Law. God bestows righteousness through grace as a spiritual condition on anyone who accepts in Faith that Christ died for the sins of the world. This internal transformation is the essential first step to becoming a new creation in Christ, which in turn leads to the development of the kinds of virtues that it is desirable for all of Christ's followers to have. Paul did not limit his list of virtues to any single writing. Instead, he wove them into the many letters he sent to the emerging missionary churches he started at various locations throughout Asia Minor.

When he received word of conflicts that threatened their internal solidarity, he responded by providing both spiritual and moral guidance. His most basic assumption is that being Christ's new creation begins with a sense of inner freedom to live according to God's Love. He employs the image of life in the Spirit to convey the power of this new freedom, which he juxtaposes to life in the flesh. As we stated in Chapter 3, in Paul's moral imagination, Love occupies center stage as the core Christian virtue. From this starting point, he branches out to include several other Character traits that all persons who become new creations in Christ ought to possess.

Paul's letters to the Galatians and Corinthians contain the best examples of the kinds of constructive virtues that nurture harmony within Christian communities. To the Galatians churches he wrote, "For freedom Christ has set us free. Stand firm, therefore, and do not submit again to the yoke of slavery" (Galatians 5:1) "The fruit of the Spirit is love, joy, peace, patience, kindness, generosity, faithfulness, gentleness and self-control. There is no law against such things." (5:22-23) "Let us not become conceited, competing against one another, envying one another." (5:26) In contrast, the destructive fruits of the flesh include "fornication, impurity, licentiousness, idolatry, sorcery, enmities, strife, jealousy, anger, quarrels, dissensions, factions, envy, drunkenness, carousing, and things like these." (5:19-21)

To the church at Corinth, he penned the best known of all his virtue passages in which he ties Love directly to other desirable Character traits. "Love is patient; love is kind; love is not envious or boastful or arrogant or rude. It does not insist on its own way; it is not irritable or resentful; it does not rejoice in wrongdoing, but rejoices in the truth." (1 Corinthians 13:4-6) "And now faith, hope and love abide, these three; and the greatest of these is love." (Verse 13)

In sum, taken together, Jesus' image of the heart as the source of good and evil deeds and Paul's lists of virtues have nourished the Christian moral imagination for centuries. When united with the wisdom insights of Proverbs and other books, plus the prophetic witness, the combined perceptions of the Old and New Testaments established the Character Ethics approach as one of the Christianity's foremost methods of moral reasoning. As in the case of the Faith-Love and Moral Law traditions, the writers of the Patristic period continued to employ the Character framework during their own time.

Two authors in particular deserve special mention, Origen of Alexandria (184-254) and Ambrose of Milan (339-397). Origen was born more than a century before Constantine's conversion to Christianity in 313 and Ambrose died only thirteen years before the Goths captured Rome in 410. Their combined contributions bridged the Church's expansion from the end of the New Testament time to the start of Medieval Christendom when Augustine defended the Church against the accusation that Christianity caused the decline of the pagan Roman Empire. The key to understanding how Origen and Ambrose elaborated the Character framework lies is grasping the degree to which Christianity evolved as a syncretistic Faith.

As the Church grew, its membership stretched across a broad range of social classes and embraced the diverse populations of Asia Minor. As a result, it gradually encountered many Greek and Roman ideas that challenged its leaders to think deeply about the relationship between several complex and potentially incompatible perspectives. The most creative thinkers of the Early Christian era responded to these new experiences by reflecting on connections between the prevailing religious and philosophical systems of thought. The writings of Origen and Ambrose epitomize the success that early Church writers had in synthesizing Greek, Roman and Jewish ideas with those of Christianity even as more Greeks, Romans, and Jews joined the Church. Christian intellectual syncretism went hand in hand with Church expansion.

The city of Alexandria, which is located along the northern coast of Africa, was one of the ancient world's major learning hubs. It attracted a broad range of scholars with interests in Neo-Platonic and Stoic philosophy as well as Jewish and Christian thought. Origen, the best-known and brightest student of Clement of Alexandria (145-215), moved comfortably within the various worldviews and demonstrated that the boundaries between them were permeable.[2] He searched for the points of intersection that would connect Christian and classical concepts. His eclectic approach established a pattern of intellectual integration that future Church scholars repeated in virtually every subsequent historical time period.

Origen viewed Christianity as compatible with the Old Testament and Greco-Roman philosophy. At the same time, he believed that Christian Faith went one step farther because it fulfilled the best tendencies of both while providing deeper insight into the nature of God. The ancient philosophers attracted him because of their belief that knowledge gave them access to the mind of God. Along with the Neo-Platonists and Stoics, he accepted that God's essence consists of divine reason through which God created the natural laws of the universe. Because we are created in God's image, we can discover these laws through human reason. He also incorporated into his Christian synthesis the Jewish and Greek wisdom traditions from the Old Testament and the writings of Plato and Aristotle.

Next, he included the Christian concept of the Trinity to tie these diverse perspectives together. Through this idea, he combines creation, rationality, and virtue: God is the creator of all things; Jesus is the divine *logos,* or word, who brings wisdom and knowledge; and the Holy Spirit is the motivator, who inspires Christians to become pure and holy. All human beings are able to gain knowledge and wisdom through rationality, but only Christ's faithful followers can receive inspiration from the Holy Spirit. Faith builds on reason. The Holy Spirit enhances the natural conditions of human existence by motivating individuals to progress toward greater goodness. Origen envisions that humanity would become more virtuous through the Holy Spirit and that over a lifetime, every Christian "may make so great an advance in holiness and purity, that the nature which he received from God may become such as is worthy of Him who gave it to be pure and perfect."[3]

Origen's writings make frequent reference to character traits such as humility, kindness, generosity, wisdom, knowledge, joyfulness, and to the human capacity for continuous moral improvement. When outsiders accused the Church of disloyalty to the Emperor, leaders like Origen defended Christianity as a religion of peace and Christians as virtuous persons who possessed no ill will toward the Empire. Origen helped pave the way for future scholars to feel comfortable with combining the best aspects of various ancient worldviews while they filtered them through the Character Ethics framework of moral reasoning.

Ambrose followed in Origen's footsteps by also developing a similar integrative approach that attracted many educated persons, including Augustine whom Ambrose converted to Christianity through his skill as an orator. By the time of Ambrose's birth in 339, the Church already occupied a privileged position in society because Constantine promoted it after his conversion and coronation to King in 313. Ambrose grew up in an upper class, non-Christian family that provided him with a superior education in Greek and Roman studies. At age thirty-four, while serving as a Roman Governor, he converted to Christianity and shortly thereafter became the Bishop of Milan. As a result of his classical education and mid-life conversion to the Christian Faith, he possessed the background necessary to see the connections between Greco-Roman philosophy and Christian theology.[4]

Ambrose based his understanding of the Christian moral life on a combination of Stoic virtues and Christian transformation. After reading the New Testament he was convinced that anyone could be forgiven for sinful behavior and subsequently could become a better person through God's grace. He accepted that the Stoic virtues of wisdom (also called prudence), courage (fortitude), moderation (temperance), and justice were part of the natural law embedded in human reason, and that God's grace could transform them to enable a person to progress toward higher levels of moral improvement.[5] Like Origen who preceded him by more than one hundred years, Ambrose left as his legacy to the Church an ethical vision of how grace can be combined with nature and at the same time enhance it.

During the era of Medieval Christendom, Thomas Aquinas more than any other writer continued the momentum that Origen and Ambrose maintained during the Patristic period. Like them he used the images of grace and nature to weave into a coherent whole the various pieces of his massive moral theology. As we discussed in the last Chapter, he is one of the major proponents of the Moral Law approach to moral reasoning. He belongs with the Character Ethics framework as well. We would not be wrong to say that the syncretistic impulse that first appeared in Paul's New Testament letters and continued in the writings of Origen and Ambrose culminated in Aquinas' *Summa Theologica* at the height of the Medieval era. Above all else, Aquinas was a master of intellectual synthesis.

During the thirteenth century, western writers rediscovered the lost works of Aristotle, which had vanished from European scholarship for centuries. Aquinas savored and used them extensively throughout his entire career as a Church theologian. Like the famous Greek forerunner, Aquinas held that virtue is a disposition of the character, a habit that causes a person to will good ends. This in turn leads to greater happiness, which is humanity's primary purpose, or *telos,* in life. The potential to achieve maximum happiness on earth comes through virtuous living. As stated in Chapter 4, Aquinas believed that the self has a natural and a supernatural destiny. The natural side includes reason and the supernatural side involves Faith that is given through God's grace.

Each side possesses its own virtues. Four exist on the natural side and three on the supernatural side. Reason discerns the four natural virtues, and Faith apprehends the three supernatural ones. Like Ambrose before him, Aquinas appropriated from the ancient Greeks wisdom, courage, moderation, and justice as the four natural, or cardinal, virtues. To this list he added from Paul (1 Corinthians 13:13) faith, hope, and love as the supernatural, or theological, virtues. These seven virtues serve as the basis for achieving goodness in the world, which leads to happiness. As human beings, we can attain a high level of happiness if we follow the four cardinal virtues; but we can reach an even higher level if we add the three theological virtues to them. Or, as Ambrose would say, grace can improve on nature.[6]

In contrast to the seven virtues stand the seven vices of sloth, lust, anger, pride, envy, greed, and gluttony. Whereas the seven virtues can increase the total amount of happiness, the seven vices can only decrease it. The vices undermine humanity's ability to make moral progress, and they prevent the achievement of both the natural and supernatural ends of life. Aquinas believed that each person possesses the freedom to decide whether to live according to the seven virtues or the seven vices, and everyone maps out their moral future through the exercise of the free will.

Aquinas' moral theology is a well-integrated intellectual system that parallels the relatively stable, hierarchical pattern that existed in feudal Europe when the Church dominated the political and social order. His view of the relationship between the natural and supernatural sides of human nature coincides with what Ernst Troeltsch calls "the ecclesiastical unity of civilization."[7] For Aquinas, the best way to achieve the human *telos* or purpose is through the Church's nurturance of Character in which the three theological virtues that exist on the supernatural side of humanity are grafted over the cardinal virtues that exist on the natural side. Aquinas' moral imagination combines the Moral Law with the Character frameworks of moral reasoning; and more than any other Christian author before or after him, he epitomizes in his seamless conceptual scheme how grace can improve nature.[8]

Next, we turn to the Reformation where we discover how Protestants continued to employ but also radically transformed the Character framework through an alternative vision of the Faith. Like all major changes that occurred during this extraordinary epoch, Luther led the way by redefining the nature of Christian vocation. Prior to the Reformation he started, Luther grew up a Catholic along with everyone else and accepted the two-tier system of religious and lay vocations that emerged in the Church shortly after the New Testament era. He joined the Augustinian order because it satisfied his desire to pursue the highest religious calling that the Church offered—the priesthood.

After 1517, Luther's thinking took a radical turn away from the vocational dualism that relegated worldly occupations to a lesser status. Eventually, he became an outspoken critic of the notion that monastic spirituality possessed greater religious value than the faithfulness of ordinary laity. He replaced the Catholic dualism with the principle of the priesthood of all believers and among Protestants effectively eliminated any sense of higher and lower callings. According to Luther, if salvation occurs by Faith alone, then it follows that all Christians stand before God as equals. What matters most is not one's occupation, but rather the faithful dedication with which one carries out its related duties.[9]

All vocations are equally worthy as religious callings. If God summons each person to righteous living in the world and not apart from it, then the need for monasteries with a separate priesthood set apart from daily life disappears. All earthly vocations are without distinction in spiritual rank, and all faithful believers can show their gratitude to God through dedication, dependability, patience, constancy, and the faithful performance of occupational obligations. In effect, Luther democratized the concept of Christian calling and removed it from clerical domination. He located the commitment to serve God through Love of neighbor in the realm of secular occupations and through the Characters of the Christians who hold them.

As Luther was separating the concept of Christian calling from clericalism, he was also moving one foot in the direction of modernity. However, his other foot remained firmly planted in the medieval structure of inherited vocations. Like his Catholic counterparts, he accepted that men would follow in their fathers' vocational footsteps and women in their mothers'. Job choice did not really exist in the largely agricultural setting of the Reformation where, as in previous centuries, occupations were transmitted to subsequent generations through family lineage. In such an agrarian economic structure, what mattered according to Luther was the manner in which Christians performed their duties irrespective of the inherited vocations into which God placed them.

Even though Luther's perspective on family centered work structures mirrored the agrarian milieu of medieval feudalism, his revision of the concept of calling was compatible with the norm of individualism that was emerging with the dawn of modernism. As industrial capitalism radically transformed virtually every aspect of post-Reformation Europe, vocational choice became a viable economic option for people who relocated from the farms to the cities. While Luther kept one foot anchored in the past, he also stepped forward, intentionally or not, toward the future. He opened the door for others to follow. John Calvin took the next step by developing a perspective on the formation of Character that contributed in no small measure to the dynamic changes that created the Modern world.

The Geneva of Calvin's time flourished like a beehive of entrepreneurial activity. More than any other Protestant Reformer, Calvin's concept of Christian calling dovetailed with the spirit of the times. As we indicated in the last Chapter, he shared many of Luther's views even though he placed greater emphasis on specific theological doctrines. Belief in predestination colored every aspect of Calvin's theology and ethical reasoning. It tilted his understanding of the development of the Christian calling toward stewardship and accountability to God.

Calvin agreed with Luther that God places all person into various vocational positions and requires that they faithfully perform their corresponding duties. Both Reformers also held that the ownership of private property is consistent with God's will. While it was commonly accepted that the accidents of birth or personal circumstances determined each individual's station in life, Calvin believed otherwise. He was convinced that from the moment of creation, before anyone had been born, God had already predetermined everyone's destiny.

Calvin stressed above all else that occupations do not exist merely to help workers make a living through their labor. Rather all economic activity in any form provides everyone, employers and employees alike, with the opportunity to serve God as faithful stewards. Christians in particular ought to seek God's glory through every vocational calling and thereby praise God for life's many blessings. When joyfully executed, economic behavior becomes a vehicle for celebrating the sovereignty of God.

Property should be viewed as a trust from God and should never be used merely to advance selfish ambitions. To become responsible stewards of their property, every Christian needs to develop the appropriate vocation-related virtues. In *Institutes of the Christian Religion,* Calvin instructs his readers to practice frugality, moderation, sobriety, honesty, humility, and abstinence in the conduct of all their worldly affairs. In like manner, they should assiduously avoid the vices of excess, vanity, ostentation, greed, dishonesty, avarice, and pride, among others. Through their diligence and expression of traits that it is desirable for hard working Christians to have, the Geneva faithful could express their glory to God for the gifts of election and eternal life.[10]

Calvin's influence quickly took root in Geneva's entrepreneurial environment because he placed accountability for virtuous behavior squarely on the shoulders of each individual. His followers perceived themselves to be personally liable for their steadfast stewardship of God given talents and possessions. Through his theology of predestination, Calvin contributed to Europe's growing democratic spirit by fostering the development of a Character disposition consistent with the prevailing ethos. In this sense, he helped shape the modern mind by stretching Luther's concept of Christian calling in the direction of individual responsibility. Ernst Troeltsch observes that Calvinism contributed to a "unique emphasis on the cultivation of independent personality, which leads to a power of initiative and a sense of responsibility for action, combined also with a very strong sense of unity for common, positive ends and values."[11]

In addition, Calvin's concept of predestination created in his followers a condition of anxiety over whether they were among God's elect. Since no one has direct access to God's mind, resolving this issue can only be inferred indirectly through behavioral clues. For Calvinists it became imperative to remain vigilant at all times and not stray from the highest moral standards of personal conduct. Max Weber refers to the Calvinist ethic as a form of worldly asceticism that leads to "systematic self control which at every moment stands before the inexorable alternative, chosen or damned."[12]

As Calvinists engaged in various entrepreneurial ventures, they accumulated vast fortunes and pumped the profits back into expanding their businesses or building new ones. In Weber's eyes, Calvin's reinterpretation of Luther's concept of the Christian calling via the doctrine of predestination created highly disciplined followers. It also led them to scrutinize the details of every action for signs of their eternal status as one of God's chosen or damned. Through hard work, frugality, sobriety, honesty, and the other character traits that comprise Calvin's ethic, they produced, earned, saved, and reinvested. As a result, they contributed to the creation of the modern urban-industrial-capitalist society.

In short, the writings of Calvin and Luther bridged two historical time periods: the fading feudalism of Medieval Europe and the emerging market place industrialism of the Modern world. Together they gave new meaning to the concept of Christian vocation. Prior to the Reformation, Christian authors who used the Character framework synthesized New Testament with Greco-Roman values. This process culminated when Aquinas combined the three theological virtues of Christianity with the four cardinal virtues of Aristotelian-Stoic philosophy. Luther, and especially Calvin, took the Character framework in a new direction.

The list of character traits that Calvin enumerated during the Reformation looked more to the future than the past. They pointed to a new kind of Christian person, one more at home in business enterprise than in philosophical discussions of ancient virtues. The Character perspectives of Paul, Origen, Ambrose, and Aquinas embodied major moral images of the New Testament, Early Christian, and Medieval eras. Luther and Calvin plowed new ground as broader social transformations called for reflecting on old traditions in light of new experiences. Together, their combined re-visioning of the Christian calling steered the Character framework toward the emerging Modern world.

Since the time of Luther and Calvin, many modern day Christians, Catholic and Protestant alike, have employed the Character approach. This should come as no surprise to Catholics who stand in a long tradition of Character Ethics that culminated in the writings of Aquinas prior to the Reformation. For centuries after his death, St. Thomas' *Summa* guided the Catholic Church and set the official standards against which its leaders measured all future theological or ethical thought. During the latter half of the twentieth century, Catholic as well as Protestant authors embraced the Character framework with renewed vigor.

During the 1960's, widespread disagreements existed between the proponents of Moral Law and Situation Ethics. At the height of this debate, the Catholic priest Robert Johann laid out the case for Character Ethics. In his view, those who favored a Moral Law perspective held that only consistent application of universal principles assured any kind of objectivity in the realm of morals. For Situationalists, the complexities of life called for making faithful or loving judgments on a case-by-case basis depending on the circumstances. According to Johann, there is a third and preferred alternative. "In the heat of their debate, both sides neglect the very ideas that might help to resolve it—those old-fashioned ideas of habit, virtue and character."[13]

Any action that is both human and moral always involves the expression of Character. Morality can never be limited simply to faithful or loving actions in specific situations or to moral codes, because first and foremost it originates in the Character of each person. The best way to bridge the gap between the two extremes is through the expression of Character and the consistency of moral choices over time. "A moral act is first of all and in its essence an act of *self-determination,* that is, an act in which the agent, beyond merely exhibiting the dispositions he has acquired through past activity, newly ratifies or modifies them, and so determines the *sort of agent* he is to be in the future."[14]

Every decision in every new situation contributes to the development of each person's habitual disposition to act in a consistent way across a broad range of circumstances. Each moral response "reinforces or weakens a habitual orientation that accords (or is at odds) with the requirements of human life, and so sets up the conditions of his future moral career."[15] At the center of Johann's approach is an image of a moral career that each person develops over an entire lifetime. It involves internalizing the kinds of virtues that it is desirable for Christians to have until they become habitual. Developing a moral career implies that a person's Character can progress so that the capacity to make moral judgments from situation to situation improves over time. "A concern for character thus looks to the concrete without getting lost in immediacy. It is mindful of universal requirements, not as external limits to personal freedom, but as really its inner accomplishment."[16]

Creating a moral career requires as much purpose and diligence as developing a vocational career. It does not happen automatically. A person becomes virtuous through the practice of virtue, by making the right moral choices and developing good habits. For Johann,

> morality is primarily a perfection of persons, not of acts; that actions are good only in relation to the goodness of persons; that this goodness of persons is a matter of habitual dispositions that have to be worked at to be acquired. Only good habits make a man good. But good habits do not just happen. They must be cultivated.[17]

Virtually all writers who use the Character framework accept Johann's view, Protestants as well as Catholics. Character development consists of internalizing desirable virtues and avoiding undesirable vices. The current author Stanley Hauerwas (b. 1940) stands squarely within this tradition. Like the Catholic Johann, the Protestant Hauerwas, whose background is Mennonite, understands that Character development occurs over the course of a lifetime. He refines Johann's insight further by distinguishing between the self-determining and non-self-determining elements involved in Character formation.

Non-self-determining elements are beyond a person's control. Self-determining elements are not. "Our character is not determined by our particular society, environment, or psychological traits; these become part of our character, to be sure, but only as they are received and interpreted in the descriptions which we embody in our intentional actions."[18] The non-self-determining elements consist of the social, natural, and historical circumstances that determine our physical and personality predispositions. Much of what we are as persons is simply given to us through birth and upbringing. We do not choose our parents, our siblings, our culture or language, our historical time period, our socioeconomic status, our political environment, our sex, race, gender, intelligence, aptitudes or other genetic features, where we reside, and so on. We are born into them. They are the "givens" of our lives, through which our Character develops.

Character emerges only as a moral agent becomes self-determining. Otherwise, Character would be little more than the effects of prior external and internal factors over which we exert no control. Character development implies the capacity for choice, which presupposes freedom. Hauerwas defines this as the qualification of our self-agency. "Our character is our deliberative disposition to use a certain range of reasons for our actions rather than others (such a range is usually what is meant by moral vision), for it is by having reasons and forming our actions accordingly that our character is at once revealed and molded."[19] Character involves intentionally making value choices and repeatedly reinforcing them. Through this process, character emerges as the "moral orientation of the self."[20]

The Church occupies a central role in the process of transforming Christians into the kinds of moral agents that Christ wants them to become and uses the Bible and tradition to identify the primary virtues that ought to comprise the self's moral orientation. The Bible also serves to define the Church's communal Character through which the Character of each Christian develops. For Hauerwas the Church, Scripture, and the development of Christian Character remain interwoven. Christian Character does not emerge in a vacuum but rather through interconnecting patterns that emphasize specific virtues and not others. Through recurring reference to Biblical stories and ethical images, Christians come to understand the character of God and thereby strive to model the development of their Character after the likeness of Christ.[21]

Along with Johann and Hauerwas, another contemporary Protestant author James M. Gustafson places character development at the center of Christian morality. Like Johann and Hauerwas he understands that traits such as consistency, predictability, reliability, loyalty, and so on are all part of the pattern of stability that constitutes Character. In Gustafson's view, the expression of Character depends on the "internalization of certain values and beliefs; there are the possibilities of habituation of motivation, and of certain dispositions toward the world, the formation of certain intentions so that persons have characteristic attitudes, or bearing toward one another and toward the world."[22]

Despite the variety of situations that individuals enter and leave during the course of any given time period, they express themselves with a high degree of consistency because their decisions about what to do emerge out of enduring patterns. There is Character stability amidst situational diversity. People act in loving ways because this is a habitual predisposition in their Characters.

> Love is so much an attitude of their wills that we expect them to do the "loving" thing in changing and differing circumstances. This "lovingness" does not come into being only on particular occasions that prompt or require a loving response; it is a readiness to respond in particular places and times in a loving way.[23]

Over time, a person's expressions of Love become intuitive and spontaneous; Gustafson's vision parallels Johann's. Becoming more loving lies at the heart of every Christian's moral career.

Gustafson also shares with Hauerwas the conviction that Character formation occurs within the context of the Church, which defines the values and commitments that are valid for Christians. Character shaping is an intentional activity that involves the transformation of the gathered community of the faithful around core Christian values, and it is purposeful in extending those values beyond the boundaries of the Church into the surrounding world. Since the Characters of people "have developed through their experiences and their convictions, the church needs to be concerned with becoming the matrix in which its values and loyalties become the marks of character."[24] The Christian community mediates God's grace as revealed in Christ by becoming the kind of people God intends for them to be; or to borrow Jeremiah's phrase, it becomes written on the heart.

We are now at the point of summarizing the Chapter. As in the case of both the Faith-Love and Moral Law frameworks, the tradition of Character Ethics sweeps across every time period from the Old Testament to the Modern world. Furthermore, like the other two, it emanates from the theological worldview set forth in the Bible. The wisdom tradition of the ancient Israelites is the starting point. Books such as Proverbs identify the kinds of traits that served as the foundation stones of Israel's communal existence. They reinforced Jewish identity and that dovetailed with their Faith in God's abiding Love for them as a chosen people and the Moral Law embedded in their Covenant.

When the Israelites drifted into disobedience, prophets such as Amos and Hosea called them to become God's people capable of making wise decisions that would secure their destiny. At the height of power, King Solomon enjoyed the reputation of being Israel's wisest King. However, even the great monarch's wisdom could not prevent the nation from sliding into rebellion against God and from splintering it into two hostile factions. As the southern Kingdom of Judah confronted catastrophe and Babylonian exile, Jeremiah soothed their fearful expectations with the consoling vision of a more hopeful future where God's Covenant would exist not only in stone but in the heart as well.

In the Synoptic Gospels, Jesus refers to the heart as the locus of all good and bad motivations. Evil emanates from the inside and leads to evil deeds on the outside. In like manner, goodness stems from good intentions. Both Jeremiah of the Old Testament and Jesus of the New Testament summarize the Character Ethics perspective in one simple and succinct moral image. The Apostle Paul envisioned an array of virtues that would accompany the transformation of Christian converts into a new creation. While Faith acting in Love comprises the core of his vision, he also includes joy, peace, patience, kindness, and so on, as hallmarks of the Christian Character.

During both the Early Christian and Medieval eras, Christian writers integrated New Testament and Greco-Roman ideas. Scholars such as

Origen and Ambrose paved the way for Aquinas, who became the Church's all-time leading synthesizer with his lists of the seven virtues (faith, hope, love, wisdom, justice, moderation, and courage) and the seven deadly sins (sloth, lust, anger, pride, envy, greed, and gluttony). More than any other, he combined Old Testament, New Testament, Aristotelian, and Stoic thought into one harmonious theological and ethical system.

The Reformation ushered in new Character Ethics images. Luther reduced the dual system of laity and religious vocations to a single vision of the Christian calling based on the doctrine of the priesthood of all believers. Calvin carried this to the next level by enumerating the kinds of traits that would enable his followers to promote the glory of God and provide clues to their eternal predestination. By emphasizing virtues such as thrift, moderation, sobriety, honesty, etc., he contributed to Europe's expanding spirit of entrepreneurship.

In the Modern world, both Catholics and Protestants have continued the Character tradition. Rather than elaborate lists of traits like their predecessors, Johann, Hauerwas, and Gustafson describe the nature of Character formation. Johann's image of the moral career captures this process well. Hauerwas and Gustafson describe both the non-self-determining and self-determining elements of character development and the important role that the Church as a moral community plays in instilling Old and New Testament virtues within its members. We would be correct in concluding that the Bible is not only the original source of the Character Ethics framework of moral reasoning. It is also the primary source through which the Church envisions and nurtures the development of the Christian Character within contemporary society.

In the next Chapter we shift to the fourth and final moral framework, which focuses on images of Justice and Liberation.

Notes

1. Barry L. Bandstra, *Reading the Old Testament: An Introduction to the Hebrew Bible,* second edition, Belmont, Cal.: Wadsworth Publishing Company, 1999, p. 394 writes, "Solomon should be considered the royal sponsor of the business of collecting and organizing family and clan wisdom. He is the one who took an official interest in it and made it the object of study and reflection."

2. See Origen's writings, "De Principiis," and "Against Celsus," in *The Ante-Nicene Fathers*, Volume IV, edited by Alexander Roberts and James Donaldson, Grand Rapids, Michigan: Wm. B. Eerdmans Publishing Company, 1977.

3. Origen, "De Principiis," *The Ante-Nicene Fathers*, Volume IV, p. 254.

4. See Ambrose, "Duties of the Clergy," in *Nicene and Post-Nicene Fathers*, Volume, X, edited by Philip Schaff and Henry Wace, New York: Christian Literature Company, 1896.

5. Denise Lardner Carmody and John Tully Carmody, *Christian Ethics: An Introduction through History and Current Issues*, Englewood Cliffs, New Jersey: Prentice-Hall, Inc., 1993, p. 67.

6. See Aquinas' *Summa Theologica* in *Basic Writings of Saint Thomas Aquinas*, edited by Anton C. Pegis, New York: Random House, 1945, Q. 61-63.

7. Ernst Troeltsch, *The Social Teaching of the Christian Churches*, Volume I, New York: Harper Torchbooks, 1960, p. 257.

8. For this reason, H. Richard Niebuhr, *Christ and Culture*, New York: Harper & Row, 1951, pp. 128-141 placed Aquinas in the category of Christ Above Culture.

9. See Martin Luther, *Concerning Christian Liberty*, translated by R. S. Grignon, in Harvard Classics, volume 36, New York: P. F. Collier & Son, 1938.

10. John Calvin, *Institutes of the Christian Religion*, edited by John T. McNeill, Philadelphia: The Westminster Press, 1960, Book III, Chapter X.

11. Troeltsch, *The Social Teaching of the Christian Churches*, Volume II, p. 619.

12. Max Weber, *The Protestant Ethic and the Spirit of Capitalism*, translated by Talcott Parsons, London: George Allen & Unwin, Ltd., 1930, p. 115.

13. Robert Johann, *Building the Human*, New York: Herder and Herder, 1968, p. 143.

14. Johann, *Building the Human*, p. 143.

15. Johann, *Building the Human*, p. 143.

16. Johann, *Building the Human*, p. 144.

17. Johann, *Building the Human*, p. 144.

18. Stanley Hauerwas, *Vision and Virtue: Essays in Christian Ethical Reflections*, Notre Dame, Indiana: Fides Publishers, 1974, p. 59.

19. Hauerwas, *Vision and Virtue*, p. 59.

20. Hauerwas, *Vision and Virtue*, p. 62.

21. See Stanley Hauerwas, *Character and the Christian Life: A Study in Theological Ethics*, San Antonio, Texas: Trinity University Press, 1985.

22. James Gustafson, *Christian Ethics and the Community*, Philadephia: Pilgrims Press, 1971, p. 169.

23. Gustafson, *Christian Ethics and the Community*, p. 169.

24. Gustafson, *Christian Ethics and the Community*, p. 172.

Chapter 6

Justice and Liberation

In this Chapter, we will direct our attention to the last of the four major ethical frameworks: Justice-Liberation. Like the hyphenated Faith-Love position, Justice and Liberation remain closely coupled in Christian Ethics. Unlike the other three major ethical traditions of Christianity, this last one is probably the least well known and most under appreciated. However, this does not diminish its importance. It is not possible to fully grasp all of the ethical dimensions of the Christian Faith apart from these two central themes. The Justice-Liberation perspective stands as an equal partner with the Faith-Love, Moral Law, and Character frameworks of moral reasoning.

As in the three previous Chapters, we start with the Old Testament where both Justice and Liberation images are woven into the very fabric of ancient Israel's theological self-understanding. First we will examine the place of Justice in the Torah and among the Jewish prophets and then tie it to God's Liberation of the ancient Israelites. The mandate for Justice is central to the Hebrew Moral Law tradition as expressed through their Covenant with God.

Deuteronomy summarizes many of the Justice stipulations that appear in the previous four books. After Moses led the Israelites from their Egyptian bondage, he guided them during their arduous journey back to the promise land. On the way he prepared them for their eventual return by announcing both the blessings and curses of the Covenant. If they obeyed, God would reward them. If not, God would punish them. In the book of Joshua, Chapter 8, Joshua places the twelve tribes of Israel around the ark of the covenant with six of them in front of Mount Gerizim and other six in front of Mount Ebal. Following Moses' instructions, he reads the Law out loud and mandates that they bind themselves to it *in perpetuity*. According to Deuteronomy, God's curse will be on anyone who violates the Ten Commandments, dishonors parents, moves a neighbor's property line, misleads the blind, deprives foreigners, orphans, and widows of their rights, commit bribery or murder, and so on. (See Joshua 8:30-35; Deuteronomy Chapters 5-11 and 27:4-5)

Earlier in Chapter 3, we indicated how from Joshua through 2 Kings, the Old Testament writers told the story of ancient Israel's rise and fall as a regional power from the perspective of the blessings and curses formula of Deuteronomy. For these authors, God eventually sent the Israelites into exile because they violated the Justice stipulations of their Covenant. Time after time the prophets pointed their accusing fingers at the growing injustice and warned the Kings and people that they courted disaster. The entire line of prophets, from Amos, Hosea, 1 Isaiah, Micah, Zephaniah, through Jeremiah, repeated the same message. They delivered their harshest criticisms as the pattern of violations deepened.

From the time of Moses until the fall of Judah, the Justice commandments of the Covenant stood as the standards of righteousness against which the Israelite prophets judged the nation. In their eyes, Israel's success as a chosen people depended on their faithfulness in fulfilling these mandates. Amos, the first of the great literary prophets, proclaimed to leaders in the north, "I saw the Lord standing beside the altar, and he said: Strike the capitals until the thresholds shake, . . . not one of them shall flee away, not one of them shall escape." (Amos 9:1) "Hate evil and love good, and establish justice in the gate." (Amos 5:16) Let justice role down like waters and righteousness like an ever flowing stream." (Amos 5:24)

The prophet Micah addressed the southern people of Judah in a similar manner. "With what shall I come before the Lord, and bow myself before God on high? Shall I come before him with burnt offerings, with calves a year old?" (Micah 6:6) The performance of ritual duties provided no substitute for Justice. God "has told you, O mortal, what is good; and what does the Lord require of you but to do justice, and to love kindness, and to walk humbly with your God?" (6:8) When the Israelite people and their Kings did not respond to the steady outpouring of prophetic warnings, the harsh consequences of God's punishment swept down on them, from north to south, with all its fury.

The combination of the Deuteronomic interpretation of Israel's history and the prophetic pronouncements allow us to see the vision of

Justice that pervaded the ancient Jewish understanding of their relationship to God through the Covenant. However, Justice does not stand by itself in the Israelite moral imagination. It is closely connected to the motif of Liberation. Both are interwoven; each one reinforces the other and together they reveal to us a rich portrait of interlocking images.

The Mosaic Covenant and the norm of Justice presuppose Liberation. Moses announced the Covenant statutes on the journey back to Canaan after he led the Israelites out of Egypt and across the Red or Reed Sea, not before.[1] The sequence of events is critical. For the twelve tribes, first came Liberation and then Justice. Or simply stated, Justice follows Liberation. Throughout the many centuries from Moses to the Joseph Maccabee, Liberation from Egyptian slavery remained the seminal event emblazoned on the shared Hebraic memory. Annually for centuries, the Jews have celebrated Passover to remember how this decisive moment forever shaped their collective identity.

The Old Testament narrative depends on God's liberating initiative on behalf of the Israelites, because without it God's promise to Abraham would have gone unfulfilled. The Jewish story of transformation never would have been told if the Israelites had perished in Egypt. Just as God's promise to Abraham preceded Israel's bondage in Egypt, Liberation from Egyptian slavery occurred prior to the Mosaic Covenant.

In a very real sense, the Biblical images of promise, Liberation, and Justice belong together: Liberation was necessary to sustain the promise, but the promise did not justify the Liberation. Liberation was the necessary precondition for the establishment of Justice, which fulfilled the promise. Without Justice, Liberation would have lacked theological or ethical meaning. God liberated the Israelites so that they could become Just, which was why God created them as a chosen people in the first place. According to the Old Testament transformation story, God chose the Jews to show the world a pathway to righteousness. This means that in the final analysis, a moral vision of Justice justified both the promise and Liberation.

The lack of Justice is what caused their continual moral corrosion and eventual political collapse in 587 B.C.E. However, national demise and expulsion from the promise land did not obliterate the memory of Liberation that the escape from Egypt had embedded in their collective consciousness. If anything, exile in Babylon created the need for an act of re-Liberation. The transforming experience of being released from the choking hand of Pharaoh was the theological image through which they interpreted subsequent moments when God delivered them from the grip of their enemies.

We cannot overstate the importance of Liberation cycles in the history of the ancient Jews and how these cycles incorporated images of Justice. When the Israelites were oppressed, God liberated them. When they were the oppressors, God punished them. However, being sent into bondage did not lead to abandonment. After their punishment, God liberated them once again and the cycle of expectation started anew.

Throughout their entire history, the foreign powers that surrounded the Israelites sought either to strip them of their uniqueness or eliminate them altogether. Even at the height of their political dominance under David and Solomon, they remained at risk; they possessed neither the size nor strength to permanently determine their destiny. When the nation divided into two kingdoms after Solomon's death, Jewish vulnerability grew until superior armies swept down from the north and forced them from the promise land.

However, their final fate was not oblivion in Babylon. In parallel to their Liberation from oppression in Egypt, God released them from their humiliating foreign exile. For the Old Testament writers, just as God chose Assyria and Babylon to punish the Israelites, God also chose Persia to liberate them. In 539 B.C.E., the Persian King Cyrus conquered the Babylonians and soon permitted the exiled Jews to return to their homeland. Under the more liberal policies of the Persian authorities, the Israelites rebuilt the Temple and renewed their Covenant faith in the land that God promised to give Abraham and his descendents.

The cycle of Liberation did not end when the Israelites returned to Jerusalem from Babylon. In 333 B.C.E., Alexander the Great and his Grecian armies conquered the Persians and imposed their power throughout the Mediterranean region. As Persian tolerance gave way to Greek intolerance, the Jewish people faced another foreign invader fiercely intent on eradicating their cultural and religious identity entirely. The controlling monarch Antiochus IV forced on them an aggressive program of Hellenization. Part of his strategy involved placing statues of the Greek gods in the Jerusalem Temple. This action, as much as any other, insulted Hebrew religious sensitivities at the deepest level.

Tyranny fueled the flames of hatred. In 164 B.C.E, Judas Maccabee and his band of Jewish followers emancipated their homeland when they drove the Greeks out of Judea and purged the Holy City of any and all polytheistic symbols and sculpture. Judas led the people of Jerusalem in celebration by re-igniting the Temple lamps to signify the return of Jewish worship and freedom from foreign domination. Like the Passover ceremony that commemorates the Moses-led escape from Egyptian slavery, Jewish leaders memorialized their release from Greek oppression through an annual festival of lights, Hanukkah. Once again, the pattern of Liberation came full circle. God had delivered them from the hands of their enemies so that they could resume their journey as a chosen people.

One hundred years later in 63 B.C.E., Pompey entered Jerusalem and exerted Roman control over the Hebrew people. Maccabean rule abruptly ended and another oppressive foreign regime returned to the region. For many Palestinian Jews, life under Roman domination remained at best an unwilling accommodation punctuated by sporadic outbursts of rebellion. The memories of former experiences of Liberation, such as escape from Egypt, return from Babylonian exile, and expulsion of the despised Greeks fueled their hope that God would free them yet another time. In 66 C.E., Jewish zealots revolted against the Roman occupation of Palestine but to no avail. Four years later, the Romans quashed their uprising. Like the Babylonian predecessors of 587 B.C.E., in 70 C.E. the Romans destroyed the Temple and expelled the Jews from Jerusalem. For the zealots, the longed-for Liberation from Roman rule ended in defeat.

However, the dream of Liberation did not die with the destruction of the Temple and dispersion of the Jews. Instead, it became transferred to the moral imagination of the Christian writers who, like their Hebrew ancestors, connected it to images of Justice. As the Old Testament era passed into the New Testament time period, Church authors transformed the Justice-Liberation tradition around their images of Jesus just as they did with the Faith-Love, Moral Law, and Character frameworks. Among these four approaches, the Justice-Liberation method of moral reasoning is the most radical. The writings that include it give special attention to the physical and social needs of the least advantaged. They call upon the rich to share their wealth with the poor; and they envision the Church as an egalitarian eschatological community where goods are held in common and distributed widely for the benefit of all.

The main New Testament source for the Justice-Liberation framework is Luke-Acts, along with occasional references to egalitarian motifs in Paul's letters. Although the Gospel of John follows the Gospel of Luke and precedes The Acts of the Apostles in the New Testament canonical order, Luke and Act exist as one continuous commentary on the life of Jesus and the growth of his Church. A single author named Luke wrote both of them.[2] More than any of the other Gospel writers, Luke explained God's movement through time as the work of the Holy Spirit; and he developed a three-stage theology of history to identify the specific time periods during which God's purposes were revealed.

In the first stage, God created the Jewish Covenant and sent the prophets to proclaim the coming of the Messiah. In the second stage, God sent Jesus to earth as the Messiah to fulfill the Old Covenant prophesies and to start a New Covenant. In the third stage, God created the Church to carry forward the New Covenant during an Interim period, the final era of history, until Jesus should come again. God accomplished all of this through the Holy Spirit, who originated the Old Covenant, guided Jesus, brought the Church into existence at Pentecost, and led disciples, apostles, and leaders like Peter and Paul on their missionary ventures throughout Palestine and Asia Minor. Like Matthew, Luke's Gospel places Jesus within the Mosaic tradition; but unlike Matthew, Luke connects Jesus to Moses through the Old Testament prophets and not the Law. For Luke, the line of the prophets starts with Moses and culminates in Jesus.[3]

Luke establishes Jesus' prophetic identity at the outset of his ministry after his baptism and temptation experiences. When Jesus returned to Nazareth, he went to the synagogue to participate in Sabbath worship. During the service, he read aloud from the Isaiah scroll. "The Spirit of the Lord is upon me, because he has anointed me to bring good news to the poor. He has sent me to proclaim release to the captives and recovery of sight to the blind, to let the oppressed go free, to proclaim the year of the Lord's favor." (Luke 4:18-19) With his synagogue proclamation, Jesus inaugurated the liberating work that his eschatological community, the Church, continued after his death. The parallel with the Old Testament is clear: Just as Moses liberated the Jews from Egypt, Jesus came to bring Justice and Liberation to the downtrodden.

Among the canonical Gospels, Matthew and Luke confer a special status on the poor in God's kingdom, but with one major difference. Matthew spiritualizes the concept of poverty and Luke does not. In the Sermon on the Mount, as recorded in Matthew, Jesus blesses "the poor in spirit, for theirs in the kingdom of heaven." (Mt. 5:3) He also blesses "those who hunger and thirst for righteousness, for they will be filled." (Mt. 5:6) Luke's renders a different interpretation of these two sayings. "Blessed are you who are poor, for yours is the kingdom of God. Blessed are you who are hungry now, for you will be filled." (Luke 6:20-21) Luke's Jesus emphasizes the immediate physical needs of the disadvantaged to whom he brings a liberating message. He comes to release the captives and let the oppressed go free. This is the language of Justice and Liberation.

From the perspective of his partiality for the poor, Luke's Gospel warns of the dangers associated with the accumulation of wealth. Some of Jesus' most challenging sayings deal with the corrosive influence that the pursuit of riches has on the human spirit. Luke records that on one occasion a devout and Law abiding rich ruler asked Jesus how to inherit eternal life. Jesus responded that he should sell everything he owned and give the proceeds to the poor. When the rich ruler became saddened at this prospect, Jesus remarked, "How hard it is for those who have wealth to enter the kingdom of God! Indeed, it is easier for a camel to go through the eye of a needle than for someone who is rich to enter the kingdom of God." (Luke 18:24-25; also see Mt. 19:24 and Mark 10:25)

Luke aims some of his harshest criticism at the complacent and wealthy rich who turn their backs on the desperate plight of the downtrodden. In the parable of the Rich Fool (12:13-21), Jesus underscores the folly of stockpiling riches and equating them with permanent security. In the story of the Rich Man and Lazarus (Luke 16:19-31), the Rich Man is the one who dies and perishes in Hades. When the Rich Man pleads with Abraham in the afterlife to send Lazarus to "dip the tip of his finger in water and cool my tongue." Abraham responds by saying that it is Lazarus who "is comforted here and you are in agony. Besides all this, between you and us a great chasm has been fixed." Luke's message to the wealthy is straightforward. Take care of the poor now or burn later. In God's kingdom, both the rich and the poor will get their just due.

Luke incorporates this same imagery into Acts through his description of an egalitarian orientation in the early Church. His account of Ananias and Sapphira offers insight into the communal sharing that was expected of the early members. Two recent converts, Ananias and his wife, Sapphira, sold a piece of property and did not give all of the earnings to the assembly of believers. Peter confronted them about holding back some of the proceeds and charged them with deception. When he accused them of allowing Satan to fill their hearts and lying to the Holy Spirit, both of them fell down and died. As a result, "Great fear seized the whole church and all who heard of these writings." (Acts 5:1-11)

Just as Jesus chose to be a servant to the needy, Luke expected the devout members of the early Church to imitate Jesus' example. Inspired by the Holy Spirit, Jesus eschewed the accumulation of wealth and gave everything he had to help the poor. So too should those who joined his eschatological community.

The Apostle Paul also focused attention on the less fortunate as he traveled throughout Asia Minor toiling to bring the word of redemption in Christ to the Gentiles. Fourteen years after he set out on his missionary ventures, he returned to Jerusalem to meet with Peter, James, and John who waited anxiously to hear about the accomplishments of this former foe of the Church. Paul reports on his meeting with the Jerusalem council in his letter to the Galatians 2:1-10 and Luke describes it in Acts 15:1-12. When Paul told the three leaders about everything that he had achieved in Jesus' name, they extended to him the "right hand of fellowship" as a sign of endorsement for his calling to the Gentiles. They threw support behind him when they heard of his plans to embark on future missionary journeys and requested only that he should remember the poor, which he expressed that he was "eager to do." (Galatians 2:9-10)

In addition to his enthusiasm to help the poor, Paul's new-creation-in-Christ theology contains egalitarian images that complement Luke's more worldly emphasis. After describing his meeting with the three Jerusalem leaders, Paul lays out the essence of Christian transformation.[4]

> In Christ Jesus you are all children of God through faith. As many of you were baptized into Christ have clothed yourself with Christ. There is no longer Jew or Greek, there is no longer slave or free, there is no longer male and female; for all of you are one in Christ Jesus. And if you belong to Christ, then you are Abraham's offspring, heirs according to the promise. (Galatians 3:26-29)[5]

In his Galatians egalitarian vision, Paul ties Christian transformation directly to the Hebrew scripture. Christ's egalitarian eschatological community fulfills the promise God gave to Abraham. God bestows an equality of righteousness on all of the faithful and frees them from the grip of the Law and the sinful ways of the old self. Christ liberates them.

Through the writings of Luke and Paul, we can discern a continuation and reinterpretation of the Justice and Liberation themes of the Old Testament. Both authors base their commitment to help the least advantaged on the example of Jesus' ministry. Luke calls upon the rich to help liberate the least advantaged from their poverty and warns that pursuing wealth can reinforce greed and selfishness. Paul adds his theological vision of a Christ-centered community of equals. Together, Luke and Paul transform the Old Testament heritage by adding an egalitarian image to the Justice-Liberation framework. Thus, by the end of the New Testament era, the four frameworks of moral reasoning in Christian Ethics were well developed and in place for future use. With the canonization of the New Testament at the end of the fourth century, all four of them became permanently embedded in the sacred Scripture.

As the dawn rose on the horizon of the Early Christian or Patristic period and the New Testament era ended, the egalitarian emphasis of Luke and Paul began to fade. The Church's missionary success outside Palestine led to continuous expansion throughout Asia Minor. This created the need for organizational structures that would help maintain and promote further growth. In response to this challenge, Church leaders created a system of male hierarchical control that concentrated authority in formal offices such as bishops, deacons, and so on. Despite his egalitarian theological imagery, the conservative rabbinical Paul contributed to this trend in a major way. The later New Testament letters of 1 and 2 Timothy and Titus, which carry Paul's name, show clear evidence of an emerging pattern that grew more formal and complex during Medieval Christendom and culminated with the male-dominated ecclesiastical unity of European Civilization.

With the ascendancy of hierarchical structures during the Early Christian and Medieval periods, the egalitarian vision of the New Testament receded into the background. It did not re-emerge with any significant force until the Reformation and Modern eras, when it became re-attached to images of Justice and Liberation, as we will discuss shortly. Prior to Reformation, writers who used the Justice-Liberation framework addressed ethical dilemmas that remained integral to Europe's agrarian-feudal system.

In spite of the gradual decline of the early Church's egalitarian vision, Church writings after the time of the New Testament continued to be inspired by Jesus' example of serving the disadvantaged. The *Didache,* which we described in Chapter 4, reminded the faithful that sharing eternity meant that they should also share everything with their brothers and sisters and call nothing their own. Clement, Peter's successor in Rome, called upon the rich to give special attention to the needs of the poor. He counseled all Christians to share their wealth to the fullest extent possible with the dispossessed members of society. As God had been generous to them, they too should show generosity to others.

With ongoing growth the Church confronted new challenges that led to important transformations in perceptions about the nature of wealth. As the number of financially successful converts increased, Christianity spread across a larger spectrum of social classes. Because Jesus had advised the rich ruler to sell everything and give the earnings to the poor, many upper strata Christians wondered whether their salvation depended on divesting themselves of all worldly holdings. As time passed, this question grew in importance and the pressure for a response from Church leaders rose. At the end of the second century, Clement of Alexandria addressed this concern directly when he published a treatise entitled, "Who Is the Rich Man That Shall Be Saved?"[6]

In this writing, Clement refers specifically to the story of the rich young ruler and cites Jesus' metaphor of the camel passing through the eye of a needle. Clement maintains that Jesus' words do not imply literally that rich persons cannot enter the kingdom of heaven. Wealth *per se* does not place the rich ruler in jeopardy. Rather, his idolatrous attachment to the pursuit of wealth does. His inner spiritual condition blocks him from entering God's kingdom. His desire to accumulate material possessions for himself alone without caring for the plight of the less fortunate endangers his prospects for eternal life. For Clement, Christian spirituality calls upon the wealthy to care for the needy.

The importance of this transformation of attitude toward the possession of wealth cannot be overstated. Clement opened the Church doors to worldly accommodation and moved the Christian moral imagination in the direction of embracing more and more members of society. This visionary extension coincided with Christianity's steady expansion throughout the Greco-Roman world and paralleled Origen's synthesis of Christian, Jewish, and Stoic thought. By the start of the third century after Jesus' birth, Origen and Clement had positioned Christianity for wider acceptance among well-educated and wealthy citizens. The former demonstrated the compatibility of theology and philosophy, while the latter reminded rich converts to act justly toward the poor.

The writings of Clement provide clear evidence of the distance the Church had traveled, both geographically and socially, since its humble start in Palestine two centuries earlier. Even though the more radical Liberation and equalitarian visions of Luke and Paul grew fainter by the end of the New Testament era, during the Early Christian or Patristic period the image of Justice persisted as one of the Church's major moral mandates, as the following example illustrates. After Constantine gained control of the Roman Empire as its first Christian King at the onset of the fourth century, he hired the well-known writer Lactantius to tutor his son. This placed Lactantius in the privileged position of having access to the eyes and ears of the Emperor.

Lactantius addressed his primary writing, *The Divine Institutes,* to his personal friend the King and advised him that he could not achieve the highest good in life through philosophy, political power, or earthy possessions. Rather, he could attain his soul's everlasting goodness only through service and the worship of God: "to serve God is nothing else than to maintain and preserve justice by good works." God is the divine parent of all, and service to God means service to all. This requires of everyone, and especially of an Emperor who is in a privileged position, "to share the bounties of the common God and Father with those who do not possess them; to injure no one, to oppress no one, not to close his door against the stranger, nor his ear against a suppliant but to be bountiful, beneficent, and liberal. . . . This truly is justice."[7] Although separated by more than a century, Lactantius' writings paralleled those of Clement. Both authors exhorted Church members everywhere from the Emperor on down, especially wealthy and powerful Christians, to bring more Justice, and thus goodness, into the world by providing for the needs of the poor.

As the Medieval era came into its own after the fall of Rome in 410, the ethical visions that Clement and Lactantius advanced during the Patristic period guided the Church's developing moral imagination. By the mid-1200's, Aquinas synthesized into his grand Moral Law-oriented *Summa* the many levels and complex interconnections of Europe's feudal system of ecclesiastical unity. In a very real sense, his writings reflected the social order that functioned from the top on down under the control of Popes and Kings. It operated as an integrated hierarchical structure in which the Church nurtured the moral sensitivities of the civilization it helped create and in time came to dominate. Justice for the poor rested on the largesse of the rich and powerful.

Within a few decades after Aquinas' death in 1274 at the height of Medieval Christendom, a radically different image of society began to emerge. It started with Marsilius of Padua (1280-1343 C.E.), who introduced the notion of popular sovereignty as a more desirable political form than governance by Kings and Popes.[8] Marsilius agreed with

Aquinas that human beings are social in nature and unite into communities in order to realize the benefits that cooperation brings. All societies experience periods of social stability, according to Marsilius; but sooner or later they all disintegrate into open hostilities when warring factions compete against each other for political control. As the chaos of warfare increases, so do the injustices that victorious groups inflict on the vanquished. Even though social calm reappears with the cessation of hostilities, it is never permanent. In due course, the cycle of injustice and disintegration always returns.

Marsilius wanted to end this cycle or reduce the frequency of its recurrence. He believed that the states exists of insure long-term social stability and set the standards of Justice, but he remained skeptical that the structures of monarchial and papal control provided the best way to achieve this. Instead he placed greater confidence in the ability of ordinary people to determine their own future course of action and to create the laws by which they would be governed. He trusted that commoners more than Kings could create a social system that would secure the peace, establish Justice, and sustain long-term social stability at the same time.

During fourteenth century feudal Europe, Marsilius' image of popular sovereignty was truly revolutionary because it struck at the heart of the monarchical order and threatened those who controlled it. Marsilius opened to door to a new image of social organization. He helped stimulate the democratic impulse by claiming that social stability could be served better through popular sovereignty. In effect, he re-connected an egalitarian vision with Justice and set the stage for developments that appeared later during the Reformation and Modern eras.

Initially the idea of popular sovereignty lacked universality because Marsilius applied it only to property owners. He excluded many groups such as women, slaves, criminals, and others. Over time, however, this embryonic democratic impulse stretched beyond property owners and inspired other groups who demanded the right to full participation in the processes that determined their future. As Medieval Christendom moved closer to the Reformation, the image of Justice as *noblesse oblige* within an agrarian hierarchical system was becoming transformed. Visions of equality that had remained out of sight for centuries started re-surfacing in the moral imagination. As the pace of change quickened, Europe stood on the edge of creating a radically different kind of democratic society from which there would be no retreat. In time, the call for Liberation would also make its reappearance.

The new egalitarian momentum that Marsilius' writings fostered during the latter phase of the Medieval era erupted into full blown, although short-lived, similar initiatives during the Reformation. The peasants' revolt in Germany plus the Levellers and Diggers groups in England demonstrated that the new energy that Luther released did not stop at the doctrinal level. These three dramatic movements comprised the radical wing of the Reformation. Even though they stood outside the mainstream changes that Luther and Calvin introduced into the Church, they contributed to the steady accumulation of moral images that an equality-oriented Justice and Liberation framework incorporates.

Thomas Muntzer, leader of the failed German peasants' revolt in 1525, transformed Luther's image of Christian liberty into Christian Liberation, which aroused Luther's ire and eventual condemnation. Through the doctrine of the priesthood of all believers, Luther envisioned that all the faithful stand as equals in heaven. Muntzer revolted in order to make them equals on earth as well. He carried Luther's ideas beyond where Luther intended to take them. Muntzer hoped to bring economic relief to the poor in his unsuccessful attempt to capture and communize the royal properties. Despite his failure, the peasants' insurrection brought together in radical combination ideas of Justice, Liberation, and equality.

To justify his revolution, Muntzer invoked Old Testament images of Daniel and Moses whom he considered liberators of the poor. He championed Jesus as the New Testament sword bearer who came to clean up a corrupt Christendom. In his "Sermon Before the Princes," he reminded the nobility that like Jesus he did not come to bring peace. He instructed the peasants on how to treat those who hindered his revolutionary aspirations. "Get them out of the way and eliminate them, unless you want to be ministers of the devil rather than of God, as Paul calls you (Rom. 13:4)."[9]

Even though the nobility quickly quashed the peasants' revolt and executed many of its followers, including its leader, nonetheless Muntzer's far-reaching image of economic Liberation for the poor presaged many radical social movements of the Modern world. Within the hierarchical structures of feudal Europe, the Church associated Justice with charitable giving, especially by the clergy and privileged classes. Muntzer stretched the idea of Justice beyond this limited form of benevolence, which he considered incorrigibly corrupt. He envisioned a transformation of the entire social order, which would directly benefit the least

advantaged. While his violence begot violence against him and his followers, nonetheless he helped paint a new portrait of Justice and Liberation that viewed society from the impoverished bottom up and not merely
from the wealthy top down.

Both Marsilius and Muntzer left a legacy that reappeared later as the
Reformation migrated to the British Isles. By the 1530's, the protest
movement that Luther launched in Germany in 1517 spread to England,
where Henry VIII broke from Catholicism and created his own Church
in order to secure a divorce that the Pope refused to grant him. After
more than two decades of Protestant-Catholic conflict, in 1559 Queen
Elizabeth I established Anglicanism as Britain's official state Church.
Nearly a century later in the 1640's and 1650's, the Reformation's radical wing surfaced once again in the form of the lesser known Levellers
and Diggers. The Levellers followed in the footsteps of Marsilius and
the Diggers in those of Muntzer. The Levellers advocated reorganizing
society around democratic principles, and the Diggers promoted collectivizing land for the common good. Unlike Muntzer, however, the Diggers remained nonviolent in the pursuit of this goal.

The Levellers derived their name from the vision that stood at the
center of their moral imagination. They sought to "level" the political
process by increasing the voice of ordinary people through a system of
elected representatives. Even though their movement lasted only three
years from 1646-1649, the Levellers stood squarely within the Justice-
Liberation framework. During these three years, their main leaders, John
Lilburne, William Walwyn, and Richard Overton, pressed their case for
the priority of the English Parliament over the Monarchy. They spoke
out for the priority of elected representation over inherited privilege,
even though like Marsilius they restricted their support of egalitarian
ideals to men and property owners.

They advocated tolerance for religious diversity, which their leadership reflected. Lilburne came out of a Calvinist background and converted to Quakerism. Overton remained a Baptist for life. They stood
outside the religious mainstream and supported an anti-clerical position.
They called for the separation of church and state and for the abolition of
a state supported church. They welcomed religious diversity and championed the right of individuals to worship according to their own conscience. According to Joseph Frank, "The Levellers preached the de-
centralization of religion, not its official subordination. The free exercise
of religion, unimpeded by clerical or magisterial interference, was, in

fact, one of the chief areas in which the individual in their brave new world could exercise his own genius inviolably and fully."[10] As Marsilius did in his time, the Levellers pointed toward a new vision of the future during theirs.

Like the Levellers, the English Diggers also imagined a different way of organizing society. Unlike the Levellers, however, they aimed their energies at the economy and not the political structures. The Diggers adopted goals similar to those of Muntzer and his peasant followers, although they eschewed violence as the means to achieve them. Their motto remained "Freedom is not won neither by the sword nor gun."[11] As the Levellers movement began to wane in 1649, the Diggers began calling themselves the True Levellers. Unlike Muntzer, the Diggers did not seize private land owned by the nobility; instead, they squatted on a common area called St. George's Hill. They acquired their name when they began to "dig" and spread fertilizer with the intent of collectivizing the land and distributing the fruits of their labors equally among all followers.

They envisioned, as had Muntzer, that God gave the earth for all to share as a common treasury. They opposed private ownership of property and the enclosure of public lands by the privileged members of society. The main leader of the Diggers, Gerrard Winstanley, claimed that like the Apostle Paul during the New Testament time he received direct revelations from God who instructed him and his followers to "work together; eat bread together; declare this all abroad. Israel shall neither take hire, nor give hire."[12] Inspired by divine revelation, the Diggers went in pursuit of a new moral vision, a "family of equals."

Winstanley viewed economic inequality as a degrading social force that created feelings of superiority among the rich who possessed property and inferiority among the poor who owned none. His ethical zeal sprang from his deep spirituality. He spoke of creation as "the clothing of God" and of "Christ as the true and faithful Leveller." He quoted Biblical prophecies that trumpeted the triumph of the "despised ones of the earth" against the rich who would one day "weep and howl." Like many passionate reformers, he was attracted to the images of tribulation depicted in Revelations and foresaw the dramatic end of the world in the Second Coming of Christ "ere many years wheel about."[13]

Like their contemporaries the Levellers, the nonviolent Diggers movement was short lived as public authorities eventually removed them from the land. However, along with the Levellers, they shared much in common. Like Marsilius, the Levellers defended democracy as the means of transforming society through popular participation in the political process. Like Muntzer, the Diggers championed a new economic image of community based on the common ownership of property. Together, they saw themselves as liberators from political and economic bondage, inspired by a vision of egalitarian Justice.

As the Reformation came to an end, dynamic forces of change continued to transform the agrarian feudal system into the modern industrial world. Growth in the use of the Justice-Liberation framework of moral reasoning paralleled this transformation as the contributions of Marsilius, Muntzer, the Levellers, and the Diggers make clear. As we indicated in Chapter 1, this framework differs from the other three by addressing ethical issues that are related more directly to group processes and structures rather than to personal moral development. There is little doubt that the Modern world has witnessed a steady growth of Justice-Liberation visions that began to surface in the late Medieval and Reformation eras, especially as societies everywhere underwent rural to urban transformations during the past two centuries.

The Justice-Liberation framework appears most frequently in the writings of Christian ethicists who address issues related to the modern political and economic order and to the struggles of oppressed groups around the world to gain freedom from unjust conditions. For the remainder of this Chapter, we will describe some of the important insights of Catholics and Protestants who have concentrated on Justice and Liberation issues. In particular, we will examine relevant Catholic encyclicals and the Social Gospel contributions of Walter Rauschenbusch. We will also turn our attention to the writings of Reinhold Niebuhr and the Liberation Theology movement of the latter third of the twentieth century. Then we will conclude the Chapter with an overall summary.

Since the end of the nineteenth century, the Catholic Church has repeatedly addressed important issues related to the status of labor under the conditions of modern capitalism and to the role of the state in securing justice for the working class. Unlike the conservative stance on human sexuality and procreation, Catholic leaders have consistently sided with progressive forces in addressing pressing needs created by modern capitalism. In 1891 C.E. Pope Leo XIII published *Rerum novarum* in which he supported the right to private property and called upon employers to provide workers with a just wage, so that they could care for themselves and their families.[14]

The Pope rejected collectivist images like those of Muntzer and the Diggers. He also refused to accept Marxism and radical collectivist solutions to the class problems engendered by industrial capitalism. While *Rerum novarum* did not call for support of labor unions, it did envision that the concepts of the common good and human dignity should guide the development of the modern economy and not merely the impersonal forces of the market place.

Leo XIII looked to the state to help solve problems that a strictly *laissez faire* form of capitalism created. At the same time, *Rerum novarum* did not endorse democracy as a preferred political means of intervening on behalf of the workers. The Pope continued support for a hierarchical approach; and he called for government to operate by the principle of subsidiarity, by which he meant that the state should address only those problems that could not be solved at a lower level. Thus, by the end of the nineteenth century, the Catholic Church made clear that public authority could be used to help improve the material conditions of life for struggling laborers.

The Popes who followed Leo XIII continued his economic and political views through the middle of the twentieth century. With the arrival of Pope John XXIII and Vatican II, 1962-1965, some significant changes began to appear. To commemorate the seventieth anniversary of *Rerum novarum,* in 1961 the Pope reaffirmed support for private property, a just wage, human dignity, and the principle of subsidiarity in his encyclical *Mater et magistra.*[15]

In *Pacem in terris,* 1963, Pope John XXIII shifted away from the Catholic Church's historical defense of the principle of hierarchy and embraced democracy.[16] In this encyclical, the Pope held that all people have a right to democratic participation in government, and he called for the creation of an effective world governing body. Vatican II brought other changes that fostered greater participation of lay people in the life of local congregations and converted the administration of the Mass from Latin to vernacular languages. The principle of popular sovereignty that Marsilius and the Levellers advocated centuries earlier found its way into in the papal encyclicals.

Pope Paul VI replaced John XXIII after his death in 1963, and in 1971 he issued *Octagesimo adveniens.*[17] This encyclical introduced the radical image of God's preferential treatment of the poor, which became a rallying cry for Liberation theologians, as we will soon discuss. During a period of eighty years from 1891 to 1971, the Catholic Church positioned itself as one of the principle proponents of the Justice-Liberation framework of moral reasoning. Starting with Leo XIII and continuing through Paul VI, papal leadership consistently applied Justice and Liberation images to ethical dilemmas that modernity and industrialism created. Catholic leaders sided with the poor and repeatedly called for an end to economic oppression. Gradually, they embraced the principle of democracy as the basis for universal political participation.

Like their Catholic counterparts, many Protestant writers used the Justice-Liberation framework to address the moral dilemmas of modern industrialism, especially those who identified with the Social Gospel theology that emerged after the American Civil War of the 1860's. The movement peaked between 1890 and 1940, and many of its authors focused on the same ethical issues that the papal encyclicals addressed. Walter Rauschenbusch (1861-1918) stood out as one of the Social Gospel's principle interpreters. Prior to joining the Rochester Theological Seminary in 1897, he spent eleven years ministering in the slums of New York City where he confronted many of the horrendous slum conditions that capitalism created. The urban misery that market competition left in its wake, along with the Darwinian survival of the fittest philosophy that justified it, appalled him.

Rauschenbusch accepted the structural view of social problems and traced the moral dilemmas of modern society to injustices in the market place. While the captains of industry enjoyed handsome corporate rewards and took the lion's share of profits, low pay wageworkers lived in squalor and earned barely enough to keep their families together. He refused to blame the poor for their penury or to label them as lazy. He rejected the explanation that New York's harsh poverty could be explained by resorting to the image of personal sin. Rather, for Rauschenbusch, capitalism caused New York's cruel inequalities, which he categorized as social sin. Like many theologians of the Social Gospel movement, he asserted that eliminating urban poverty required altering the economic arrangements that created it.

Unlike the Catholic encyclicals, Rauschenbusch and many Social Gospel Christians advocated a socialist solution to the problem of urban poverty. Both Catholics and Protestants shared a common vision of Justice, but they differed on how to achieve it. The Popes supported the principle of private property, but Rauschenbusch and his followers rejected it. Despite this difference, Catholics and Protestants alike staunchly opposed Marxism and its atheist-materialist-autocratic philosophy. Unlike Catholicism, which grounded its Justice convictions in Aquinas' natural law theology, Rauschenbusch based his support for democratic socialism on an ethical image of the Kingdom of God that the German theologians Albrecht Ritschl (1822-1889) and Adolf Harnack (1851-1930) articulated.

Social Gospel writers like Rauschenbusch employed the Kingdom image to depict a moral society founded on the principle of the intrinsic worth of each person and common good will. Unlike Paul, Augustine, Luther, and Calvin, they were optimists about human nature. Like other socialists of their day, they shared the conviction that evil outcomes stem from evil institutions and not from innate corruptions of the human will. Capitalism causes greed, and greed engenders gross economic disparities that produce slums. They lived by the motto: Change institutions that create greed and social sin will disappear. Human goodness remains repressed beneath the capitalist struggle for survival. Eliminate the source of repression by socializing the factory system and goodness will start flowing into society.

Motivated by the Kingdom vision, Rauschenbusch believed that any society could be measured morally by the degree to which it was becoming "Christianized." In 1912, he confidently wrote that America had made considerable progress in Christianizing the family, church, education, and political democracy.[18] Powerful Kingdom forces had already changed these institutions for the better. Economics remained the last social holdout. Narrow self-interests dominated the motives of industrial leaders rather than concern for the general welfare. Only socialism could alter the horrible inequalities that capitalism generated because it could convert cutthroat competition into collective cooperation. For Rauschenbusch, socialism would result in Christianizing the last unconverted structure of the Modern world, which in turn would bring more goodness, in this case Justice, into the social order.

By the end of the nineteenth century, the liberal spirit of optimism shared by Rauschenbusch and other Social Gospel advocates prevailed throughout Europe and the United States. In 1900 many looked forward to the next one hundred years as the Christian century, a time when the coming Kingdom that Jesus proclaimed would finally arrive on earth. By 1940, a mere four decades later, this expectation had all but disappeared. After the brutalities of World War I and the rise of Communism and Fascism, the Social Gospel assumption about the innate goodness of humanity lost its credibility. The times called for a new moral vision that could account more profoundly for the depths of human evil.

By the middle of the twentieth century, Christian Realism superseded the Social Gospel as the main theological template for interpreting these dramatic global transformations. The Social Gospel left a rich residue of images regarding the social nature of sin. While Christian Realists rejected the naivety about human nature, they shared the Social Gospel's passion for Justice. In the midst of changing world conditions, Reinhold Niebuhr (1892-1971) emerged as the most influential Christian Realist of his generation. While serving as a new pastor in Detroit during the 1920's in the shadow of the Ford Motor Company, like Rauschenbusch had done earlier in New York, Niebuhr observed first hand capitalism's harsh inequalities as well as the horrors of Hitler and Stalin.

As the young Niebuhr searched his Social Gospel assumptions for an explanation into the root causes of human greed and evil, he found them lacking. During the mid-1930's he briefly embraced the socialist alternative on his pathway to Christian Realism, which he first presented in his 1939 Gifford Lectures and then maintained for the rest of his life.[19] His greatest contribution lay in his ability to grasp how human beings could soar to incredible heights of goodness and yet plunge into the pit of moral degradation.

Niebuhr's Christian Realism is best described as a paradoxical approach to problem of Justice. Twentieth century European Neo-orthodox theologians like Karl Barth (1886-1968) inspired Niebuhr to think in new ways, just as nineteenth century European liberal theologians influenced Rauschenbusch. The theological images of Neo-orthodoxy nurtured Niebuhr's moral imagination and gave him new insights into understanding the tensions inherent in the human condition, especially the capacity for both good and evil. He recognized that Christians and others often divide into optimists and pessimists in their perceptions of human nature and destiny; but he refused to accept one without the other. His ingenuity lay in his ability to see the tensions and ironies that interconnected good and evil.

The human potential for both good and evil stems from self-transcendence, which presupposes human freedom. According to Niebuhr; this endows everyone with the ability to make specific moral choices among alternative possibilities. As human beings, we exist as the only species that can think about our origins and destiny, place in the universe, and purpose in life. We can imagine unlimited possibilities and project perfect worlds. At the same time, we know ourselves as biological creatures that will die some day like all other living things. We experience pain, suffering, disease, old age, injustice, and maltreatment at the hands of others.

Niebuhr believed that the finite side of our human nature produces in us an unspoken anxiety that we seek to overcome by creating personal, racial, religious, economic and political systems that will protect us from our finitude. We trust that the cultural and material artifacts of own making will keep us secure and safe from harm. We rely on our own capacities rather than on the Love of the God who created us. Even though our self-transcendence gives us the option of turning to God in Faith, inevitably we do not. Instead, we yield to the temptation to trust ourselves above all else. We possess the freedom to follow God's will, but we live with the illusion that we can protect our future against all potential misfortune by human-will alone. This is the very essence of our sin.

For Niebuhr, an image of persistent human sinfulness enabled him to move beyond the Social Gospel's shallow optimism that left his generation unprepared for the harsh inhumanities of the twentieth century. By the early 1930's his writings started to signal movement away from the Social Gospel. He needed deeper insights. In 1932 he wrote *Moral Man and Immoral Society*[20] in which he began to lay out a vision that he eventually incorporated into his Christian Realism in 1939. In this book, Niebuhr observed that all humans succumb to the temptations of sin, but groups more than individuals remain particularly vulnerable. Nations, races, corporations and other large collectivities pursue their own self-aggrandizement even if it leads to inflicting moral abuse on others. From the perspective of its impact on society as a whole, social sin is far more catastrophic than personal sin.

Niebuhr criticized religious liberals for being naïve and sentimental in the face of Nazism and Stalinism. He rejected the belief that pacifism or Love alone could eradicate their horrendous sinfulness. At the same time, he did not swing to the opposite pole of cynicism because he recognized that evil actions could be offset by the opposite tendency toward human goodness. From the perspective of Christian Realism, Niebuhr envisioned that proximate Justice, although not perfect, could be established through the creation of power balances between competing groups.

Despite his overriding interest in Justice and the role power plays in society, Niebuhr made room in his theology for Love's creative possibilities, but with limitations. He believed that human beings could achieve a higher level of loving self-sacrifice through interpersonal relationships that through group interaction, where the highest form of moral development would always be restricted to Justice. In his typical paradoxical manner he claimed that Love could make Justice more just and prevent it from becoming more unjust. He considered it a dangerous form of wishful thinking to imagine that the need for Justice would some day disappear; and he did he accept that the Kingdom of God would ever appear in history as the Social Gospel writers envisioned. He called this an impossible possibility because as long as people remain sinful, Justice and power balancing will be necessary to keep the predatory strong from preying on the vulnerable weak.

More than in any other arena, he aimed his paradoxical views at politics where he exerted his greatest influence. He wrote in his 1944 book on the nature of political behavior, *The Children of Light and the Children of Darkness,* that democracy was possible because of the human capacity for good but also necessary because the capacity for evil.[21] For Niebuhr, the Social Gospel completely lacked any real understanding of tensions involved in human nature, which he sought to rectify through Christian Realism. Just as freedom and finitude are paradoxically related to each other, so are good and evil as well as Justice and Love.

Despite the disagreements that existed between the Social Gospel and Christian Realism, an image of creating greater social Justice motivated both. Rauschenbush sought to Christianize economic structures and Niebuhr envisioned that fairness would increase through power sharing among the world's nations and in management-labor-government relationships. On balance, little doubt remains that the Social Gospel and Christian Realism helped forge many of the broad structures of Justice during the twentieth century and benefited millions of people. They also laid the foundation for the final expression of the Justice-Liberation framework in the last third of the twentieth century and prepared the way for the twenty-first.

By the 1960's Christian Realism started losing its grip just as the Social Gospel had done decades earlier. Two main reasons contributed this decline. First, during the middle third of the twentieth century, the once mighty colonial empires of England, France, and other Western countries began declining as the subjugated nations of Asia, Africa and South America threw off foreign domination and established their own political independence. Country after country rejected the injustices of the colonial system and called for Liberation from external oppression. Second, in the industrial nations of the West, minorities and women rose in protest against unfair social arrangements that systematically excluded them from full participation in the economic, political and social benefits of their societies.

Despite the contributions of both the Social Gospel and Christian Realism, the door of Justice remained closed for many individuals and groups. While Christian Realism helped establish greater Justice, it also contained the seeds of its own limitations. Someone like Niebuhr would appreciate this irony. If all structures of Justice remain proximate, then eventually they will need to be changed to allow for greater Justice. However, by itself the pursuit of greater Justice does not guarantee its achievement because the level of Justice that has already been gained might decrease. In sum, no guarantees exist that the desire for more Justice will necessarily produce it.

Christian Realists had struggled mightily to establish structures of Justice in industry and during the Second World and Cold Wars. As a result of this concentration of effort, they possessed limited awareness of the injustices that many groups continued to suffer because of their enduring exclusion from those arrangements. In a very real sense, success in achieving proximate Justice also embodied, as Niebuhr would say, imperfect Justice and continuing injustices. By the 1960's, the doors of Justice that the Social Gospel and Christian Realism wedged open began to swing ever more widely.

During the last third of the twentieth century, excluded peoples found their voice by combining previous visions of Justice with the call for Liberation. They reunited in a dramatic way the Justice-Liberation images that appeared in the Old and New Testaments, became separated during the Patristic period, and began to reemerge during the late Medieval and Reformation eras. Just as Christian Realism compensated for the limitations of the Social Gospel, Liberation Theology moved beyond some of the shortcomings of Christian Realism.

The central focus of the late twentieth century Liberation perspective was on God's preferential treatment of the poor. Both Catholic and Protestant writers from the United States and other countries drew heavily on this image. As we have already mentioned, this language appears in

Pope Paul VI's 1971 encyclical *Octagesimo adveniens*. In particular, people of color, oppressed groups in developing countries, and women embraced this method of moral reasoning in order to express their dissatisfaction with traditional theologies they claimed embody the biases of privileged white males from Western countries.

All Liberation writers share a common framework. They view Justice and Liberation from the bottom up. That is to say, they always begin with specific conditions of injustice as experienced by oppressed groups that occupy the bottom rung of the social ladder. They possess a moral bias toward the disadvantaged on whom oppressors impose all manner of hardships and maltreatment. They critique the cultural and structural supports that reinforce this oppression and call for a dramatic reordering of society. By using images from both the Old and New Testaments, their goal is to set the "captives free" and bring greater Justice into the world.

James Cone's book, *Black Power and Black Theology*, epitomizes the Justice-Liberation framework of moral reasoning and incorporates all of its main characteristics. This milestone work published in 1969 departs in major ways from the central concerns of earlier Christian Realists. "Black Power, even in its most radical expression, is . . .Christ's central message to twentieth-century America."[22] Cone issues a radical demand to eliminate all forms of injustice against African-Americans. "The work of Christ is essentially a liberating work, directed toward and by the oppressed. Black Power embraces that very task."[23] He invokes the Exodus story in Old Testament, the words of the prophets, and the liberating presence of Jesus in the New Testament to support his clarion call.

Cone aims his harshest rhetoric at those who depict Christ with white skin, wavy brown hair, and blue eye. He substitutes a radically different image by associating Black Power with Christ as the liberating Lord. For white people, to find Christ "with big lips and kinky hair is as offensive as it was for the Pharisees to find him partying with tax collectors. But whether whites want to hear it or not, *Christ is black, baby,* with all of the features which are so detestable to white society."[24]

Blackness symbolizes African-American oppression and Christ identifies with the oppressed. "The event of Christ tells us that the oppressed blacks are his people because, and only because, they represent who he is."[25] Cone does not restrict the reality of oppression to skin color only. "Being black in America has very little to do with skin color. To be black means that your heart, soul, your mind, and your body are where the dispossessed are."[26] Nonetheless, his goal is not Liberation in general but Liberation for African-American in particular. "The goal of Black Theology is to prepare the minds of blacks for freedom so that they will be ready to give all for it. Black theology must speak *to* and *for* black people as they seek to remove the structures of white power which hover over their being, stripping it of its blackness."[27]

Cone's application of the Justice-Liberation framework to Black Power and African-American oppression mirrors the approach used by other Christian writers. Many Liberation voices have emerged from other oppressed groups. Letty Russell writes, "Christian women make use of the ideology of women's liberation, Black liberation theology owes much of its perspective on reality to the ideology of the black-liberation movement. Many Latin Americans look to some socialist ideology to provide helpful conceptual tools for change."[28]

As the Liberation momentum took root in multiple sub-populations of disadvantaged people, it produced a plethora of angry voices that demanded an end of all forms of discrimination. Inevitably, this raised questions about the long-term relationship between oppressors and oppressed. At the heart of the matter lies the concern over whether the Christian Liberation image can stretch beyond the immediate needs of specific groups and rise to the level of envisioning Justice throughout the whole social order rather than for only narrow segments of it. It comes down to whether Liberation means merely reversing patterns of oppression or reconciling oppressors and oppressed.

Cone moves toward a larger vision of Liberation when he writes, "Christ, in liberating the wretched of the earth, also liberates those responsible for the wretchedness."[29] Christian feminist Rosemary Ruether builds on this more encompassing perspective. When oppressed groups initiate revolutionary change, they must confront the question of how to deal with oppressors. They run the risk of dehumanizing the oppressors in the same way that the oppressors dehumanize them. This is understandable given the hatreds that revolutionary subgroups feel toward dominant groups. However, according to Ruether, "One cannot dehumanize the oppressors without ultimately dehumanizing oneself, and aborting the possibilities of the liberation movement into an exchange of roles of oppressor and oppressed."[30]

Ruether remains acutely aware that oppressor groups will defend their privileges against bottom up social change movements and will falsely identify the structures that they control with the "Kingdom of Righteousness." They will also seek to portray the oppressed as the "evil ones." The responsibility not to demonize the opposition falls on the shoulders of both the oppressor and oppressed or social conflict will lead either to a continuation of the pattern of oppression or only to power reversal. "All theologies of liberation, whether done in a black or feminist or a Third World perspective, will be abortive of the liberation they seek, unless they finally go beyond the apocalyptic, sectarian model of the oppressor and the oppressed."[31]

Ruether recognizes that this is no easy task; but for those who call for Justice for oppressed people everywhere, inclusiveness should stand as their cornerstone image. "The oppressed must rise to a perspective that affirms a universal humanity as the ground of their own self-identity, and also to a power for self-criticism. The alienated oppressor must learn what it means to be truly responsible for whom and what he is."[32] Liberation for all cannot be achieved unless both oppressors and the oppressed abolish their mutual hatreds. Thus, in Ruether's view, even for those Christians who use the Justice-Liberation framework for the purpose of demanding radical social transformations, reconciliation and not reversal should guide their moral visions.

We are now in a position to conclude this Chapter with an overall summary. As with the Faith-Love, Moral Law, and Character frameworks of moral reasoning, we began our discussion of the Justice-Liberation tradition with the Old Testament. The stories of Moses and the Liberation of the Israelites from Egyptian slavery provide the core images of this framework. Liberation kept alive God's promise to Abraham and gave the ancient Hebrews the opportunity to progress toward the goal of creating a Just society. The Mosaic Covenant defined God's Justice expectations for the entire Jewish community. Many cycles of Liberation characterized their history as they confronted nations that sought to enslave them, especially the Babylonians, Greeks, and Romans.

During the time of the New Testament, Christian writers transformed the Old Testament image of Liberation by applying it to Jesus. Luke's Jesus proclaims release to the captives and brings good news to the poor. Luke called upon the rich to act justly toward the disadvantaged members of society by sharing their bounty. He warned about the corrosive effects of greed on the human spirit. The Apostle Paul always remembered the poor in his missionary travels. Although his conservative side helped promote the emerging male hierarchical patterns of the early Church, he also envisioned an eschatological community of equals as Christ's new creation.

Concern for Justice continued well beyond the New Testament era. As Christianity expanded throughout the ancient Roman Empire, many well off citizens joined the Church. During the Early Christian or Patristic period, Clement of Alexandria reassured the rich that the possession of wealthy *per se* did not jeopardize their chance to attain eternal life, although their idolatrous attachment to it would. Lactantius counseled King Constantine that he could assure his soul's everlasting goodness through Justice and the performance of positive works. Together Clement and Lactantius instructed the Church leaders and fostered a charitable impulse among the nobles who controlled Europe's feudal order.

During the Medieval and Reformation eras, Marsilius and the Levellers began envisioning new democratic procedures for reordering society, which would enable citizens to govern from the bottom up rather than Popes and Royals from the top down. Muntzer and the Diggers sought to create a new communal economic order based on the common sharing of all the goods of the earth, even though the Diggers eschewed violence as the means of achieving it. Although short lived, these initiatives introduced egalitarian and Liberation images into the hierarchical structures of Medieval Europe and foreshadowed many of the radical changes that occurred in the Modern world.

By the nineteenth century, the newly emerging capitalist order pitted the wealthy factory owners against the impoverished mass of workers who inhabited the urban slums. The times called for a new vision of Justice. For more than eight decades, Catholic Popes issued successive encyclicals that reminded industrial leaders of their responsibility to end exploitation and restore human dignity to laborers by providing them with a just wage. Protestant Social Gospel writers like Raushenbusch joined the Popes in seeking ways to bring greater Justice to modern society, although they disagreed on the means. The papal leadership endorsed the principle of private property, and Rauschenbusch advocated socialism as the only way to Christianize the economic order.

Christian Realists like Niebuhr approached Justice as a paradoxical problem where both good and evil remain intermixed in history. He believed in the possibility of proximate but not perfect Justice and that power balances among competing groups could enhance the chance to achieve it at progressively more inclusive, although not necessarily permanent, levels. Love could increase mutuality in the pursuit of common goals but never eliminate the need for Justice. Justice and Liberation are radically joined in the writings of James Cone and other Liberation theologians. Their focus is on the special needs of minorities, women and impoverished populations around the world. Ruether's image of Justice combines the call for Liberation with an inclusive vision based on the reconciliation of the oppressor and the oppressed. From the Old Testament to the Modern era, writers have used Justice-Liberation framework repeatedly with depth of insight.

We have now completed our survey of the four major frameworks of moral reasoning in Christian Ethics. In Section 3, we will combine their strengths and apply the transformation perspective to three pressing ethical problems of our time.

Notes

1. Barry L. Bandstra, *Reading the Old Testament: An Introduction to the Hebrew Scripture,* second edition, Belmont, California: Wadsworth Publishing Company, 1999, p. 141, writes, "Most English Bible versions locate Israel's miraculous escape at the Red Sea, but the underlying Hebrew phrase *yam suf* might better be rendered Reed Sea."

2. John and Kathleen Court, *The New Testament World,* Englewood Cliffs, N.J.: Prentice-Hall, Inc., 1990, p. 134, write, "It is an axiom of modern scholarship that the gospel of Luke and the Acts of the Apostles belong together, the work of a single author."

3. See especially Jesus' conversation with his disciples in Luke 24:13-27.

4. New Testament scholars disagree on the authorship authenticity of some of Paul's letters. However, virtually all of them accept that he wrote Galatians. As an example see Edwin D. Freed, *The New Testament: A Critical Introduction,* Belmont, California: Wadsworth Publishing Company, 1991, Chapters 10-13.

5. Similar images appear in Colossians whose authorship is disputed. Becoming transformed into the "new self" means that "In that renewal there is no longer Greek and Jew, circumcised and uncircumcised, barbarian, Scythian, slave and free; but Christ is all and in all!" (Colossians 3:11).

6. Clement of Alexandria, "Who Is the Rich Man That Shall be Saved?" in *The Ante-Nicene Fathers,* edited by Alexander Roberts and James Donaldson, Grand Rapids: Wm. B. Eerdmans Publishing Co., 1977, XXXVII.

7. Lactantius, "Divine Institutes," in *The Ante-Nicene Fathers,* V.7.

8. Marsilius of Padua, *The Defender of Peace,* edited by Alan Gewirth, Volume II, New York: Columbia University Press, 1956, Discourse I, Chapter 4.3

9. Thomas Muntzer, "Sermon Before the Princes," in *Christian Social Teachings,* edited by George W. Forrell, Garden City, N.Y.: Doubleday/Anchor Books, 1966, p. 189.

10. See Joseph Frank, *The Levellers,* Cambridge, Mass.: Harvard University Press, 1955, p. 248.

11. Quoted in H. N. Brailsford, *The Levellers and the English Revolution,* Stanford, California: Stanford University Press, 1961, p. 656.

12. Quoted in Brailsford, *The Levellers and the English Revolution,* p. 660. Winstanley published his most important pamphlet, *The Law of Freedom in a Platform,* in 1652.

13. Brailsford, *The Levellers and the English Revolution,* pp. 663-665.

14. See *"Rerum novarum"* in *Seven Great Encyclicals,* Glen Rock, N.J.: Paulist Press, 1963.

15. See *"Mater et Magistra"* in *Proclaiming Justice and Peace: Documents from John XXIII to John Paul II,* edited by Michael Walsh and Brian Davies, Mystic, Conn.: Twenty-third Publications, 1984.

16. *"Pacem in terris,"* in *Proclaiming Justice and Peace: Documents from John XXIII to John Paul II.*

17. *"Octagesimo adveniens,"* in *The Documents of Vatican II,* edited by Walter M. Abbott, New York: America Press and others, 1966.

18. Walter Rauschenbusch, *Christianizing the Social Order,* New York: Macmillan, 1912.

19. Reinhold Niebuhr published his Gifford Lectures as two book, *The Nature and Destiny of Man,* Volumes I and II, New York: Scribner's, 1941 and 1943.

20. Reinhold Niebuhr, *Moral Man and Immoral Society,* New York: Scribner's, 1932.

21. Reinhold Niebuhr, *The Children of Light and the Children of Darkness,* New York: Charles Scribners' Sons, 1944, p. xiii.

22. James Cone, *Black Theology and Black Power,* New York: Seabury, 1969, p. 1.

23. Cone, *Black Theology and Black Power,* p. 42.

24. Cone, *Black Theology and Black Power,* p. 68.

25. Cone, *Black Theology and Black Power,* p. 118.

26. Cone, *Black Theology and Black Power,* p. 151.

27. Cone, *Black Theology and Black Power,* p. 118.

28. Letty Russell, *Human Liberation in a Feminist Perspective—A Theology,* Philadelphia: Westminster Press, 1974, p. 59-60.

29. Cone, *Black Theology and Black Power,* p. 42.

30. Rosemary Ruether, *Liberation Theology,* New York: Paulist Press, 1972, p. 13.

31. Ruether, *Liberation Theology,* p. 16.
32. Ruether, *Liberation Theology,* p. 16.

Section III

Moral Imagination and the Transformation Framework

We take our first step in moving toward a Transformation Ethics by reiterating that the major ethical images of the four frameworks flow from both the Old and New Testaments, as the preceding four Chapters clearly illustrate. Visions of Faith, Love, Moral Law, Character, Justice, and Liberation all have deep roots in the moral imagination that appears in the pages of the Bible. In truth, none of the four frameworks can claim to be more Biblically oriented than any of the others, because they all share an identical starting point in the Old and New Testaments. This means that Transformation Ethics is also first and foremost Bible-based because it integrates the primary images of the Bible-based four frameworks.

What differentiates Christian writers from each other in all four frameworks is not the presences or absence of a Biblical perspective, but how they interpret the Bible and what weight they give it in relationship to the other three sources of authority, namely, experience, tradition, and reason. For our purposes, we will not presuppose that some writers are Bible-Christians while others are not. Instead, we will start with the assumption that the Old and New Testaments inform the perceptions of the authors of all four frameworks, even though they combine their views of the Bible with experience, tradition, and reason in different ways. We see these diverse approaches as positive and believe that all of them contribute constructively to our understanding of the Christian moral life. As stated in Chapter 1, our goal is not to argue for the superiority of one framework over the others but instead to combine their strengths.

In Chapter 7 we will describe how many of the authors identified in Chapters 3 through 6 use more than one framework. Not all writers incorporate all four frameworks, but some do. Others include only two or three. This does not mean that Christians who employ two or more have made superior ethical contributions to those who limit themselves mainly to one. Extensive and targeted use of one framework can yield extraordinary insights, as we have seen in the case of Origen and Clement of Alexandria, St. Francis, Marsilius and the Levellers, Johann, Cone, and others. At the same time, it is remarkable how many of the greatest theologians and ethicists integrate multiple perspectives. We will also include in Chapter 7 a discussion of the essential elements of the Transformation framework.

In Chapters 8 through 10, we will focus on three of the most important ethical issues facing the Church and modern society and use the Transformation approach to analyze them. Our goal will be to identify moral choices that hold out the possibility of bringing the greatest amount of goodness into the world in terms of Faith and Love, Moral Law, Character development, and Justice and Liberation. The three issues and their related ethical challenges are capital punishment, genetic modification, and homosexuality.

Chapter 7

Transformation Ethics: Combining Strengths of the Four Frameworks

Multiple Use of the Four Frameworks

We begin this Chapter by describing how many of the writers discussed in the previous Section employed two or more of the four frameworks. For all intents and purposes, the practice of using multiple perspectives has gone on for centuries. It dates to the two Biblical eras that gave rise to the four frameworks in the first place. Thus, we would expect to see evidence of how Old Testament and New Testament authors engaged in multiple applications. For the sake of illustrating the predominance of the four ethical frameworks throughout Judaic-Christian history in Chapters 3 through 6, we selected writers whose images and language fit firmly within each framework. We also mentioned several of them in more than one Chapter as we described how the frameworks differ. Now we will bring together what we previously separated.

The historical time period covered by the Old Testament spanned several centuries. As we have shown in previous Chapters, the ancient Israelites gave expression to their moral concerns through the four frameworks. The greatest of all leaders Moses used all of these perspectives. His repeatedly reaffirmed that God's Love guided the Jewish people after their Liberation from Egypt and instructed them to remain faithful to God's summons. Through the Covenant he provided them with the Moral Law that defined the mandates of Justice. He counseled them to become wise as befitted their status as a chosen people. He was an integrator who wove moral images together into a seamless whole.

The northern prophet Hosea followed in the Covenant footsteps of Moses. By remarrying the prostitute Gomar he declared that God would not only punish the errant Israelites but would also continue to Love them despite their failure of Faith, lack of wisdom, and disregard for Justice. The southern prophet Jeremiah similarly accused Judah of unrighteousness and warned of pending destruction and exile to Babylon. Like Hosea he also brought comfort by announcing that at some future date God would write a new and everlasting Covenant on their hearts. Moses, Hosea, and Jeremiah all exemplify how the moral imagination integrates disparate moral frameworks irrespective of their conceptual differences.

Together the New Testament Gospels incorporate all of the four ethical frameworks even though different Gospel writers emphasize some of them more than others. Matthew and Luke incorporate most of Mark, but they also differ from each other. Matthew combines the Faith-Love, Moral Law, and Character traditions, while Luke merges the Faith-Love and Character traditions with Justice and Liberation. He employs the Justice-Liberation framework in Acts as well. John's Gospel and letters place primary emphasis on the Faith-Love perspective and show little interest in the other three, especially Moral Law and Justice-Liberation. Collectively the four Gospels of the New Testament further demonstrate their commonality by transforming the Old Testament's four ethical approaches through images of Christ.

The greatest New Testament integrator of them all was the Apostle Paul. He found a place for both the Faith-Love and Moral Law frameworks. While he asserted that salvation could be achieved only through Faith and not the Law, nonetheless he retained the Old Testament accent on obedience to the Law by subsuming it under Love. In addition, more than any one else, he enumerated the virtues that comprise the Christian Character. He also demonstrated his ongoing concern for the poor throughout his missionary ventures into Asia Minor. Despite his socially conservative rabbinic male hierarchical tendencies, he envisioned that everyone stood as a theological equal, that is, as an identical new creation, in Christ's eschatological community. This does not mean that Paul balanced all of the frameworks in his moral imagination. He did not. However, he found space for all of them.

The integrating impulse did not end with the New Testament. The *Didache* combines two frameworks by enumerating lists of Moral Laws and counsels the faithful to show their gratitude to God by sharing justly the goods of the earth with the less fortunate. Augustine's images of the heavenly and earthly cities flow directly from the Faith-Love framework. His articulation of the Just War doctrine places him in the Moral Law tradition that Aquinas used as the foundation for his *Summa*. St. Thomas also borrowed extensively from Aristotle's understanding of Character development and integrated both Greek and Pauline virtues into his moral theology. His Divine Law of salvation through Christ ties directly into the Faith-Love framework.

Both Luther and Calvin accentuated Faith and Love as the cornerstones of the Reformation. Like Paul, they underscored the necessity of obeying the Law in order to contain the innately sinful tendencies of the human will. They also embraced Character Ethics in their enumeration of the virtues that characterize the Christian concept of calling or vocation. Calvin in particular contributed to the emerging entrepreneurial spirit of the Modern world.

Nineteenth and twentieth century Catholic encyclicals embody the Moral Law, Character, and Justice-Liberation frameworks in full measure. During the 1960's, Vatican II's commitment to give greater priority to the Bible moved the Catholic Church closer to Faith-Love traditions of the Old and New Testaments as well. The Protestant Social Justice emphasis of the twentieth century reinvigorated Biblical images of Justice and Liberation. Paradoxical approaches like Reinhold Niebuhr's combine both Love and Justice as does Ruether who calls for reconciliation in the midst of Liberation. Through reconciling Love, God sets both the oppressor and oppressed free even as the voices of the poor and dispossessed cry out for Justice.

As the above examples illustrate, combining the strengths of two, three, or all four of the frameworks in the moral imagination is not new. From Moses to Ruether, this integrating activity has continued without end. Transformation Ethics follows this long-standing tradition of synthesis.

The Transformation Ethics Framework

The process of combining the varying strengths of the four frameworks starts by recognizing that they all share a common point of departure: the conviction that God's grace has been fully revealed in Christ. In the simplest terms, Christianity understands that God gives grace, human beings receive it through Faith, and Christ mediates it through the Cross and resurrection. God's grace transforms both persons and community and serves as the foundation stone of the Christian Church, which in turn sustains itself through the ongoing experience of the gift of grace. The Bible provides the Church with its primary theological and ethical images through the stories of ancient Israel and the testimonies surrounding the life, death, and resurrection of Jesus as the Christ.

The Church's main mission is to proclaim to the world that God's amazing grace as revealed in Christ is available to all through the simple act of receiving it in Faith. Bonhoeffer understood well this aspect of Christianity by affirming that the Church exists to bring the world into the presence of the ultimate, God's grace, and that everything else is penultimate and exists to serve this purpose. At the same time, writers like Augustine have always recognized that the experience of grace and the emotional intensity associated with it remain enigmatic. From Faith's human side, grace comes easier and more often to some persons than to others. At one level, mystery remains at the heart of the experience of grace. At another level, the consequences of the experience can be profound. From its inception, Christianity has always affirmed that persons who truly receive God's grace in Faith become new creations in Christ. Transformation Ethics begins by assuming that God's grace received in Faith through Christ transforms lives.

Given this assumption, the next question involves the nature of the transformation and its implications for ethical beliefs and behavior. As our analysis of the ethical frameworks in Section II shows, the line from Faith to Ethics does not follow only one direction. It is multidirectional. It goes in four directions—consistently over time for centuries. Even though considerable diversity exists within the four frameworks, the frameworks themselves reappear with amazing regularity. To borrow an analogy from music, Christian Ethics consists of four themes with many variations.

Why should this be so? In part, we can answer this question by combining knowledge, that is, new experiences, from the contemporary Behavioral Sciences with the four ethical frameworks that emanated from the Biblical traditions. The following diagrams pulls together in a visual format how the major elements of previous Chapters flow together. Following the diagram, we will combine the main elements of the four frameworks, describe their interconnections, and integrate them with ideas developed by the twentieth century Social Psychologist George Herbert Mead.[1]

Transformation Ethics Diagram

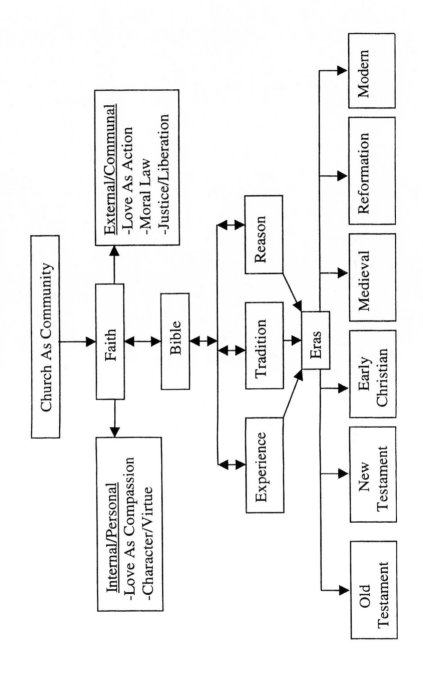

The above diagram depicts the Church as Christ's ongoing community of Faith in the world. The Church grounds its existence in the Bible, which provides the primary theological and ethical images of the four frameworks. The Church nurtures Faith by creating the communal context within which the experience of God's grace enters personally into the life of each member. Given the diversity of Christian confessions and institutional forms that exist around the world, the Church can mediate the experience of grace in diverse ways, ranging from the still small voice within to enthusiastic expressions of music, dance, or joyous shouts of hallelujah. The Church as a living community must exist in the heart of each Christian person or else it becomes merely a moribund institutional shell. Its distinctiveness derives ultimately from the deep reservoir of shared Biblical Faith that flows from God's grace and penetrates to the committed core of each individual's social, emotional, and spiritual identity.

From this combination of Church, Faith, and the Bible, we move horizontally from Faith to its Internal/Personal and External/Communal forms of expression. At this point Mead's insights into the nature of the social self become particularly relevant in helping explain the existence and persistence of the four ethical frameworks. For Mead, every individual possesses a central core of identity that is both intensely personal and innately communal. He refers to this dual reality as the "I" and the "Me" within the social self. The "Me" is the socialized part of the self and is based on internalizing shared group norms, which he called the "Generalized Other." The "I" is the core of each person's unique identify and source of self-transcendence.

Each self possesses a distinctive "I" while simultaneously sharing collective values and perceptions that comprise the "Me." To reduce the social self to either the individual or collective side exclusively is to distort the true nature of what it means to be human. The self is simultaneously and inseparably both individual and social. Each person possesses an "I" and a "Me" at the same time, all the time. This paradoxical duality is a permanent part of the human condition.

From the perspective of Mead's two dimensions of the social self, we can fold in the four frameworks of moral reasoning as they appear in the diagram within the two boxes labeled "Internal/Personal" and "External/Communal." Faith ties these two sides of the self together. Through Faith, God's grace evokes the capacity for compassion on the personal side of the self. Faith and Love unite to create empathy for human suffering and for a desire to improve the well being of others. In combining ethical images of Christianity with the language of Mead, we can say that Faith and Love join together at the center of the transformed "I" within the Christian social self. Starting with the Old Testament and continuing into the Modern period, this close coupling has cut across all the eras summarized at the bottom of the diagram.

In addition to Love as internal compassion, it also motivates the self to initiate actions in the world outside the self, as indicated in the diagram under External/Communal. It motivates behaviors that have concrete consequences for community life. Love exists not only as a personal emotion; it also manifests itself in the form of social activity. It inspires individuals to make sacrifices for the well being of others. As Fletcher would say, loving God in the neighbor means that Christian Faith is inherently communal in nature. Or to use Mead's term, Love translates into action on the "Me" side of the social self.

The Bible witnesses to God's nature as *agape*, as pure self-giving Love that reveals itself through the history of ancient Israel and in Christ whose redemptive sacrifice reunites humanity back to God through Faith. The Church rests on the cornerstone conviction that Christ's reconciling action binds together all believers into a loving community. Once again, to borrow from Mead, Love flows from Faith and resides in the unique "I" that sits at the center of the self and in the collective "Me" that mirrors society's norms. In short, Faith transforms the self into a new creation in Christ and gives rise to Love that encompasses both the Internal/Personal and External/Communal sides of selfhood.

From this point forward, we need take only a short step to show how Faith and Love relate to Character, which the diagram indicates belongs on the Internal/Personal side of the social self. As we described in Chapter 5, both the Old and New Testaments contain numerous images of the ideal virtuous person. The Love that flows from Faith also connects Faith to Character. The New Testament repeatedly reminds readers of the centrality of Love for Christian Faith, as John's Gospel and Paul's letters indicate. John's Gospel and letters define Love as the new commandment that Christ gives to his followers. Paul starts his virtue list in the fifth Chapter of Galatians with Love and then proceeds to joy, peace, patience, kindness, and so on. In the thirteenth Chapter of 1 Corinthians, he places Love in a superior position to all other traits. In short, Character stands in direct relationship to Faith and Love because the New Testament defines Love as the quintessential Christian virtue that connects to all the others.

We demonstrated the adaptability of the Character tradition throughout Christianity's long march through time. Early Christian writers such as Origen and Ambrose combined Biblical Character references with Greco-Roman philosophy. Such intellectual dovetailing culminated when Aquinas combined wisdom, courage, justice, and temperance with faith, hope, and love to create his list of the seven great virtues. Luther and Calvin reshaped this tradition by specifying traits consistent with the Christian sense of vocation. Calvin in particular stressed the importance of honesty, frugality, sobriety, and other business compatible virtues. Johann, Hauerwas, and Gustafson deepened this framework in the twentieth century by exploring the nature of Character development.

From the time of the Old Testament wisdom traditions, visions of virtue have remained at the center of the search for how to *be* in the world as a faithful person. Mead's view of the social self helps us gain insight into why this should be so. Desirable virtues are nurtured on the internal side of the self, in the "I." While they are shared communally as well and therefore exist in the "Me," in the final analysis, for Christians they must become internalized personally in the Character of each faithful member of the Church.

Love not only serves as a bridge to the entire range of virtues on the internal side of the self. Love also spans into the communal networks that exist outside of the self. While Love has an individual dimension, it is not just "individualistic." That is to say, as persons we do not exist as unattached atoms or merely bump into each other like discrete billiard balls. Rather, we are enmeshed in social webs and relationships; and we participate in external institutions that exert powerful influences over our lives. When Love shifts from the personal to the communal side of the self, it penetrates into social structures where it takes the form of Moral Law, Justice, and Liberation. In this way, the transforming power that begins with God's grace received in Faith on the personal side extends into the larger society that surrounds the self.

Law exists to regulate human interactions within group settings and provides the legal framework for defining acceptable and unacceptable behaviors. However, by itself law does not necessarily contribute to ethical outcomes. Powerful groups use the law to advance their self-interests over others and can justify almost any cruelty by manipulating the law and appealing to its grandeur. History reeks with such examples.

Prior to the American Civil War in the 1860s, legal codes reinforced the institution of slavery that bound kidnapped Africans to perpetual servitude under the control of southern white landowners. After the Civil War Jim Crow laws buttressed the structures of segregation.

Dominant groups have repeatedly used the law to maintain positions of power and privilege over subordinate classes of people and to perpetuate patterns of discrimination. Prior to the passage of labor legislation, laws prohibited factory workers from organizing collectively and bargaining with management for improvements in working conditions and employment benefits. Restrictive covenants and red lining in housing have kept neighborhoods separated by race, ethnicity, religion or some other arbitrary demographic factor. Historically the law has been used to deprive women of the right to own property or to have access to the same educational, political, or economic opportunities that men took for granted. Tyrants everywhere, and forever, have always justified their social and political abuses through lofty sounding legal language that served no other purpose than to oppress some dehumanized "other."[2]

However, just as the law can be grossly manipulated for harmful purposes, it can also serve as a powerful force in bringing greater goodness into the world. In can be a vehicle to enhance human well being as well as to diminish it. At this point, we can connect Love to law through the Moral Law tradition dating from Moses, when God called the Israelites to show their Faith in God and Love of one another by obeying the Law of the Covenant. From the beginning, a profound ethical vision of God's Love and of the Covenantal ordering of communal Justice through Moral Law nurtured the moral imagination of the ancient Israelites and became appropriated by Christians.

Standards of Justice permeate the Old Testament through the Covenant. As we described in Chapter 6, a Christian focus on Justice has appeared in every subsequent historical period. During the Modern Era especially, the class antagonisms of industrial capitalism, conflicts among nation states, patterns of colonial domination, and the systematic discrimination of some groups toward others forced Justice issues into high relief. The visionary horizon of Justice as individual *noblesse oblige* that characterized much of Medieval Christendom stretched to include power relationships between groups as well, as the Catholic encyclicals, Social Gospel writers like Raschenbusch, and Christian Realists like Niebuhr reveal. By the end of the twentieth century, Liberation theologians had reshaped images of Justice once again, this time around relationships between oppressors and the oppressed.

According to the diagram, as Love travels from personal compassion to external action, it becomes transformed into Moral Law according to Biblical images of Justice. Throughout the long sweep of Christian history, Church leaders and writers have adapted Justice images to a variety of changing circumstances and new experiences. They have expanded Justice to include not only acts of individual charity that continue as important markers of Christian witness in the world but power relationship among competing groups as well. In a world where egregious and unjust inequalities remain entrenched, a Christian vision of Justice also implies Liberation for oppressed peoples of the planet and the universal reconciliation of all.

This means that just as the Christian image of Love ties together the Internal/Personal and External/Communal aspects of the social self, so does Justice. Also like Love, Justice exists as one of Christianity's major Character traits. Justice is a virtue that predisposes a person to act in a particular way, which makes the nature of Justice inherently social. Like Love, Justice bridges both personal identify and social action; it defines a way of both *being* in the world as well as *acting* within it. By its very nature, Justice conjures up a moral image of distributing the burdens and benefits in a fair manner. Another way to say this according to Mead's language is that while the virtue of Justice exists within the Internal/Personal side of each person's Character (I), it has no meaning apart from External/Communal applications (Me). There is no such thing as Justice for only one. Justice applies to all, which means that as an ethical image it transforms the moral imagination toward a vision of *inclusion*. .

Love and Justice cannot be confined to only select groups or individuals. At its core, a Christian understanding of Love and Justice based on doing the will of God as revealed in Christ pushes toward the universal because Christian Faith affirms that every person is a neighbor for whom Christ died. As its central image, Christianity proclaims that God's Love encompasses all of creation, which by definition includes all of humanity. No one is excluded. As Love expands from personal compassion (the I of Mead's social self) to Justice through communal action (the Me), it embraces everyone.

For Christianity, reaching toward inclusiveness started with the Apostle Paul's vocation as Christ's emissary to the uncircumcised and in

Peter's realization in Acts 10:45 that God had poured out the Holy Spirit on the Gentiles. Paul's emphasis on Faith in Christ as the source of salvation for all made Christianity portable. Faith does not depend on biological lineage or cultural inheritance. Anyone, any time, and anywhere can become transformed spiritually into a new creation through Faith in Christ. With Paul and all the disciples and apostles who followed his lead, as described in the New Testament, the long trek toward universal inclusion began.

This does not mean that the path toward inclusiveness has always gone smoothly, as the history of Christianity's relationship to society makes clear. The Church encountered many pitfalls and setbacks along the way, and more than once it joined with the forces of injustice. In contradiction to its highest vision of inclusive Love and Justice, knowingly or not, it has all too often helped perpetuate the conditions of oppression rather than Liberation.

However, despite the historical ups and downs, the Church's innate drive to increase goodness in the world has never ceased even as it went through historic cycles of decline and regeneration. The reason seems clear. When the Church remains true to its commitment as Christ's community on earth, God's grace nurtures it through an enduring spirituality of self- renewal. Grace transforms the moral imagination by awakening visions of personal compassion and social Justice. The grace of God that Faith receives facilitates the cultivation of Christian Character and the inculcation of virtuous dispositions. It leads to the creation of Moral Law inspired by an image of Justice that settles for nothing less than the constant expansion of the circle of inclusion.

For example, in the United States slavery formerly survived under the sanction of legality. Today, virtually everyone would label such human exploitation as inherently immoral and oppressive. Around the globe, groups guided by visions of Justice confront the historic patterns of discrimination based on race, religion, ethnicity, nationality, or other arbitrary factors and cry out for their eradication. Worldwide pressures for gender equality go head to head with the centuries old patriarchal patterns that deny women rights and privileges men have always taken for granted. An international system of independent states has replaced the previous system of colonial conquest and domination. Even though the September 11, 2001 attack on New York's World Trade Center and the persistence of a global terrorist network remind us that the vision of a peaceful world still remains a distant dream, the very existence of the

United Nations holds the promise of eventually resolving international conflicts without resort to war. Its Human Rights Declarations for men, women, and children offer a universal image that encompasses the whole of humanity.[3]

Underneath the widening circle of inclusion lies a universal vision of compassion and Justice. As this has gained momentum around the world, old laws that promoted bigotry or protected the privileges of some groups at the expense of other have been modified, reinterpreted, or eliminated altogether. These include Biblical laws or passages that have been invoked to justify slavery, the maltreatment of Jews and other religious groups, discrimination of minorities, the oppression of women, and so on. By appealing to the Bible's most comprehensive ethical visions, the Bible becomes the source of its own self-critique. It contains both broad and narrow images of how God works in the world. The momentum toward universal inclusion within the context of global pluralism offers Christianity the opportunity to lead in the future with its broad visions of God's inclusive Love and Justice.[4]

When the Church remains faithful to its commitment to Christ, it nurtures within the Character of each faithful follower the whole range of Christian virtues. Through Love it kindles human empathy and through Justice it seeks to reorder society. Through its actions, it extends God's mercy throughout the world and struggles to liberate everyone from the artificial barriers that prohibit the development of their human potential. It searches for ways that lead to personal and social transformation, through both belief and behavior, in order to bring more goodness into the world.

Before proceeding to the final section of this Chapter, based on the above discussion we can summarize as succinctly as possible the major elements of Transformation Ethics, which combines the strengths of the four frameworks of moral reasoning. We start with the core images of Faith and Love, which easily incorporate the cultivation of Character. We define Justice as one of the major virtues of the Christian as a moral agent. When viewed from the Biblical tradition, Justice lies at the center of the Church's Moral Law images. By it very nature Justice within Christian Ethics is a social virtue that gives preferential treatment to the least well off members of society and seeks their Liberation from conditions that disadvantage them. Justice also aims toward the creation of universal laws that reflect the highest moral standards and the elimination of patterns of bias that benefit some people at the expense of others.

Justice posits equality of treatment before the law; and this invokes an image of inclusion compatible with our point of departure, Faith acting in Love.

We do not want to suggest that combining the strengths of the four frameworks into a combined perspective eliminates the differences, or even the tensions, that exist among them. Nor do we assume that we can necessarily resolve complex moral dilemmas more easily through an integrative framework. Our goal remains simply to develop a Christian approach to Ethics that will help increase goodness into the world even though we know that we will not achieve perfection. While becoming morally perfect is no simple historical possibility, continuing to strive toward the goal is. This means that given any moral dilemma and its potential solutions, the one that transforms the world toward greatest goodness through the combined strengths of the Faith and Love, Moral Law, Character, and Justice and Liberation traditions of the Church is the preferred choice.

In the next three Chapters, we will apply our integrative approach to moral dilemmas related too capital punishment, genetic modification, and homosexuality. However, before doing so we need to clarify further some of the possibilities and limitations of the Transformation viewpoint. Three come to mind. First, whatever method we use, we cannot eliminate the need for human judgment. Another way to say this is that no ethical approach can be made "judgment proof. " Ethical choices do not emerge automatically by themselves out of any method of moral reasoning. Making moral choices requires an act of the human will. Choosing a course of action always involves making judgments about which of the many possible alternative outcomes of any particular moral problem would be preferred. From our perspective, the judgment that contains the highest number of potentially good outcomes based on the strengths all four frameworks is the best.

The second concern involves whether we can rank order the many virtues that comprise the Christian Character. At one level, we might feel the need to identify *the* Christian virtue and then arrange all the remaining virtues, assuming we know what they are, on a hierarchical scale. Given the complexities and diverse viewpoints within Christian Ethics, most likely this is not possible. Nor is it desirable. However, we can safely conclude that two Biblical virtues more than any others stand at the center of the Christian moral imagination. As we have insinuated in the above discussion, they are Love and Justice. These two primary

Christian virtues are mutually reinforcing, exist coextensively, and cross the boundaries between the Internal/Personal and External/Communal sides of the social self.

Any moral judgment or action that combines both Love and Justice will create more goodness than judgments or actions that include only Love or Justice. For example, people can express their heartfelt Love for others at a deeply personal level; but if the structures of society perpetuate unfairness, especially toward the least advantaged, then they should be changed in the direction of Justice. On the other hand, people can act to create social structures that embody bold visions of Justice but lack personal compassion. In such cases, the absence of Love diminishes their Character and leads to jeopardizing the broader possibilities of reconciliation and inclusion. Moral choices need not be restricted to either Love or Justice. While human behavior based on one or the other will increase goodness in the world, actions that combine both will result in even more goodness.

We further expand our moral imagination, and hence human goodness, by combining Love and Justice with other virtues such as hope, joy, peace, patience, kindness, gentleness, self-control, wisdom, courage, moderation, honesty, fidelity, and so on. By doing so, we weave ethical images together like threads in a carpet. The virtues of Love and Justice occupy the center of this fluid and flexible mosaic of virtues because they connect in the most direct manner the self and society. To use the language of Mead, they bridge the "I" and the "Me," the internal and the external, the personal and the communal sides of the social self and of society as a whole.

In brief, for Transformation Ethics, Love and Justice are the most encompassing Biblical virtues that fuel the Christian moral imagination and integrate all of the others into a seamless tapestry. Thus, a preferred image of the relationship of Love and Justice to the other virtues is not a scale of ranked priorities. Rather, it is more like a circle where Love and Justice exist at the center and radiate out to embrace the rest in a fluid and flexible manner. This is a wholistic, pliable, and at the same time, integrated vision rather than a hierarchical one.

Our third and last concern deals with the question of how far we can go in transforming the world in the direction of increasing goodness. In truth, the answer is we do not know. Several reasons support this assertion. The most important is that the future remains developmentally open. That is to say, the future has not been determined yet, which means that we can move toward either more or less goodness. The pathway into the future is not unidirectional. Nor is only one possible future inevitable. In our imagination we can envision not just one but several alternative futures; and the decisions we make will determine the direction we will take.

Also, from the perspective of Christian Faith, the future will emerge out of some combination of God's grace and human response, which always involves both prospect and constraint. Through grace, God inspires us toward expressions of greater goodness. If we respond with authentic Faith, then God will direct our beliefs and behaviors in the direction of bringing more Love and Justice into the world. Whenever and wherever Christians remain Christ's faithful followers, then those who share the Faith believe that the world will become a better place in which all humanity can live in peace and Justice.

However, no guarantee exists that this will happen. The sinful side of human nature can always pull Christians, as well as others, in the direction of confusing narrow-minded moral visions with God's, as Reinhold Niebuhr's writings repeatedly remind us. Christian Faith affirms that it is our human condition to live somewhere between God's grace and human sin, between God's possibilities and humanity's limitations. There is no sure, inevitable, or irreversible trajectory toward bringing greater goodness into the world. We can always backslide.

At the same time, Christianity proclaims that by being loyal servants of Christ, Christians can transform the world for the better. Authentic Christian Faith produces deeper and more inclusive visions of Love and Justice along with the other virtues of Christian Character. It inspires images of a universal Moral Law of Justice, the Liberation of all oppressed people, and global reconciliation. While we still have a long way to go and the ultimate outcome of the future remains unclear, the Transformation Ethics point of view affirms that God's power is forever moving in the present moment and making all things new.

Notes

1. All references to George Herbert Mead are from his book, *Mind, Self, and Society,* Chicago: University of Chicago Press, 1967.

2. For an excellent analysis into the nature of tyranny, see Daniel Chirot, *Modern Tyrants: The Power and Prevalence of Evil in Our Age,* New York: The Free Press, 1994.

3. See *Human Rights: A New Consensus,* London: Regency Press, 1994, pp. 253-299.

4. This applies to the other religions of the world as well.

Chapter 8

Capital Punishment

In this Chapter we will apply the Transformation viewpoint to the issue of capital punishment. Substantial moral challenges surround this issue, and widespread disagreements exist over how to deal with them, especially among Christian persons in the United States. Throughout this Chapter, we will compare and contrast the major disputes that divide supporters and non-supporters of capital punishment. At the end, we will form our own moral judgment based on the alternative that most likely will bring the greatest amount of goodness into the world. The most desirable option will incorporate the strengths of the four ethical frameworks that we have described in the previous Chapters and that comprise the integrated core images of Transformation Ethics.

For Christian Ethics, capital punishment can be characterized as an innately ambiguous moral problem because Christians can and do legitimately disagree on whether or not to support it. By capital punishment we mean putting a person to death in accordance with a legally imposed sentence based on an egregious crime, that is, execution by a legitimate political authority. Normally we reserve punishment by legal death for the "worst crimes," however we might define them. Premeditated murder and treason usually stand at the top of the list. Some persons might also include rape, kidnapping, or some horrendous act of cruelty against another human being.

For the sake of this discussion, we will limit our definition of capital punishment to situations involving premeditated murder. This definition excludes the killing of another person based on self-defense or protecting innocent life, such as a parent or any other person defending children. It also excludes the loss of life that results from accidents or other behaviors that are not motivated by premeditated malice of forethought to kill. The law recognizes that important distinctions exist between first- or second-degree homicide and involuntary murder or manslaughter depending on the motivation of the person(s) responsible for causing death.

Since premeditated murder involves the intentional taking of human life, it appears on everyone's list of worst crimes and all societies universally proscribe it. In the United States, the serial killings of Ted Bundy, Jeffrey Dahmer, and John Wayne Gacy and the Oklahoma City bombing by Timothy McVeigh belong in the category of worst crimes. Serial killers who repeatedly engage in the premeditated destruction of human life or one time mass murderers commit many of humanity's worst evils. Except for Dahmer, whom a fellow inmate killed in prison, all of them were caught, convicted and executed for their crimes. They represent the extreme end of malice of forethought with intent to murder.

Despite the enormous loss of life that these and other murderers inflict on innocent victims, the morality of capital punishment should not be reduced to a numbers game or driven by gruesome cases that receive sensationalist news coverage, as horrifying as they might be. We raise more questions than we answer when we try to decide the merits of capital punishment based on the number of victims or the barbarous behaviors surrounding their deaths. To build a consensus on where we should mark the cut off point and why seems like an impossible task. For this reason, we will assume that even one death by premeditated murder is one too many.

Also, we will not examine the morality of capital punishment in regard to killing that occurs within the context of war. To do so would require an analysis of the Just War doctrine as Augustine, Aquinas, and others expressed it. This is an important but separate moral topic. We would need to investigate how changes in military technology have altered the conduct of war and whether the original premises of Just War doctrine still apply. We would also have to consider the role of international terrorist activities like those that destroyed the World Trade Towers, and this would take us in a different direction from the one that concerns us here.[1] We will limit our examination of the morality of capital punishment to acts of premeditated murder under normal social conditions that do not involve special circumstances such as self-defense, war, or threat to survival.

Among Christians, disagreements over the morality of capital punishment normally operate at two levels. The first involves the empirical and the second the ethical. Both proponents and opponents of capital punishment appeal to the Bible, tradition, experience, and reason to support their positions. While we do not want to over simplify this debate, we can characterize capital punishment arguments among Christians as a "battle over Bible verses" supported by appeals to experience, tradition, and reason. We will begin by examining the empirical pros and cons and then move to the ethical ones.

Empirical Perspectives

The empirical arguments generally involve emphasizing the social, psychological, and economic outcomes associated with capital punishment. They appeal to experience and reason and are frequently couched in the language of modern Behavioral Science. One of the most hotly debated issues is whether capital punishment is a deterrent to murder. Both proponents and opponents try to demonstrate this empirically. Both sides use some form of correlation analysis to bolster their positions. Opponents demonstrate that there are situations where not having capital punishment laws is associated with low murder rates and situations where having them correlates with high murder rates.[2] On the other hand, advocates of deterrence point to opposite situations where the existence of capital punishment laws correlates with low murder rates and their absence relates to the opposite.[3]

Who is right? The answer is that we do not know for sure, because correlation does not equal causality. It is a basic statistical principle that the simultaneous existence of two events does not imply that a necessary causal relationship exists between them. To conclude that gender inequalities in the workplace and income differences between racial groups are caused by the genetic superiority of one group over another is to confuse correlation with causation. By analogy, whichever way they argue, both the proponents and opponents of capital punishment lack indisputable knowledge about how the presence or absence of capital punishment laws affects deterrence. In the final analysis, empirically grounded pro or con arguments based on experience, reason, and statistical correlations are weak because they show no consistent pattern across all cases or over time. For this reason, we do not find them helpful, one way or the other, in deciding whether or not to support capital punishment.

The psychological argument comes next. As with deterrence, proponents and opponents appeal to experience and reason. Opponents claim that capital punishment leaves psychological pain and causes a sense of re-victimization when the families who oppose capital punishment must endure the execution of the killer of their murdered loved one.[4] Proponents claim that executing convicted murderers offers psychological relief by releasing pent up feelings of revenge associated with brutal acts of murder. Ernest Van den Haag expresses this position clearly. "Vengeance is a compensatory and psychologically reparatory satisfaction for an injured party, group, or society. I do not see wherein it is morally blameworthy." He states further that legal vengeance is "socially useful" because it "solidifies social solidarity against lawbreakers."[5]

In addition to the social deterrence and psychological perspectives, both opponents and proponents of capital punishment also use various forms of economic analysis. These include the financial benefits versus costs of keeping convicted murderers in prison instead of executing them. Short of eliminating or radically reducing the expensive and lengthy appeals process that exists to protect innocent people from wrongful conviction and execution, it is widely recognized that the expense of maintaining the capital punishment system is substantially higher than imprisonment—even for life with no chance of parole.[6] Reducing the costs of the capital punishment system, as many advocate, by shortening the appeals process would only increase the probability of wrongful death by legal means. If we decide to continue the capital punishment system and protect the innocent at the same time, then we will have to keep paying for it despite the fact that eliminating it would save money.

As the disagreements over the social, psychological, and economic aspects of capital punishment reveal, both proponents and opponents interpret the empirical findings differently. On the questions of whether or not capital punishment deters murder, provides psychic relief, or is worth the added cost, both sides can muster strong arguments. Despite these many disagreements over the empirical evidence, this book offers an alternative perspective: Society does not create, continue, modify, or eliminate a capital punishment system because of empirical evidence but rather because of its moral sensibilities through which it selects, filters, and interprets such evidence. We should not be surprised that both the opponents and proponents of capital punishment advance their convictions by claiming that the "data" support their positions. In the final analysis, we cannot appeal primarily to experience and reason to justify or reject capital punishment. We must penetrate to a deeper level—to Christianity's moral visions.

Ethical Perspectives

In this section, we will employ three ethical perspectives to examine the pros and cons of capital punishment, just as we used three empirical perspectives in the preceding one. They are Love, Justice, and revenge. All three of them have Biblical roots. We begin with revenge, follow with Justice, and end with Love. From a Christian perspective, psychological arguments based on the expression of vengeance are the least acceptable of all, because they pull the moral imagination down to the lowest realm of human emotions—the desire for retaliation. The New Testament position seems clear on this issue. "Never avenge yourselves, but leave room for the wrath of God; for it is written, 'Vengeance is mine, I will repay, says the Lord.'" (Romans 12:19)

Revengeful passions leave little room for reconciliation in human relationships that have been radically ruptured through an act as atrocious as premeditated murder. This does not mean that feelings of vengeance are not understandable. They are. The emotion of revenge is as old as humanity itself. The desire to "get even" is a normal human reaction when people believe they have been harmed. While seeking vengeance in the case of murder is one possible moral response among many possible responses, it is not the one that the Transformation perspective would consider the most ethical.

Next, we turn to Justice. As we have discussed, Justice visions appear frequently in the moral imagination of both the Old and New Testament writers and cross all six historic time periods. Two central themes dominate these images. The first is fairness and the second is God's preferential treatment for the disadvantaged, as modern Liberation theologians remind us. This seems clear enough. However, when we apply these two Justice images to the issue of capital punishment, conflicts arise, as the following discussion demonstrates.

The best known vision of Justice in the Old Testament appears in Exodus 21:23-25, "If any harm follows, then you shall give life for life, eye for eye, tooth for tooth, hand for hand, foot for foot, burn for burn, wound for wound, stripe for stripe." This is straightforward measure for measure—*quid pro quo*. It is pure reciprocal equivalency that is grounded in the idea of fairness. Whatever you do to others shall be done to you. When translated into capital punishment, it means that when someone takes away the life of another person through premeditated murder, the state through its legal authority will take away the murderer's life. The mind grasps this image easily and Scripture provides direct support for it. Christians who defend capital punishment always quote the Exodus passage to justify their position.

We find a variation on this viewpoint in the principle that each person has an inherent right to life because human life is sacred. People who violate this principle through murder relinquish their own right to life. Murderers cannot defend themselves against capital punishment by invoking the principle that life is sacred if they have shown disregard for the principle through the premeditated and willful killing of another person. From the perspective of Exodus, justice requires fairness, and in this case fairness calls for reciprocity of treatment. If one kills through murder, then one shall be killed through execution, which is nothing other than a government using its legal authority to balance the scale of justice: life for life.

At the deepest level, the idea of Justice as fairness implies equality of treatment, first in morality and then in law. In the former case, persons who want others to respect the sacredness of their lives must also honor the principle that they must equally value the lives of others. Reciprocity requires equal treatment; and treating everyone equally is the essence of fairness. Anyone who violates this moral principle becomes subject to legal action that reinforces the moral principle.

This means that we can affirm as innately immoral any irrational mob action against an alleged murderer because such action violates the principle that life is sacred. Mob action does not give the accused an opportunity for self-protection or self-defense. Furthermore, in the past, many accused murderers have been proven not guilty after being convicted in a court of law and sentenced for execution. Between 1973 and January 2002 in the United States, ninety-nine people or an average 3.4 persons per year have been released from death row because of evidence of their innocence.[7] The use of new DNA techniques along with acknowledged flaws in criminal justice procedures have contributed to such dramatic reversals.

While we have no way of ever knowing for certain how many incorrectly accused persons have been put to death, little doubt exists that the criminal justice system has erred, and continues to err, in convicting innocent persons of murder. States such as Illinois have declared a moratorium on further executions pending a thorough review of all criminal justice procedures. For these states, elected officials have concluded that the criminal justice system must contain numerous shortcomings if so many innocent people have been falsely convicted of capital offenses.

However, despite three decades of almost one hundred wrongful convictions, other states such as Texas continue to execute convicted murderers after they have exhausted all appeals and legal safeguards. Imperfections notwithstanding, such states assume that convicted murderers have had their "day in court" and thus have received fair treatment. Unless new evidence exonerates them, their executions proceed as scheduled. Despite the lingering possibility of error, many capital punishment states continue their legal execution of convicted murderers in order to satisfy the Justice principle of "life for life."

Does this mean that when a legally constituted political authority executes an innocent person, the action is in some way more moral than when a murderer takes away the life of another person? Should we conclude that the legal execution of an innocent person is morally acceptable if a government provides that person with full legal rights, even though a murderer's killing of an innocent person is not justified? Clearly, the answer is no. In the case of execution, a political authority is not above morality, especially when it carries out the law in violation of the very moral principle that the law is suppose to protect.

Nor does the defense of "making a mistake" dismiss the immorality of executing someone who has been falsely convicted of murder. It is no less unethical for the state to kill an innocent person under the sanctity of the law, legal safeguards notwithstanding, than for a murderer to kill an innocent person in direct violation of the law. Both the murderer and the state violate the same moral principle of the sanctity of life. Both commit an injustice even though the state does so while attempting to satisfy the principle of justice. Both actions are inherently immoral.

The widespread propensity for error in the U.S. criminal justice system has led many thoughtful persons to question whether we should conduct any further executions until we have eliminated all the system's imperfections that result in wrongful verdicts. Despite call for caution, many others continue their support for carrying out scheduled executions. They defend their position with the following argument. No human system will ever be error-free. Perfection is not a human possibility. If we do not impose this expectation on other social arenas such as the family, economics, politics, and so on, then we should not do so on the criminal justice system. It is always a tragedy when we wrongly execute innocent people, and we should avoid this as much as it is humanly possible. Nonetheless, in the name of Justice, guilty murderers deserve death by legal execution.

On the other side, opponents of capital punishment respond that death is different. A wrongly executed person has no chance of regaining life if later found innocent; and this only adds to the injustice of the case, which thereby renders such an error-prone system unacceptable.

In addition to emphasizing the unfairness of a system that wrongly condemns innocent persons, opponents of capital punishment point out another unfairness. People who sit on death row are disproportionately poor, racial minorities, and mentally retarded. For example, since 1976, 35% of all executed persons have been Black even though Blacks constitute only 12% of the U.S. population.[8] In 1990, the U.S. General Accounting Office concluded in its study, *Death Penalty Sentencing,* "In 82% of the studies reviewed, race of the victim was found to influence the likelihood of being charged with capital murder or receiving the death penalty, i.e., those who murdered whites were found more likely to be sentenced to death than those who murdered blacks."[9]

While many possible reasons exist for sentencing and execution inequalities, no doubt lack of financial resource necessary for expensive legal council affects poorer persons more adversely than wealthier ones who can afford it. From the Justice-Liberation perspective of Christian Ethics, this means that any attempt to remove the unfairness embedded within the criminal justice system must begin with the preferential treatment of the disadvantaged, because they suffer the most. The system not only convicts innocent people; it also disproportionately convicts racial minorities who are disproportionately poor. If Justice means equality of treatment, then the poor obtain less Justice because of their unequal treatment within the system.

We would not be oversimplifying to say that the opponents of capital punishment decry the U.S. criminal justice system for its inherent injustice. It falsely condemns innocent persons to death and discriminates against the disadvantaged. This makes it self-contradictory. The capital punishment system cannot be defended because it violates the very principle of Justice that proponents use to justify it. As a result of gross injustices, opponents conclude: it should be abolished.

The defenders of the capital punishment system respond to this allegation by claiming that we must continually strive for improvements within the system so that no innocent person will ever be wrongly convicted. At the same time, convicted murderers like Bundy, Gacey, and McVeigh were in fact guilty of their crimes. Therefore, according to the demand for Justice, they deserved to die by execution. Most important of all, the very image of Justice stimulates the search for ways to reduce injustices. The goal is not to abolish capital punishment for those who deserve it but to keep improving the system so that those who are innocent are not wrongfully convicted. In this way, we continue to serve Justice while progressively eliminating injustice. They point out that even those state officials who call for a moratorium on executions do not necessarily want to abolish capital punishment. Instead, they want to improve it by correcting defects in the criminal justice system so that at some point in the future, when they end the moratorium and restart the system, they can reasonably be assured that only the truly guilty will be executed.

Opponents respond that we merely deceive ourselves if we believe we can ever eliminate completely the possibility of error within the criminal justice system. It is simply not realistic to think we can reduce to zero the chance that we will never execute an innocent person. While modifications might cut away some of the systemic defects and racial biases that conspire against the innocent and disadvantaged, it is a pipe dream to expect perfection. Since perfect Justice is not possible, we should not settle for a system that perpetuates even the smallest injustice when an innocent person's life is on the line.

It seems clear from the above discussion that both the opponents and proponents appeal to the idea of perfection to bolster their positions and tie it directly to an image of Justice. Opponents claim that the impossibility of ever achieving perfect Justice obviates the entire system. Proponents stress that the lack of perfect Justice in the system ought not keep us from executing truly guilty murderers while we continually strive to eliminate the injustice of false convictions. Which position seems more persuasive? In truth, neither does. The Justice argument by itself, one way or the other, leads to deadlock. Can we move beyond it?

For many the answer is yes. Christian opponents claim that an Old Testament vision of Justice is not adequate enough for dealing with the thorny moral issues related to capital punishment. They contend that in order to move beyond the bottleneck created by Justice arguments, it is necessary to shift the direction of the moral imagination. Instead of Justice, we should examine the pros and cons of capital punishment from the New Testament image of Christ's Love. This means that many Christians do not oppose capital punishment because of the impossibility of ever achieving perfect Justice; they oppose capital punishment *per se* because it violates their most deeply held moral visions.[10] While they do not deny the validity of the Justice principle, for them Love takes priority over Justice.

Christian opponents of capital punishment insist that they have no other option because their ethical commitment to the norm of Love mandates that they seek an end to legal executions. However, others point out that despite their passionate dedication to Love, they cannot so easily set Justice aside. In the case of murder, the demand for Justice does not disappear. It must be satisfied. Any attempt to resolve the difficult moral dilemmas surrounding capital punishment by resorting to Love alone is inadequate, because both Love and Justice are fundamental Biblical images that nurture the Christian moral imagination. How do Christians who oppose capital punishment based on New Testament images of Love make their case? What role does Justice play in the process?

We have already described many of the pros and cons of capital punishment based on Justice. We can say much in its favor, especially when compared to vengeance, which appeals to the lowest level of the moral imagination. As an ethical vision, Justice is morally superior to revenge. How does an ethic of Love measure up against Justice?

Many Christians who oppose capital punishment begin with the theological assumption that the life, death, and resurrection of Christ reveal God's ultimate nature as Love, or mercy, and not Justice. The New Testament repeatedly underscores this conviction. In the Gospels, Jesus' parables of the lost sheep (Luke 15:1-7), the prodigal son (Luke 15:11-32), and the unmerciful servant (Mt 18:23-35) are prime examples. Paul writes in his letter to the Romans, "All have sinned and fall short of the glory of God." (Romans 3:23) Furthermore, "Christ died for the ungodly," and "while we still were sinners Christ died for us." "For if while we were enemies, we were reconciled to God through the death of his Son, much more surely, having been reconciled, will we be saved by his life." (Romans 5:6-10)

If God has shown ultimate mercy toward humanity by sending Christ to forgive and reconcile a sinful world, then Christians should imitate this same mercy in all aspects of their lives. Their theological commitment to a vision of God's ultimate nature as merciful Love nurtures their moral sensitivities at the deepest level. For Christians who apply mercy to the morality of capital punishment, no alternative exists but to reject all forms of legal execution. This includes death by lethal injection, which leaves a false impression that the executed person dies in a humane and peaceful way by entering a permanent sleeplike state. For Christians committed to the Church's long theological heritage of mercy, such a silky picture of state sponsored death is dishonest, deceptive and inherently abhorrent. While Justice takes priority over revenge, God's supreme act of redemption through Christ means that Love takes precedence over Justice.

Christian opponents of capital punishment believe that the mercy option provides several moral advantages over the logjam created by the Justice position. To begin, ending legal executions removes the dilemma of arbitrary "line drawing" to determine whether some convicted murderers deserve death more than others. It eliminates both the numbers game and the worst crimes problem. It takes government out of the business of legally killing citizens and removes the state from reinforcing the obsession for retaliation and psychological release through the convicted murderer's death.

In addition, showing mercy by eliminating capital punishment gets rid of the problem of potentially executing innocent persons. It removes all the ambiguities and uncertainties in this area. It eradicates completely all injustices resulting from wrongful death. The mercy option especially favors minorities, the poor, and mentally retarded persons who disproportionately sit on death row and cannot afford costly legal help. It ends the impossible quest for an illusive perfection that continues to contribute to executions resulting from persistent biases and patterns of discrimination against minorities and those who can least afford to defend themselves.

This means that an approach based on Love holds an advantage over other alternatives because it combines both mercy and Justice. Ending state executions brings greater Justice to the least advantaged and liberates them from a disproportionately higher risk of wrongful conviction and execution. Simply stated, in terms of the morality of capital punishment, stopping legal executions in the name of Christian Love improves Justice for the poor. Furthermore, abolishing capital punishment removes the need to justify the death of innocent people by claiming that, "although we can never remove all the imperfections, we want to make as few mistakes as possible." From the mercy perspective, good and noble intentions do not justify even one wrongful death at the hands of a system that in all probability will never be perfect.

Thus, it would seem that the Love as mercy option moves beyond many of the impasse problems that the Justice position creates, while it also enhances the possibility of bringing more Justice to those who are victimized by the imperfections and injustices that the capital punishment system perpetuates. On the whole, this conclusion seems morally compelling. However, this is not necessarily so. The Love position is not entirely free of ethical ambiguities that could lead to greater immoral consequences than those associated with the Justice alternative. By itself, a Love approach to capital punishment does not necessarily guarantee a superior moral outcome. It depends on how it is applied.

Little doubt exists that persons guilty of criminal behavior deserve punishment. The only question is what it should be. While showing mercy by eliminating capital punishment protects the innocent and disadvantaged, and in this sense holds the higher moral ground than Justice, being merciful does not necessarily lead to greater Justice. In order for the mercy option to be morally superior to Justice, it must not only eliminate the injustices that the capital punishment system perpetuates, it also must not create greater injustices. If abolishing capital punishment in the name of mercy does not lead to more Justice, then maintaining and modifying the system of capital punishment based on Justice would be the preferred ethical choice.

Anyone who favors Love over Justice should carefully examine this possibility and the ethical vulnerabilities of the mercy position. Unfortunately, all too often, disputes about the morality of capital punishment devolve in the direction of Love versus Justice, which leads to an impasse similar to the one associated with the pure Justice position. Justice proponents readily take aim at mercy advocates who minimize or even ignore the importance of Justice. Just as mercy advocates criticize the Justice position because of its inadequacies, Justice proponents point out deficiencies of the mercy option, which they claim leads to excessive leniency and release of murderers back into society where they can kill again. This is a serious issue.

The question that mercy advocates have to consider involves alternative forms of punishment: If not execution, then what? In calling for the abolition of the death penalty, mercy proponents also must satisfy the moral mandate for Justice. One way for Christian Love advocates to respond to the charge of excessive leniency is to support tough sentences that couple confinement with rehabilitation. Some convicted murderers might need to be locked up for life without the chance of parole. Others might receive less severe sentences depending of the nature of their crimes and the circumstances under which death occurred.

In malice of forethought cases of premeditated murder the maximum penalty might be confinement in prison until death. Killing committed in an act of passion might be adjudicated differently depending on the setting. For mercy proponents, a maximum sentence of imprisonment with no parole is more loving than death by execution even if it does not eliminate completely the chance that convicted murderers might kill again while being confined. For opponents of the death penalty, lifelong imprisonment is not only merciful, it also adequately satisfies the need for Justice. On the other side, for many Justice purists, nothing short of execution fulfills the need for Justice.

Mercy advocates also claim that eliminating capital punishment allows maximum time for uncovering mistaken convictions. It keeps open the opportunity for healing, rehabilitation, and reconciliation, which Christians opposed to capital punishment hold as their core ethical images. Supporters of the mercy alternative see no moral advantage in taking yet another life under the authority of the state, especially in a system that is riddled with false convictions and that places minorities and the poor at higher risk of wrongful execution. They prefer life to death even in horrendous murder cases where one person's injustice, no matter how morally depraved this might be, destroys another person's life.

On the other side of the debate, advocates of capital punishment respond that the elimination of the death penalty violates the mandate for Justice that society owes the murder victim's living loved ones. They have been offended egregiously and have a deep craving for emotional relief. Executing the convicted murderer gives them psychological closure. Opponents of capital punishment reply that they profoundly empathize with the devastation that murder produces in the personal lives of loved one, where emotions run the gamut from incomprehension and seething anger to depression and deep sorrow. However, despite the ravaging anguish that murder imposes on victims' families, the death penalty ought not be used because it might provide psychological release.

For Christians whose base their Faith on the conviction that God responded with Love to Christ's death on the cross, morally superior ways other than execution exist for dealing with grief caused by murder. God's mercy does not extend only to convicted murderers. It encompasses everyone; and it especially embraces the loved ones whose lives a murder shatters. Their urgent needs require that Christians reach out with extraordinary compassion and sensitivity. In addition, God calls upon the faithful to go one step farther. In a world torn apart by sin, the ultimate image of divine mercy involves reconciliation between murderers and their victims' families. For many proponents of this position, apart from a profound Faith that God's ultimate Love has been revealed through Christ's reconciling sacrifice on the cross, it is not even possible to imagine such an act, especially within the moral framework of Justice or revenge.

Finally, from the mercy perspective, we have one more concern to consider. It involves the long-term effect of the capital punishment system on the development of personality and culture. This issue penetrates to the heart of the Christian understanding of Character and to the deepest transformations within the moral imagination. It relates to creating an ethical image of the kind of world we want to become. In any society that glamorizes violence and reinforces it through popular culture, film, video games, television, and public media of all types, killing becomes normative. When a culture maintains an easy tolerance for violence, legal executions become just one more expression of the norm. In such a community, any attempt to transform the imagination through a moral vision based on mercy confronts enormous challenges because killing engenders more killing and images of violence beget more images.

In such a culture, opponents of the death penalty will have an uphill battle because the act of execution, which by definition means legal killing, strengthens the culture of violence. In turn, this affects the development of Character and the normative structures of society within which killing behaviors become common and routine. In a word, repetitious patterns of governmentally enforced killing degrade the moral imagination and corrode the spirit of a people. According to Judge Richard L. Nygaard, "We as Christians must also confront what institutionalized killing is doing to our attitudes toward ourselves. . . . It is difficult to feel pride in a culture that has become so inured to violence that death is an acceptable element."[11] For Nygaard, the prevalence of the death penalty begs the question for Christians. "Should we not as Christians strive to exemplify the grace and mercy of Jesus? And should we not desire this quality likewise in our society?"[12]

We are now ready to draw some conclusions. How do we evaluate the alternatives in terms of both the integrated elements of Transformation Ethics, that is, Faith, Love, Moral Law, Character, Justice, and Liberation and the four sources of authority? We begin with the Bible. It is clear that Christians who either support or oppose capital punishment interpret the Scripture differently to defend their points of view. Those who favor the death penalty use the Old Testament Moral Law passages of life for life, while opponents focus on New Testament images of God's mercy as revealed through the cross of Christ. Both sides argue their well-reasoned positions by appealing to either the Justice or Love traditions of the Christian Faith.

Thus, given these disagreements, we are left with the question: from the Transformation perspective, which alternative is most likely to create the greatest goodness in the world and why? No doubt, support for capital punishment based on Justice has considerable merit. It is consistent with a basic universal human reciprocity norm. Doing like for like, giving measure for measure, tit for tat, or however we express it, has deep appeal within the social conscience of humankind. The idea of proportional treatment in the conduct of everyday affairs has deep roots in human experiences that cut across diverse cultures and religious traditions. In a nutshell, the idea of Justice rests on the golden rule of "do unto others as you would have them do unto you."

When we apply the Justice position to capital punishment, no doubt many convicted murderers like Bundy, Gacey, and McVeigh were guilty of the crimes they committed. From the Justice perspective, they deserved to die. Executing them removed all possibility that they would ever kill again. Their legal deaths served the cause of Justice by balancing the scale of life for life. However, as we have indicated, a weakness in the Justice position is not that it results in executing guilty murderers but that leads to supporting a system that subjects non-guilty persons to the possibility of wrongful execution or, at a minimum, to the indignities of sitting on death row until their release due to innocence. In a perfect world, Justice would be administered perfectly. However, the world is not perfect, and the capital punishment system contains many imperfections that violate the very Justice ideal on which it rests.

Nonetheless, the existence of such imperfections does not necessarily mean that capital punishment should be abolished if no other alternative can be shown to be morally superior. This leads directly to the question of whether the Love or mercy option creates more goodness in the world than one based on Justice. The answer is not simple because we can say much in favor of the Justice position. The mercy option is *not* the preferred alternative unless we can show that it satisfies both the need for Justice and goes beyond it at the same time. Stated differently, Justice is morally preferable to Love unless Love incorporates Justice. This means that the less Love incorporates Justice, the more it loses credibility as a defensible moral position. Murderers must be punished in order to satisfy the need for Justice. The only meaningful question is the form of punishment.

The main advantage of the Love option is that we will never execute an innocent person, especially vulnerable minorities and the least advantaged. When we couple non-execution with tough punishment, such as the possibility of life imprisonment without parole, we act mercifully and justly through permanent confinement. Being merciful also leaves open the possibility of repentance, rehabilitation, and uncovering mistaken convictions. In addition, the virtue of mercy instills within the Christian Character ethical images that do not embrace violence as normative. Nor does it glamorize killing for financial, political, or any other gain. Love transforms the Christian moral imagination and gives rise to a spiritual commitment to seek reconciliation wherever possible, even in the worst cases such as murder.

Given the potential for the long-term transformation of the core cultural values of society, it appears as though the combination of mercy with Justice would create the greatest amount of goodness in the world. This means that both the Justice and Love perspectives by themselves are morally less appealing. Justice alone increases the potential for injustice. Mercy by itself does not satisfy the need for Justice and could contribute to greater injustices. *Thus, Love with Justice is the best moral choice.*

For Transformation Ethics, this means placing the Biblical view of the grace of God as revealed in Christ at the center of Christian Faith and life. The combination of mercy with Justice would satisfy the Old Testament fairness norms and at the same time transcend rigid legalism by tempering the pursuit of Justice, which is grounded in the Moral Law tradition, with mercy. Ending capital punishment in the name of Love with Justice would also send an important anti-violence message that society no longer accepts a legally reinforced culture of killing, even when carried out in the name of Justice. For minorities, the poor, and the mentally retarded, this would be a message of Liberation. Finally, Character development that stresses Love with Justice would help create a community environment where mercy would be a dominant norm, fairness would apply equally to all, and vengeance would have no place. As a result, the total amount of goodness in the world would increase.

Notes

1. We will define Timothy McVeigh's bombing of the Federal Building in Oklahoma City on April 19, 1995 as an act of premeditated murder even though the form of the crime qualifies as an act of domestic terrorism.

2. See Hugo Adam Bedau, "The Case Against the Death Penalty," in *Moral Issues and Christian Response*, edited by Paul T. Jersild and Dale A. Johnson, fourth edition, New York: Holt, Rinehart, Winston, Inc., 1988, pp 282-286. Also see "Facts About Deterrence and the Death Penalty," published on the Home Page of the Death Penalty Information Center, http://www.deathpenaltyinfo.org/deter.html, January 14, 2002.

3. Ernest Van den Haag, "The Collapse of the Case Against Capital Punishment," in Paul Jersild, and others, editors, *Moral Issues and Christian Response,* sixth edition, New York: Harcourt Brace College Publishers, 1998, pp. 255-265.

4. See Rachel King and Barbara Hood, editors, *Not In Our Name: Murder Victims Families Speak Out Against the Death Penalty,* Cambridge, Mass.: Murder Victims' Families for Reconciliation, 2001.

5. All quotes from Van den Haag, p. 263.

6. Matthew L. Stephens, "Instrument of Justice or Tool of Vengeance?" in *Moral Issues and Christian Response,* fifth edition, New York: Harcourt Brace Javanovich College Publishers, 1993, pp. 237-238.

7. See "Innocence and the Death Penalty," Death Penalty Information Center, http://www.deathpenaltyinfo.org/innoc.htm.

8. See "Race of Defendants Executed Since 1976," Death Penalty Information Center, http://www.deathpenaltyinfo.org/dpicrace.html.

9. Quoted in "Persons Executed for Interracial Murders," Death Penalty Information Center, http://www.deathpenaltyinfo.org/dpicrace.html.

10. See books like Helen Prejean, *Dead Man Walking,* that incorporates Love as the central value and that Hollywood turned into a movie with the same title.

11. Richard L. Nygaard, "'Vengeance Is Mine' Says the Lord," in Jersild, and others, *Moral Issues and Christian Response,* sixth edition, 1998, p. 254.

12. Nygaard, "'Vengeance Is Mine' Says the Lord," p. 254.

Chapter 9

Genetic Modification

In this Chapter, we will examine the morality of genetic modification, which is also called genetic manipulation or engineering. We have chosen to use the word modification because it implies permanently altering the genetic structures of life through scientific manipulation. Recent controversies surrounding cloning and stem cell research have received widespread media coverage and contain many of the same ethical dilemmas involved in genetic modification. All three of these issues confront humankind with extraordinary challenges that will engage our post-industrial moral imagination for decades to come. Among the many bioethical issues that emerged during the last third of the twentieth century, our growing ability to modify the genome, that is, the genetic blueprint of life, casts the longest shadow into the future because it deals with changing the most fundamental foundations of plant and animal existence. In this sense, it stands as one of the most revolutionary changes of our time.[1]

Background Issues

The moral controversies related to genetic modification stem from developments that occurred over the past century or so. Because of modern scientific research, we have discovered that the map of organic and biological life consists of the DNA (deoxyribonucleic acid) that encodes the genetic information necessary for perpetuating all living forms. These include plants, humans, and every non-human species. The monk Gregor Mendal gets credit for being one of the most successful early pioneers in this area. During the mid-nineteenth century, he began studying the genetic structures of plants. Since then molecular biologists have progressed steadily toward the holy grail of genetic research, uncovering the DNA patterns that direct the course of evolution on the earth.

In this Chapter, we will concentrate on the ethics of genetic modification as it pertains to human life and not plant or non-human life. This does not mean that moral concerns connected to the alterations in these latter two areas are insignificant. They are, especially as they affect the future of the entire biosphere and respect for all the diverse manifestations of life. Nonetheless, we will not examine the uses of biotechnology as they affect agriculture and non-human animal genetics. The recent outcries over animal abuse and the fear of creating freaks or "frankenfoods" show that altering non-human species and plants through scientific and technological intervention remains controversial. At a minimum an atmosphere of caution surrounds these initiatives, which in some cases produces harsh criticism.[2] Despite the deep ethical questions connected to altering plants and non-human species, we will focus our discussion elsewhere—on the morality of modifying the human genome.

In one importance sense, a Transformation approach dovetails with an examination of the morality of genetic modification because to modify something means to transform it from on state to another. One of our most universal experiences is that life changes constantly. It never stays stagnant. This observation cuts across virtually every aspect of human existence. The most cursory study of history reveals that social, political, and economic conditions in the modern world differ dramatically from pre-modern eras. Many of the structural arrangements and ideas that once dominated entire civilizations no longer exist. Many prosperous ancient societies have disappeared altogether or have been modified through contact with other cultures. Life in all its forms *is* transformation.

Our scientific understanding of the human genome has expanded very rapidly during the past fifty years. In 1953 James Watson and Francis Crick identified the double helix DNA structure that contains all the genes of the human body. Every human cell houses a complete set of genes that are distributed on the 46 chromosomes, except for the germ cells. After 1953, scientists set about the task of completely mapping and sequencing the human genome as rapidly as possible. In 1989 the U.S. Congress weighed into this effort by committing millions of dollars to the Human Genome Project with the goal of creating a comprehensive genetic map by 2005. In 1999, the private corporation Celera Genomics entered the chase.[3] One year later through the combined public and private sector initiatives, scientists completed the mapping process five years ahead of schedule.

For all intents and purposes, we start the twenty-first century and the third millennium with the map of the human genome in hand. It would not be an overstatement to say that we have entered into a new stage of human evolution without knowing where we will go or how far. Unlike all previous generations, we now possess the knowledge and power to permanently modify the genetic foundation of human life. Along with this new capacity, we confront many vital ethical questions that range all the way from whether we should intrude into the human genome at all or, if we do, in what way and to what end. During the past two decades, we have begun to address some of these questions as we have improved our capacity to conduct screening tests that reveal any person's genetic makeup. Throughout the rest of this Chapter we will examine the genetic challenges of the present with the goal of transforming the future into a world of maximum goodness.

We begin by laying out the four alternative forms of possible genetic modification. The ethical issues that we will address relate directly to these possibilities as depicted in the following diagram.[4]

Genetic Modification Diagram

	Somatic	Germ-Line
Therapy	1	2
Enhancement	3	4

The diagram contains four cells and each one identifies a different type of genetic modification. First we will describe the characteristics of the cells and then examine their ethical aspects. As public awareness of our ability to alter the human genome grows, we will inevitably confront the concern of whether we should draw the line somewhere by sanctioning some forms of genetic modification but not others. This issue lies at the heart of the matter. We need to have a clear image of all the possibilities and of their moral implications for the future.

As the left side of the above graphic shows, we can distinguish between genetic therapy and genetic enhancement. Therapy refers to curing, preventing, or eliminating diseases that genetic deficiencies cause, such as hemophilia, cystic fibrosis, and so on. Enhancement intervention differs from therapy because it involves not just curing, etc., but improving the genes that contribute to the development of specific human capacities, such as intelligence, physical size and appearance, aptitudes, and so on. We can label therapeutic modifications as negative eugenics, and enhancements as positive eugenics. In the most basic sense of the word, negative eugenics equates to getting rid of bad genes and the positive eugenics to improving good ones.

Across the top of the diagram we can separate somatic cell from germ-line cell interventions. Somatic cell manipulation refers to altering in some way the genome of a single person without transferring the change to future generations. In short, it involves changing genes one person at a time. On the other hand, germ-line alteration involves genetic modifications in the reproductive cells and can be passed to future generation through procreation.

With these basic distinctions, we can identify four alternative forms of genetic modification: somatic-therapy (cell 1), germ-line therapy (cell 2), somatic enhancement (cell 3), and germ-line enhancement (cell 4). Cell 1 (somatic therapy) is the least controversial of the four types of modification because it involves only single individuals and does not permanently affect the human gene pool. Cell 4 (germ-line enhancement) is the most controversial because it seeks to improve humanity through genetic modifications that can be passed along through reproduction.

Cell 2 (germ-line therapy) and cell 3 (somatic enhancement) lie somewhere in between these two extremes. They are more controversial than cell 1 (somatic therapy) because they involve either germ-line intervention or enhancement, but they do not go as far as cell 4, which is the most extreme form of genetic modification because it leads to germ-line enhancement. Which of these four forms of genetic modification are morally acceptable? Should we draw the line somewhere? Basically, we have three options. We can reject all four, accept some and not others, or accept all four. Which option will most likely lead to the greatest goodness?

Ethical Perspectives

In order to answer these questions, we start with the core images that for Transformation Ethics lie at the center of the Christian moral imagination, Love and Justice. As we have shown, both have their origins within the Biblical heritage of the Church. No direct Scriptural references exist on the application of Love and Justice to modifying the human genome for the obvious reason that the science of genetics did not exist at the time the Bible was written or canonized. This means that we must draw our conclusions about the morality of genetic modification on the basis of inferences from specific verses or moral visions. This also applies to the traditions of the Church, although the Bible takes precedence in guiding our interpretations.

Love and Justice complement each other by moving between persons and social structures. As we have seen, Justice is the External/Communal side of Love. Moral Law and just public policies direct the distribution of collective burdens and benefits throughout the whole of society, but ultimately they exist to enhance the welfare of each person. From an ethical perspective, policies that apply to everyone are preferable to those that benefit some at the expense of others. In this sense, Justice reinforces Love and Love leads to Justice. Which of the three above options would we most likely choose by applying these two standards to the morality of genetic modification?

In addition to Love and Justice, the Christian view of Character also relates directly to whether or not we should consider altering the human genome in some way. We need to give careful consideration to the role that virtues such as compassion and empathy would play in steering our decisions in the most ethical direction. At a minimum, a vision of liberating people from the ravages of genetic diseases might motivate us to pursue specific medical goals. We also need to address the concern that all needy persons have equal access to the benefits that modifying the human genome might bring to humankind. In the final analysis, we will move into the future of genetic modification based on the ethical vision we possess in the present.

We begin by presenting the perspectives of those who oppose interventions into the human genome. In general, two main viewpoints exist. The first is based on nature and the second on theology. We will begin with the naturalist perspective and then turn to the theological one. According to the most vocal opponents, genetic modification produces more harm than good and is damaging, dangerous, and inhumane.[5] The naturalist critics envision a kind of forbidden zone of inquiry. They fear that if we venture into it, then in no time at all we will become mesmerized by the erroneous idea that we can genetically engineer the human species at will. They share a profound suspicion that we could visit great harm on future generations through misguided intrusion into the gene pool. They place greater confidence in the superiority of biological evolution over human intervention and perceive that human beings lack the wisdom necessary for making the right choices.

This critique is not frivolous; it offers us much food for thought. Careless human manipulation of the biological foundations of life could undo the genetic structures that took millions of years to evolve and that sustain all forms of life. Nature has demonstrated time and again its inherently self-sustaining strengths. We should not take genetic intrusion lightly or smugly assume that we can force our will on nature without running the risk of doing irreversible damage to natural processes that sustains us. Given that humankind has already destroyed many non-human species through reckless technological assaults on the environment, we would be wise to leave nature well enough alone. It would seem that nature is able to care for itself better than we can. Thus, we should refrain completely from entering the biological or moral terrain of genetic modification.

Despite the well-taken cautionary tone of this position, in the final analysis it is untenable because it proceeds from a false view of the relationship of humankind to nature. As humans, we do not live apart from nature as disembodied spirits. We cannot exist in our earthly form without physical bodies. At the same time, we are self-transcendence and possess the capacity for Faith and reasoned self-reflection. In truth, as a biological species, we have been altering nature since the first human being planted a seed by poking a digging stick into the ground. We do not go against nature when we change some aspect of it. Rather, it is our nature to alter nature. Genetic intervention is merely an extension of what we have been doing for thousands of years. In the case of modifying the human genome we are nature changing itself at the most basic level of life. The real issue is not whether we should intervene in nature but rather why, how, and to what end.

Even though we reject the hidden zone viewpoint, we need to consider one more crucial concern that the naturalist critics of genetic modification raise. In all fairness, they recognize that human beings have been altering nature in one way or another throughout the long march of biological evolution. At the same time, for opponents of genetic intervention, this is but a steppingstone to a more significant issue: Natural selection has created the best of all possible worlds. Simply stated, over eons of time, nature has demonstrated that it knows best. It has weeded out all the inferior life forms and has guaranteed the survival of only the superior ones. Therefore, humankind should not tamper with biological evolution because in doing so we will probably only bring greater harm into the world.

We recognize the strength of this point of view and acknowledge that nature has created millions of amazingly beautiful, well-adapted and diverse life forms. At the same time, nature is not perfect; and humankind has been intervening to improve it as long as humans have walked on the earth. From the earliest of times, we have been modifying nature in one form or another to transcend its limitations. This applies especially to our efforts to improve the human condition. We have been practicing medicine for centuries on the assumption that it is morally acceptable to intervene into the malfunctions of the human body for the purpose of enhancing health. We have learned how to fix broken bones, eliminate dreaded diseases like small pox, and perform open-heart surgery. When it comes to the operations of the human body, we have *never* assumed that nature knows best, especially when its imperfections cause pain and suffering.

For those persons who inherit biological weaknesses that can cause or lead to more than 5,000 genetic diseases, ample room exists to modify nature for the better. According to one source, genetic diseases linked directly to DNA deficiencies "are responsible for much human suffering."[6] The list of disabling genetic diseases is a long one; it includes early and late-in-life degenerative conditions like Tay-Sachs and Huntington's, cystic fibrosis, sickle-cell anemia, muscular dystrophy, cancer, cardiovascular weaknesses, and many more. From the perspective of anyone victimized by genetic disabilities over which they have no control, nature not only does not know best, it causes the problem in the first place.

Therefore, we can assume that it is morally acceptable to reduce human suffering through genetic modification if we can do so without creating harm. While the opponents are correct to emphasize the dangers of interfering with evolution and of the potential to damage or even destroy the biological underpinnings of life, if we can make nature better by intervening directly into the processes of natural selection, then we should do so. Only one question remains. Given the four alternatives defined in the Genetic Modification Diagram, which one(s), if any, should we choose? Before we take up this question, however, we need to review religious reasons for opposing genetic modification.

The theological argument is straightforward: If we attempt to direct the course of human advancement through genetic modification, we usurp divine authority over the evolution of life. By intervening into the human genome, we are trying to "play God." All such initiatives are inherently sinful because they encroach on God's prerogative as the creator and sustainer of the universe. God has created the world with permanent biological boundaries. God remains sovereign over the created order and governs through divine providence. We should trust that God knows best when it comes to determining the future of human evolution. We sin when we try to direct our own destiny by changing the human genome.

For those who hold this perspective, God created us with certain but restricted capacities and held on to prerogatives that have not been delegated to us. We sin when we inappropriately assume an authority that only God possesses. James J. Walter describes this viewpoint in the following way. "When humans take it upon themselves to usurp God's rights, for example, those rights to determine the future and to change the universal laws that govern biological nature, they act from the lack of a right . . . and thus they act in a sinful manner." In this view, God relates to humankind from the top on down. The freedom that God gave us exists mainly for the purpose of discovering God's fixed laws and following them. In the area of the human genome, any attempt to modify the genetic blueprint is an expression of "human arrogance."[7]

This theological position is a variation of the naturalist point of view; but instead of saying nature knows best, we would state that God knows best. Like the argument from nature, we recognize the value of caution regarding any human genome intervention. At the same time, by turning the theological lens to another setting, we can perceive in a different light how to approach the moral dilemmas related to the morality of genetic modification.

We can still affirm that God created all that is but that the universe does not remain a static order. God created a biological system within which change constantly occurs. Stable patterns exist, but they become transformed over time. The destiny of humankind has not been predetermined or defined with complete finality. Furthermore, God has imbued us, as human beings, with the freedom to participate in creation's continuous evolution through the capacity for choice. The moral judgments we make today will help shape the course of the future tomorrow. We can act with good or evil intent. We can use our freedom responsibly or irresponsibly.

These assumptions about God lead to a different conclusion about our relationship to nature than the previous theological perspective. We understand ourselves not merely as responders in a universe of divinely crafted unchanging physical or biological structures. *We are co-partners with God* and can make responsible decisions that lead to improving on the imperfections of the natural order. The main moral challenge that stands before us involves deciding how we should use the freedom that God has given us. Walter writes that if one reasons that God has left the "material nature unfinished and believes that the future is mainly indeterminate, then one would be more inclined morally to justify attempts at genetic manipulation."[8] With divine guidance as defined through the Biblical witness and in combination with experience, tradition, and reason we can participate with God in making changes that will bring greater goodness into the world, including transformations in the human genome.

All this sounds good in theory. However, according to both the religious and naturalist opponents of genetic modification, history teaches us that we should not place much confidence in humanity's capacity to make wise choices in this area. Virtually all of the eugenics experiments of the past have taken us down the wrong path. They point especially to how Hitler's genetics programs during the 1940s brutalized Jewish and other innocent victims. For many, even the word "eugenics" conjures up dehumanizing images like those depicted in *Brave New World* and *1984* or in movies like *Blade Runner*. Critics remain skeptical that we can ever safeguard ourselves against such exploitation. For them, history demonstrates the opposite: In our enthusiasm to enhance humankind through eugenics, we have only succeeded in eroding the fragile moral fabric that protects us from sliding down the slippery slope of moral degradation.

Few would deny that the perpetrators of the Nazi eugenics programs visited anything but horror on their victims and scarred the conscience of humanity forever. At the same time, many changes have occurred since the 1940s. Starting with the 1949 Principles of the Nuremberg Code, we have enumerated ethical principles and created medical procedures designed to prevent the recurrence of such brutalities. All of them rest on the moral principle of respect for human dignity. All medical research or therapeutic interventions require the informed consent of participants and patients. Over the past fifty years we have developed safeguards to protect vulnerable populations, such as children, prisoners, the poor, the terminally ill, and so on. We have created rigorous review protocols for all biomedical research involving human subjects.[9] A sacred moral principle sits at the center of all these initiatives: No one should be forced to participate in any medical procedure or research program against his or her will.

The Biblical images of Love and Justice tie directly to these changes and help nurture the moral imagination through virtues such as compassion and fairness. For bioethics in general and genetic modification in particular, these values serve to protect all persons from mistreatment caused by careless procedures and overzealous researchers. It is moral to use medical knowledge for the purpose of improving human health, but it is not moral to obtain such understanding through procedures that violate informed consent protections, ignore careful research protocols, and place patients or participants in harm's way. Good outcomes do not justify the use of evil methods to obtain them. The only ethically defensible position in the field of biomedicine, including genetic modification, is one that incorporates both means and ends.

In theory this sounds right, but in practice it is difficult to implement. We recognize that genetic science and medical practice are extraordinarily complex and challenging for many laypersons to understand. Nonetheless, we believe that medical researchers and providers have a moral obligation to help patients and research subjects comprehend these complexities as fully as possible before they consent to participate in any procedure. At a minimum medical practitioners and scientists should provide information, take time to answer questions, and wherever necessary hold education sessions to promote understanding.

In this way, lay patient-subjects will achieve a level of sophistication that accurately and adequately informs their voluntary consent, even though they might not fully grasp all the scientific facts.

We are now in a position to address the question of which of the four forms of genetic modification, if any, we would consider morally acceptable. Based on the medical codes of ethics, review protocols, and informed consent procedures that have been developed during the past half-century, we can conclude that rejecting all four forms of genetic modification is not ethically defensible. While we must never forget the depth of moral deterioration to which humanity can plunge, as witnessed in the Nazi eugenic experiments, we should not be so immobilized by fear that we fail to use our knowledge of the human genome in beneficial ways. If we follow the safeguards that we have created, then we can proceed with caution in making genetic modifications that will bring greater goodness into the world.

In fact, we have already taken the first steps in this direction. The only remaining question is how far we will go. In effect, we have rejected the position that we should avoid any and all forms of genetic modification. The first officially approved genetic intervention in the United States occurred in 1990 when researchers inserted a modified gene into a four-year old girl in order to correct a malfunctioning one. W. French Anderson, one of the early pioneers in genetic research and medicine, and his associates successfully added genes to a type of white blood cell called T cells. In this case the cells lacked ADA (adenosine deaminase) without which the body cannot ward off infections. Since 1990, over 100 different experiments have been conducted on a wide variety of defective cells that cause diseases like cystic fibrosis and cancer.[10]

In effect, since 1990 we have been performing one of the four forms of genetic modification, which is somatic-therapy (see cell 1). This form of intervention is the most conservative because it involves altering single genes one person at a time and does not subject the human gene pool to possible harm. The early successes in somatic therapy are encouraging because they have alleviated diseases caused by the defects of nature. Little doubt exists that we will continue to expand this form of genetic modification in the future in order to eliminate as many genetic diseases as possible for persons who have them.

Given a decade of success with cell 1 genetic modifications involving somatic therapy, we can turn our attention to the remaining three cells. We begin by asking whether it is moral to move beyond cell 1 and cross the line into cell 2, germ-line therapy. Germ-line intervention is far more controversial than limited somatic treatment because it carries the potential to cause irreversible damage to the human gene pool. Germ-line manipulations (cell 2) might leave future generations vulnerable in ways we do not yet understand. It is risky to attempt permanent alterations of the human genome, even if we are motivated by the noblest of moral visions: the Liberation of humanity from the ravages of genetic disease.

While we would be wise to proceed with great caution, this does not mean that we should never move from cell 1 to cell 2. At the same time, it does imply that we should not engage in germ-line therapy until we are sufficiently certain, based on the best scientific evidence, that we will not endanger the human genome. We recognize that no medical intervention is one hundred percent risk free, even with such commonplace occurrences as taking an aspirin. Nonetheless, we can reasonably assume that if future germ-line therapies become as medically safe as somatic therapies are now, then in principle germ-line genetic modifications would be morally permissible. Given the rapid advancements in genetic medicine, we can assume that germ-line interventions will occur in the not too distant future. Using the worldwide eradication of small pox as an analogy, we can conclude that if it is ethical to eliminate diseases one person at a time, then it is also ethical to remove them permanently for all humankind.

To some extent we have already begun to move in this direction with advances in genetic screening and counseling. Genetic examinations already exist for couples who suspect that they are carriers of hereditary diseases, such as Tay Sachs, Huntington's, and many others, that they might pass on to their offspring. Through such pre-fertilization testing, we are asserting *de facto* that a moral preference exists for perpetuating only the healthiest genes. If persons test positive as genetic disease carriers, then they must decide whether or not to have children who would risk being affected. If they choose not to reproduce, in effect they are deciding to remove from future generations a gene that could potentially cause much suffering.

By whatever name we call this type of decision, it is a form of negative eugenics because it stops the perpetuation of a bad gene. In the moral imagination, we need only to take a small step to go from the choice not to reproduce under these circumstances for the sake of future generations to actively altering the human genome for the same reason. The science of genetics is still young. However, future progress in this area will most likely lead toward greater understanding of both the possibilities as well as the limitations of germ-line therapy. At some point in the future, given the choice of 1) not having children in order to avoid subjecting them to the risk of genetic disease or 2) having children after eliminating disease-causing genes, most couples will probably opt for the latter.

Thus, from the perspective of Christian Ethics, we find no basis for limiting genetic modifications to cell 1. If germ line therapies (cell 2) result in bringing future healthy children into the world without permanently damaging the human genome, then like somatic therapies that improve the health of already living people, in principle they are morally acceptable.

Next question: If we can justify both somatic and germ-line therapies, how should we think about genetic enhancements? Should we cross from cells 1 and 2 into cells 3 and/or 4? If it is permissible to remove or modify bad genes that cause genetic diseases for both living and future populations, is it also acceptable to improve good genes through somatic or germ-line alterations? According to geneticist W. French Anderson, who pioneered somatic-therapy, we should not cross over into genetic enhancements. In his view, we should avoid both cells 3 and 4. "Our society is comfortable with the use of genetic engineering to treat individuals with serious disease. On medical and ethical grounds we should draw the line excluding any form of enhancement engineering. We should not step over the line that delineated treatment from enhancement."[11]

In Anderson's view, we lack scientific knowledge of the effects of genetic enhancement. We do not comprehend the interconnections between specific genetic traits and the dispositions that might derive from them, especially in areas as complex as intelligence, aptitude, emotion, character traits, and so on. We lack understanding of the interaction effects between single and multiple genes and between single or multiple genes and the environment. It is one thing to cure hemophilia by modifying the genetic building blocks that cause it, but it is quite another to attempt to enhance the genetic foundations of intelligence, aptitude, emotion, or tendencies toward developing specific character traits. Furthermore, as we stated earlier, past positive eugenics programs have always ended in moral degradation.[12]

Given the current status of medical knowledge, we might do well to heed Anderson's caveats. However, despite these scientific observations and strong words of caution, this does not mean that we should permanently exclude the possibility of making genetic enhancements in the future. While it is unclear when this might occur, it seems certain that genetic research will inevitably thrust us in this direction, which in turn means that we need to prepare ourselves for this eventuality.

According to J. Hughes, in one important sense we have already started down this road. Even though we have drawn an important dividing line between therapeutic and enhancement interventions, in effect this distinction is not as clear as some might think. Upon closer examination, the line becomes fuzzier. For Hughes, our effort to reduce the potential for genetic diseases is in fact an attempt at improvement. By eliminating or changing genes that cause diseases we prevent future suffering. As W. French Anderson noted, we are comfortable with the idea of treating individuals who have genetic diseases or of removing the potential to get them later in life. Hughes claims that strengthening the body's resistance to genetic disease is a form of enhancement.[13]

Except in those clear cut cases like hemophilia, Tay-Sachs, cystic fibrosis, and so on, we cannot give a simple yes or no answer to the question of whether any given person's genes will cause a genetically predisposed disease like cancer. In many cases, getting or avoiding such a disease is not like flipping a toggle switch on or off. Rather, whether any single person gets some form of cancer or cardiovascular disease is a matter of probability depending on a combination of many influences such as genetic makeup, family history, personality, habits, environment, and so on.

This implies that from the perspective of human health, if we can enhance the body's potential to resist genetic diseases and do so safely, then we have a moral obligation to do so. If the genes that predispose a women to breast cancer are weak, and we can strengthen them to resist the disease, then we should. By analogy, we routinely inoculate people for protection from air born contagious illnesses. Vaccination is one of most universally accepted practices of modern medicine. If we can justify strengthening a person's capacity to resist deadly diseases through immunization programs, we can do so through genetic modification as well. According to one sources, "health-related enhancements by genetic means are morally justifiable in principle."[14]

Thus, we can conclude that crossing the boundary from therapy into enhancement is morally permissible. Are both forms of enhancement acceptable, that is, cells 3 and 4, or only one and not the other? We can give a straightforward answer this question. If it is ethical to do somatic therapy (cell 1) and germ-line therapy (cell 2) to improve human health, then it is also ethical to do somatic and germ-line enhancements (cells 3 and 4), assuming of course that we can do so safely. Therefore, from the perspective of improving the health conditions of humanity, *in principle* all four forms of genetic modification (cells 1, 2, 3 and 4) are morally acceptable.

One final question remains. Is it ethical to engage in genetic modifications for non-health related reasons, such as enhancing intelligence, aptitudes, physical size or strength, character, and so on? In this case, we are not just eliminating bad genes or strengthening weak ones. We are modifying the human genome to enhance certain human traits we consider desirable. Admittedly we have a deep discomfort with this prospect given the history of past eugenics experiments like those in Nazi Germany. Nonetheless, it seems reasonable to conclude that if we can justify enhancing the human genome in order to eliminate or resist disease, we can justify enhancements that would strengthen human potential in other areas as well. The issue is not whether we should enhance or not enhance. We have already concluded that genetic enhancement is morally acceptable. The only real concern involves deciding which human capacities we want to strengthen and for what reasons.

If the goal of recent genetic discoveries, as envisioned by Christian Transformation Ethics, is to increase goodness in the world, then we can identify numerous character traits that we ought to strengthen through genetic modification and others that should weakened. This might sound farfetched given that our current scientific understanding of the operations of the human genome is still at an early stage. Even though we do not comprehend how genetic inheritance interacts with social learning or moral development, one aspect of our human potential is clear. There is a genetic foundation underneath all of the conditions and activities of human life.

What is the next step? Given that we are on the cutting edge of one of the most profound turning points in human history, we must stretch our moral imagination beyond the near-term future of ten, twenty, or even fifty years. We need to expand our visionary horizon to encompass the twenty-second century and even farther into the future. There is no reason why we should not engage in enhancements and germ-line alterations if they are medically safe, follow approved scientific protocols, are performed under conditions of informed consent, and transform the world in morally positive ways. What appears outlandish now might become routine at some distant point in the future. In due time, would it not a step in the right ethical direction if humankind could modify the human genome to enhance the capacity for Love and Justice and weaken the predisposition to greed and violence?

For many Christians and others, this sounds preposterous if not downright scary. While we accept and are already doing somatic therapy (cell 1), we remain anxious about drifting toward germ-line enhancement (cell 4). We agree that we are morally justified in eliminating or modifying defective genes to improve physical health, but we are dubious about enhancing genes not directly related to this goal. Fear is a normal reaction to the unknown. Plus, given that we do not understand well enough the science of genetics at this point in time to predict the long-term outcomes of reproductive cell modifications, we freeze in fright at the thought, and understandably so, that we might bring more evil into the world than good. Nonetheless, there is no reason in principle why we should not accept all four forms of genetic modification for the purpose of improving health as well as enhancing other desirable and positive traits.

For theological reasons, many Christians might disagree with this conclusion and emphasize that our attempt to exert greater influence over our biological evolution through genetic modification merely expresses our human sinfulness. They contend that only God can direct the course of the future. From the Transformation perspective, this theology is inadequate. We are not just passive responders. God has created us with freedom and the capacity for choice. We are called through Faith in Christ to be God's co-partners. The future is not something that just happens to us while we wait for providence to push us forward or blind chance to pull us into the unknown. Rather, God provides us with the privilege of being co-initiators and co-decision makers in helping create a future filled with greater Love and Justice. Genetic modification helps open the door to this possibility. If the human genome is imperfect and we can transform it for the better, then for Christian Faith, no reason exists why we should not do so.

Can we guarantee that genetic modification will not take us in the direction of yet another eugenics nightmare? In the final analysis, we cannot. No failsafe method exists to prevent backsliding into evil. If history teaches us any lesson at all, it is that human progress is not inevitable. There is no once and for all assurance that we will evolve irreversibly toward a more humane future. We can always regress. The potential for the demonic to reemerge in the midst of moral advancement seems to be permanently implanted in the human condition.

In order to avoid ethical backsliding, we must transform the human Character in the direction of goodness. For writers like Ted Peters, the essential Christian virtue that holds out the greatest promise for preventing genetic dehumanization is compassion, which is of course one of the essential aspects of Love. He cautions that we run the risk of losing our sensitivity toward imperfect persons as we advance in our ability to eliminate genetic deficiencies.

At the center of the genetic modification controversies stands a moral paradox: The desire to eliminate nature's defects might become transformed into the imperative to do so. Simply stated, the "can do" of genetic modification might become a "must do." As we develop our capability to alter the human genome, we could run the risk of self-dehumanization and of developing the delusion that we could create the perfect person.[15] As a result, our intolerance of imperfection would grow, which in turn would diminish our capacity for compassion. Would we expect that all prospective parents be tested for genetic defects before conceiving children or encourage abortion if their growing fetuses carry "bad" genes? Would parents and their "imperfect" children become objects of disdain or discrimination as portrayed in the movie *Gattaca?*

These are serious questions; and anyone who contemplates a future where genetic enhancement will probably become common practice must deal with them. For the Christian moral imagination, the key defense against dehumanization is the cultivation of compassion toward the suffering of others. This does not remove the difficult choices that will have to be made in both the present and the future on the cutting edge of genetic modification. However, it does provide a context of deep caring in a world where the removal of all imperfections is no simple possibility. The goal of Transformation Ethics is not human perfection but rather to use genetic science to maximize Love and Justice in the world through co-partnership with God.

While compassion may serve to guard us against the drift toward dehumanization, serious concern still remains over how to distribute the benefits of genetic modification in a fair and equitable manner. At core, this is a matter of Justice, where the question of who gets what and why is always of paramount importance. Would only wealthy persons benefit because they could pay the high costs of genetic therapies or enhancements? Would disparities worsen between the rich and poor? Would society's least advantaged members fall back even further in their ability to close the gap? For some critics, we should focus our energies on assuring that everyone has access to a basic standard of health before we start modifying genes based on wealth.

This perspective has merit, but it is too restrictive. Providing universal health coverage and improving humankind through genetic modification are not mutually exclusive goals. If altering the human genome is good for one group, then it is also good for all groups. Our best Justice alternative is not to stop the forward momentum of genetic research and treatment but rather to create public policies through which we can more equitably distribute their benefits to all needy persons.

Along with distributing the benefits of genetic modification in a fair manner, another Justice issue involves the need for privacy and keeping confidential each person's genetic medical records. The potential for abuse in this area is enormous. Persons with disease prone genetic conditions run greater risk of discrimination and rejection for employment and insurance coverage. Employers would be reluctant to hire new workers whose genetic predispositions might cause diseases that would increase future medical expenses. In many cases, insurance companies that already reject applicants with pre-existing medical conditions would turn away others with genetic weaknesses.

The concern for fairness requires protecting the confidentiality of all medical records in order to eliminate the potential for genetic discrimination. Persons who are vulnerable to their own disease producing genes need moral and legal safeguards in order to gain access to jobs and health coverage. In our post-industrial, computer networked, information-oriented society where data retrieval is easy, we need to remind ourselves constantly of the need for ongoing public policies that reflect the highest standards of Justice and that insure each person's privacy.

We are now ready to summarize this Chapter. Clearly, we have entered the brave new world of genetic modification, where the potential to bring benefits as well as harm challenges us at every turn. We have already begun to modify ourselves through somatic healing, and widespread support exists for this type of alteration. As we gain more scientific knowledge about the inner workings of the human genome and how to alter it, we will confront other questions. How far will we go? Will we stop somewhere between cell 1—somatic therapy and cell 4—germ-line enhancement? If we move toward enhancement, what traits will be try to improve and for whom?

At this point in time, we lack a consensus on numerous aspects of genetic enhancement. Disagreements range all the way from not doing it at all to not knowing what traits to enhance should we develop the scientific expertise to do it. Despite our current lack of consensus on these issues, as stated earlier we believe that all four forms of genetic modification, that is, somatic therapy, germ-line therapy, somatic enhancement, and germ-line enhancement, are morally acceptable in principle.

We also recognize that no guarantee exits that we will not take a turn for the worst in our efforts to bring about either healing or enhancement. However, we should not be immobilized by the thought that we might do more harm than good. We cannot sit on the status quo or return to an earlier place in time. The human genome train has already left the station. As we head toward the future of genetic modification, we will see dramatic changes. The only issue is the direction we will take and who will benefit.

While the horrible eugenics lessons of history teach us to go cautiously down the path toward tomorrow, we must also remind ourselves that the potential to do good exists at every moment in time even though it is not automatic or inevitable. From the perspective of Transformation Ethics, human beings can better the world. If not, then we can rightly question why Christian Faith even exists at all. Through Biblical visions of Love and Justice, the development of virtues like compassion and empathy for suffering, the creation of fair and equitable laws, and Liberation from the ravages of genetic disease, in co-partnership with God, we can transform the future in the direction of greater goodness.

Notes

1. In addition to cloning and stem cell research, other issues include the development of reproductive technologies, *in vitro* fertilization-embryo transplant, using fertility drugs, surrogacy, fetal research, abortion, treating impaired infants, organ transplants and allocating scarce medical resources, euthanasia, and so on.

2. One of most outspoken critics is Jeremy Rifkin, *Entropy: Into the Greenhouse World,* revised edition, New York: Bantam Books, 1989. Also see Joel Keehn, "Genetic Engineering Harms Agriculture," pp. 74-81; Wes Jackson, "Biotech Agriculture is Inefficient and Destructive," pp. 88-93; and Andrew Kimbrell, "Genetically Altering Animals Is Dangerous and Inhumane," pp. 102-107, in *Genetic Engineering: Opposing Viewpoints,* edited by Carol Wekesser, San Diego, Cal.: Greenhaven Press, Inc., 1996.

3. Ronald Munson, *Intervention and Reflection: Basic Issues in Medical Ethics,* sixth edition, Belmont, Cal.: Wadsworth/Thomson Learning, 2000, p. 560.

4. This diagram also appears in LeRoy Walters and Julie Gage Palmer, *The Ethics of Human Genome Therapy,* New York: Oxford University Press, 1997, p. xvii.

5. See B. Julie Johnson, "Genetic Engineering Is Dangerous," in *Genetic Engineering: Opposing Viewpoint,* pp. 17-21.

6. Walters and Palmer, *The Ethics of Human Genome Therapy,* p. 15.

7. Both quotations are for James J. Walter, "Presuppositions to Moral Judgments on Human Genetic Manipulation," in *Moral Issues and Christian Response,* edited by Paul T. Jersild, and others, sixth edition, New York: Harcourt Brace College Publishers, 1998, p. 347.

8. Walter, "Presuppositions to Moral Judgments on Human Genetic Manipulation," p. 347.

9. See Ronald Munson, *Intervention and Reflection: Basic Issues in Medical Ethics,* pp. 463-494.

10. Walters and Palmer, *The Ethics of Human Genome Therapy,* p. 20-26.

11. W. French Anderson, "Genetics and Human Malleability," *The Hastings Center Report,* January/February, 1990, p. 24.

12. Anderson, "Genetics and Human Malleability," p. 24.

13. J. Hughes, "Embracing Change With All Four Arms: a Post-Humanist Defense of Genetic Engineering," *Eubios Journal of Asian and International Bioethics,* June 1996, 6(4):94-101.

14. Walters and Palmer, *The Ethics of Human Genome Therapy,* p. 131.

15. See Ted Peters, *For the Love of Children: Genetic Technology and the Future of the Family,* Louisville, Kentucky: Westminster/John Knox Press, 1996.

Chapter 10

Homosexuality

In this Chapter we will examine the issue of Christianity and homo-sexuality. Like capital punishment and genetic modification, Christians of good will disagree on the morality of sexual beliefs and behavior. During the past thirty years, the disagreements among Christians have reached stentorian levels and in some cases threaten to divide entire denominations in the same way that conflicts over slavery split the Church during the mid-nineteenth century. Even the question of its importance relative to other weighty moral matters such as the persistence of poverty or vast global economic inequalities is debated. Nonetheless, rapid transformations characterize the Modern world where one of our dominant challenges involves changes in sexual mores. Given the traditionally conservative stance on this topic, these changes strike at the heart of some of Christianity's most deeply entrenched ethical beliefs.

Definitions and Background

We begin with definitions so that we are clear in our focus by sharing a common vocabulary. We need to distinguish homosexuality from the other types of orientation and activity that comprise the spectrum of human sexuality. For the purposes of our discussion, we will differentiate the more general concept of human sexuality from the more specific idea of sex. Human sexuality embraces the broad expressions of maleness and femaleness and includes all the emotions, beliefs, and behaviors that we associate with gender differences. Sex involves a narrower focus on genital activity, stimulation, or intercourse.

We consider sexuality between humans and non-humans and between adult human beings and children to be inherently unethical. For this discussion, human sexuality applies only to adult human beings capable of consenting to participate in sexual activities and of understanding the consequences. Three types of sexuality exist among humans and can best be understood as separate positions along a continuum. The three types are heterosexuality, homosexuality, and bisexuality. Heterosexuality stands at one end of the continuum; homosexuality is at the other end; and bisexuality occupies the middle. The word heterosexual refers to someone who is attracted to persons of the opposite sex; homosexual denotes an individual who is drawn to others of the same sex; and bisexual incorporates those who express interest in both sexes.

Any person's sexuality can range along the continuum from being exclusively at one end or the other or can include varying degrees of both with one or the other being dominant. The word "straight" applies to heterosexuals and "gay" or "same-sex" to homosexuals. "Gay" and "lesbian" further distinguish male and female homosexuals, and "bi" stands for bisexual. These definitions exclude both transsexuals who prefer to be members of the opposite sex and transvestites, or cross-dressers, who take pleasure in wearing the clothing of the opposite sex. These two forms of human sexuality require a separate discussion that will not be included in this Chapter.

In addition to defining the three main types of human sexuality, we need to distinguish between sexual orientation and sexual activity. Sexual orientation involves the feelings of attraction that a person has for someone of the opposite sex, the same sex, or for both sexes. It refers to an individual's sexual preferences that attach themselves to other persons as potential sexual partners. While in the minority, there are asexual persons, both male and female, who possess no sexual orientation at all, one way or the other and who do not desire to have a sexual relationship with anyone. However, the vast majority of persons have a sexual orientation. The only issue is whether they are straight, gay, or some combination of the two.

Sexual activity refers to the genital behavior of sexual partners. Sexual activity goes beyond desire and expresses itself in practice. Any person can have a sexual orientation without engaging in sexual activity. Nonetheless, most people with some type of sexual orientation also engage in one or more of the four main forms of sexual behavior that involve manual, oral, vaginal or anal stimulation with or without orgasm. Unlike asexual persons who have no desire to engage in sexual activities, sexually oriented persons have sexual desires that they usually express through sexual activities, although this is not inevitable. By choice, individuals can remain celibate for life without being asexual, although non-asexual celibacy requires extraordinary control and dedication that most sexually oriented people find either too demanding or not even desirable.

Thus, except for a minority of asexual or celibate-by-choice persons, most human beings engage in sexual activities that are an extension of their heterosexual, homosexual or bisexual orientations. In all societies, heterosexuality is the dominant form of sexual expression, although homosexuality and bisexuality appear to be present in all societies as well. The causes of human sexual orientation are disputed along with the precise numbers of persons who fall into each of the three categories of sexual orientation and activity. Thus, we can conclude that sexual diversity exists universally and while most people in all societies are heterosexual, a minority is exclusively homosexual or bisexual with estimates ranging from two to ten per cent.[1]

Despite this diversity of sexual orientations and activities, Christianity has traditionally accepted one principle standard of sexual behavior: celibacy in singleness and fidelity in marriage. We will call this the celibacy-fidelity heterosexual norm. From this perspective, the only legitimate form of human sexual expression is sexual intercourse within heterosexual marriage and sexual abstinence outside of heterosexual marriage. All forms of homosexual and bisexual behavior, as well as non-marriage heterosexual activity, are sinful by definition.

The current dispute over homosexuality within Christianity turns on the question of whether the celibacy-fidelity heterosexual norm can still be defended ethically. Many contemporary Christians have risen to challenge it. They point out that our understanding of the origin and nature of human sexuality has changed so dramatically during the past one hundred and fifty years that the traditional norm no longer applies. In its place we must evolve a new standard that more consistently builds on this new knowledge. On the other hand, supporters of tradition reject this initiative and maintain that the Church's celibacy-fidelity heterosexual norm is ethically defensible. We will call those who support this norm "conservatives" and those who call for changing it "liberals."

When we review the pro and con arguments surrounding the homosexuality debate, we discover that advocates on all sides incorporate the four ethical frameworks and four sources of authority to advance their positions. They draw variously from the Faith and Love, Moral Law, Character, or Justice and Liberation perspectives. Their disagreements rest on different interpretations of both the Old and New Testaments. They diverge in their reference to tradition, experience, and reason as non-Biblical sources of authority and how these three can be combined with relevant passages from the Bible.

For conservatives, the Biblical Moral Law and stories that condemn homosexual acts carry the greatest authority. For liberals, the Biblical images of Faith and Love and of Justice and Liberation take priority. Both sides incorporate Character development concerns but accentuate the virtues that are most consistent with their different interpretations. Based on experience and reason, liberals accept the modern scientific understanding of human sexuality and use it normatively to critique the Biblical verses that conservatives quote to condemn homosexuality. On the other hand, conservatives maintain and correctly so that the Bible consistently opposes homosexual behavior. Liberals counter that the Bible passages conservatives like to quote are as irrelevant to the modern discussion of human sexuality as the Genesis seven-day creation story is to any scientific discussion of the origin of the universe.

How might tradition shed light on disagreements over how to interpret the Bible? According to John Boswell, throughout its long history Christianity has vacillated in its attitude toward homosexuality.[2] Boswell has conducted the most thorough examination of the Church's historical traditions on the issue of homosexuality. His findings reveal a pattern of oscillation between periods of disapproval and acceptance. The Church's historical views of homosexuality often varied with normative shifts that occurred in the surrounding culture. For example, from the third to the sixth centuries, widespread antagonisms toward homosexuals arose. During periods of tolerance, such as the eleventh century, gay and lesbian persons even held positions of leadership among the clergy. Thus, despite the current support among many Christians for the celibacy-fidelity norm, from the perspective of two thousand years of Christian history, the Church's condemnation of homosexuality has been neither consistent nor linear.

As the above discussion suggests, Christians have disagreed and continue to disagree on moral matters related to human sexuality and use the Bible and tradition differently to defend their claims about the morality of homosexuality. The result is gridlock. How might we move beyond this impasse?

In the next section, we will describe how knowledge about the origins and nature of human sexuality has changed in the past century and a half. In the process we will include references to heterosexuality as well as homosexuality. In the final analysis, any examination of homosexuality will inevitably lead to questions about other forms of sexual expression, including bisexuality. We will focus mainly on heterosexuality and homosexuality because these two types of sexuality stand at the center of the dispute. By definition, if homosexuality is morally unacceptable, so is bisexuality.

We will also discuss the Biblical perception of human sexuality and how it differs from the modern point of view. Next we will examine the major Bible passages that include references to homosexuality. Finally, we will look for ways in which we can combine an acceptable view of sexuality with relevant Biblical images in order to identify a Christian moral position that will contribute to increasing goodness in the world.

Origin and Nature of Human Sexuality

The current debate about the morality of homosexuality might not exist at all if our understanding about the origin and nature of human sexuality had not changed so dramatically during the past one hundred years. Prior to the latter part of the nineteenth century, it was automatically assumed that all human beings were born heterosexual and that they became homosexual by choice. Nature created us from the moment of birth to be heterosexuals, which meant that homosexuality became defined as a deviation from nature's norm. Homosexuality was considered unnatural, a distortion, or at worst a perversion from the design of the universe. The Bible reinforced this perspective through the Genesis account of creation. God did not create only males or females to inhabit the earth but rather males and females. Furthermore, God created them as heterosexuals and instructed them to be fruitful and multiply (Genesis 1:28). Since God created human beings for this purpose, anyone who disavowed the heterosexual intention contradicted the divine mandate. Therefore, homosexuality was by definition contrary to the will of God.

This view of the origin and nature of human sexuality began to change during the latter third of the nineteenth century. Although we now routinely divide humankind into various sexual orientations, the word "homosexual" did not even appear until 1869 when Dr. Karoly M. Benkert in Germany used it for the first time to identify males and females who are born with an erotic orientation toward their own sex.[3] When Dr. Benkert postulated that homosexuality might be as natural for some persons as heterosexuality was for others, he started a perceptual revolution. His findings directly challenged the Bible's assumptions about the origin and nature of human sexuality in the same way that Galileo challenged the Genesis view of the origin and nature of the physical universe.

For all intents and purposes, the current controversy within Christianity over the morality of homosexuality rests on a classic confrontation between an ancient understanding that Biblical writers took for granted and a modern viewpoint that challenges it. At core, it is part of the science versus religion debate that has gone on for centuries since the emergence of modern science. At the same time, it is not as easy to determine the origins of sexual identity by using the tools of science as to verify that the earth revolves around the sun rather than vice versa. Despite advancements in this area, scientific disagreements still exist about the precise origins of any given person's sexual identity, which only adds lack of clarity to the debate.

We know that sexual identity emerges through a very complex process of personality development that involves the interaction of physiological, psychological, and/or social forces. It cannot be said with complete confidence what impact each of these factors has on the others. Nor can it be determined totally whether a person's sexual orientation is learned (nurture), given genetically at birth (nature) like skin color, or arises from some combination of both. While modern researchers are not able to specify with pinpoint accuracy the causes of a person's sexual identity, their studies point toward some fairly firm, although tentative, conclusions.

Sexual orientation, whether heterosexual or homosexual, emerges very early in life and remains stable over time. The causes of this early emotional development are not completely understood. However, it appears as though individuals do not make their sexual orientation but rather discover it as they move from youth into adolescence. During most the early twentieth century modern psychiatry, following Sigmund Freud's psychosexual theories, classified adults who possessed a homosexual identity as developmentally abnormal. As a result of believing they were sick, many homosexual persons turned to psychiatric treatment to change their sexual orientation to heterosexuality. After several decades of counseling, the success rate among homosexuals who tried to convert to heterosexuality has been virtually zero. This suggests that once a person establishes a sexual identity, it probably remains permanent for life.

In 1973 the American Psychiatric Association removed homosexuality from its official list of pathologies. Today, very few people who work in the fields of psychiatry and psychology follow the Freudian view and regard homosexuality as a disease or an unnatural personality aberration. Chandler Burr writes, "Five decades of psychiatric evidence demonstrates that homosexuality is immutable, and nonpathological, and a growing body of more recent evidence implicates biology in the development of sexual orientation."[4]

While it cannot be stated conclusively that biology is destiny in the case of sexual orientation, it seems increasingly evident that physiological or genetic factors play a significant role, maybe even greater than psychological or social ones. If this is the case, then it is reasonable to conclude that it is just as normal for some persons to be homosexual in their orientation as it is for others to be heterosexual. This means that we are not all born heterosexuals as the Biblical writers assumed according to the then prevailing view of nature and God's orders of creation. The modern scientific view implies that whatever a person's sexual orientation, whether heterosexual or homosexual, in all probability he or she is born with it; and even if this cannot be asserted with certainty, once it is "locked in," so to speak, early in life, it usually does not change.

While both liberals and conservatives might agree with the modern view of the origins of sexual identity, nonetheless they would soon part company over what this implies for the morality of homosexuality. For conservatives, accepting that it might be natural for persons to be either heterosexual or homosexual in their sexual orientation does not mean that heterosexual and homosexual activities are equally moral. According to conservatives, the Bible consistently denounces homosexual behavior, and this leads to only one conclusion: Even if a person is born with a homosexual orientation, although this cannot be known with complete scientific certainty, he or she should refrain from engaging in homosexual behavior. The only acceptable moral choices for persons who possess a homosexual orientation are lifelong celibacy or conversion to heterosexuality, where God permits sexual activity but only within marriage.

For many liberals, to draw the line between sexual orientation and sexual activity for homosexuals but not heterosexuals is an unacceptable double standard. From this standpoint, if it is as natural for some persons to be homosexual as it is for others to be heterosexual, then it is as moral for homosexuals to engage in sexual activity as it is for heterosexuals. The only serious issue is the context within which engaging in sexual activity can be morally justified from the perspective of Christian Ethics for either heterosexuals or homosexuals.

This leads to the next question of whether homosexuals should have the same marriage or legal partnership rights that heterosexuals do and thereby receive the same lawful protections and privileges, including adoption rights, insurance coverage, social security benefits, and so on. For conservatives, since any homosexual relationship that involves sexual activity is sinful, legalizing homosexual relationships through marriage or legal partnerships is unacceptable. Liberals do not share this perspective. If sexual activity is acceptable for both heterosexual and homosexual people, then homosexuals should have access to the same legal rights as heterosexuals.

Thus, the line that divides conservative from liberal Christians on the morality of homosexuality seems clear. Liberals who challenge the celibacy-fidelity heterosexual norm build on the modern scientific understanding of human sexuality, which they believe implies a need to revise the norm. They maintain that it is no longer credible to support the Biblical view that that everyone is born heterosexual or that being homosexual is sinful, perverse, or contrary to nature. At the same time, while they critique the Bible's heterosexual assumptions, they also use the Bible as the basis for moving beyond the celibacy-fidelity heterosexual norm, which we will discuss later in this Chapter.

On the other side, conservatives take the Bible's condemnation of homosexuality at face value as contrary to God's will. They also reject the liberal suggestion that it is not necessarily immoral for same-sex oriented persons to engage in sexual activities. They flatly reject any suggestion that gays and lesbians have a civil right to marriage or legal partnerships. Even though their homosexual orientation might be as natural as someone else's heterosexual orientation, although this cannot be known with scientific certainty, homosexual persons should not cross the line into sexual activity.

Since much of the current debate involves different interpretations over what the Bible actually says about the nature and morality of homosexuality, it is essential that we examine the relevant passages and the varying interpretations that surround them. For Transformation Ethics this is especially important because of the Bible's central role in forming the Christian moral imagination. After we have completed this review, we will return to the question of whether supporting the celibacy-fidelity heterosexual norm or revising it in some way would most likely bring greater goodness into the world in terms of the combined strengths of Christianity's four frameworks of moral reasoning, Faith-Love, Moral Law, Character, and Justice-Liberation.

Biblical Perspectives

While the Bible does not develop a systematic sexual ethic, it is not silent on sexual issues. Based on the assumption that heterosexuality is inherent in God's natural order of creation, various Biblical passages address the morality of both heterosexual and homosexual practices. Only a few direct references to homosexuality exist in both the Old and New Testaments, but the writers of these passages are consistent in their condemnation. This presents Christians who perceive that Christianity and homosexuality are not necessarily incompatible with a quandary. They must confront directly the Bible's consistent disapproval of such behavior. For conservative Christians, this uniform Biblical witness is proof enough that homosexuality is morally unacceptable.

On the basis of the Bible alone, it would appear that conservatives who support the "heterosexuality only" viewpoint have the weight of evidence on their side. However, liberals contend that this is not necessarily so. Many scholars have examined the Scriptural references to homosexuality in the context of the ancient world's heterosexual assumptions and related cultural practices. They have concluded that these references are no longer relevant to the modern world's perception of the nature of human sexuality or gender relationships. Conservatives disagree. Let us examine these passages in detail.

The conservative position combines Biblical references that both support heterosexuality and condemn homosexuality. They point out that Genesis 2:24 asserts that God made male and female to be of "one flesh" not male and male or female and female. From this Biblical starting point, they move to those passages that portray the sinful nature of homosexuality. Given the intensity of the debate that surrounds homosexuality, we might conclude that the Bible discusses it extensively. However, this is not the case. Only four references appear in the Old Testament and three in the New Testament for a total of seven altogether. We will start with the Old Testament and follow with the New Testament. The four Old Testament passages appear in the Genesis 19 account of Sodom and Gomorrah, in the Judges 19 story of the Levite's concubine, and in the Leviticus Holiness Code in Chapters 18 and 20.

In the well-known Genesis 19 narrative about the demise of Sodom and Gomorrah, the Lord rains sulfur and fire on the sinful inhabitants because of their moral wickedness. Lot, the main character in the story, invites two male angels to spend the night in his house before they venture on their way the next day. The men of the city surround Lot's house and demand that he send the two angels outside so that they might "know them," (Gen 19:5), that is, gang rape them. In order to protect his two guests, Lot offers to substitute his two daughters, but they persist in wanting the two men. Before harm comes to anyone, the two angels blind the potential rapists so that they cannot find the door. The next day God destroys the two cities because of their sinfulness.

This story has become a battleground of interpretation for both sides of the homosexuality debate. Conservatives focus on the homosexual intent of the sinful male citizens as reason for God's ire. Liberals oppose this interpretation and point out that God did not destroy Sodom and Gomorrah because of the intended homosexual rape by the male citizens but because they failed to show hospitality to strangers. This egregious discourtesy violated one of the ancient world's most sacred norms and inflamed the Lord's fury against them.[5]

While conservatives and liberals debate their different interpretations of Genesis 19, few disagreements exist over another aspect of the Sodom and Gomorrah story. The narrative exposes the deep patriarchal cruelty that men in the ancient world inflicted on women. Females were considered property and possessed few rights of protection against male arbitrariness. The intensity of the homosexuality versus inhospitality debate surrounding Genesis 19 veils this story's extraordinary abuse of women. In pleading with the inhospitable rapists not to harm the two males, Lot makes a counter offer. "I have two daughters who have not known a man; let me bring them out to you, and do to them as you please; only do nothing to these men." (Gen 19:8) Apparently without qualm, the father Lot offers his daughters to be gang raped in place of his two male guests.

One of the ironies of the homosexuality versus inhospitality debate over Sodom and Gomorrah is that so little criticism is directed at the heterosexual maltreatment that is an inherent part of the narrative. In an effort to gain theological and ethical insight into the causes of divine judgment, should we not give as much attention to the idea the God might be equally enraged, or possibly even more so, by a father who offers his virgin daughters to be violated so horrendously under these or any other circumstances? On this issue, the debate over the meaning of the Sodom and Gomorrah story is largely silent.

In a similar narrative in Judges 19, a Levite's concubine is not as fortunate as Lot's daughters. In this story a male Levite and his concubine are traveling through the city of Gibeah, where they spend the night at the home of a generous old man. In parallel to the males in the Sodom and Gomorrah story, the men of Gibeah call to the old man to give them the Levite so that they might have sexual intercourse with him. Instead, the Levite gives them his concubine and throughout the night they collectively rape her to death.

Both Genesis 19 and Judges 19 are not just about homosexuality or inhospitality but rather homosexuality, inhospitality, *and* violent heterosexuality. At the deepest level, these two stories expose the ancient world's male cruelty against women. In the tradeoff between homosexual or heterosexual rape, Lot offers his daughters and the Levite's concubine loses her life. This means that if we limit our interpretation of Sodom and Gomorrah to the current homosexuality versus inhospitality debate, we cut ourselves off from the narrative's deeper brutality: Both this story and the account of the Levite's concubine in Judges 19 are about gang rape and patriarchal violence against women.

In short, neither one says anything meaningful about the nature of long-term loving relationships and shared commitments among consenting adults whether they are homosexuals *or* heterosexuals. If we want to gain greater understanding of why God created us as sexual beings, then we need to move beyond the homosexuality versus inhospitality impasse in order to grasp how the Bible's deeper moral insights can be applied to human sexuality—in all of its forms. We will say more about this in the last section of this Chapter.

The third and fourth Old Testament references to homosexual acts appear in the Holiness Code of Leviticus, chapters 17-26, which was written during the post-exilic period. Chapters 18 and 20 contain the two references to homosexuality. After the Persians conquered the Babylonians in 538 B.C.E. Emperor Cyrus allowed the Israelites to return to Jerusalem where they struggled to reestablish their Jewish identity after several decades of foreign captivity. In order to disentangle themselves from surrounding cultural influences, the priests prescribed a rigorous Code of behaviors designed to prevent cultic and religious defilement. This Code includes food preparation procedures, purification rituals after menstruation, childbirth and encounters with lepers, rules for planting crops and choosing fabrics for clothing, and so on.

For the Israelites who disobeyed the Holiness statutes, the Code imposed various forms of punishment ranging from mild to severe. According to Leviticus 18, uncovering the nakedness of one's father, mother, father's wife or sister, or other closely related kin was considered depraved behavior, but it called only for a lesser punishment of ritual purification. Other violations were deemed so serious that the only acceptable penalty was death, including cursing one's parents. (Lev 20:9)

The Holiness Code also prescribes death for various sexual violations. For example, if a man has sexual intercourse with his wife and her mother, all three of them shall be burned to death. (20:14) When a man or a woman has sexual intercourse with an animal, they shall be put to death along with the animal. (20:15, 16) Adultery also requires the death penalty for both the adulterer and the adulteress (20:10). The regulation forbidding homosexuality is found among these defiling forms of sexual behavior. "If a man lies with a male as with a woman, both of them have committed an abomination; they shall be put to death." (20:13) Also see Lev 18:22. An alternative translation of verse 20:13 or 18:22 is that a male should not "lie as though lying with a women."

Conservatives who hold that the Bible condemns homosexuality quote the Holiness Code to support their position. Liberals respond that they arbitrarily select only those verses that support their prejudices and ignore the Code's other violations that mandate the death penalty, such as cursing one's parents or adultery. Liberals further claim that conservatives routinely reject requirements related to food production, purification rituals, agrarian practices, and so on. Nor do they ever explain why some Holiness statues should continue to be morally binding but not others.

In addition, liberals argue that the Code's authors opposed homosexual behavior for cultural reasons: It contravened the norm of male superiority that the ancient world believed was inherent in the natural order. The ancient Jewish priests assumed that God created men as the dominant partner in male-female relationships. Because they could not imagine that an egalitarian heterosexual relationship might meet with God's approval, they assumed that when a man took the passive female position during sexual intercourse he defiled his manhood and breached one of the most fundamental orders of creation. For the writers of the Holiness Code, God created human society to be heterosexual and patriarchal.

While valid at one level, the liberal critique of ancient patriarchy and the modern conservatives' predilection for arbitrarily selecting Biblical passages, while excluding others, without reference to their historical context, does not obviate the fact that Leviticus condemns homosexual behavior. In addition, even though liberals reject the conservative's approach of quoting specific Bible verses out of historical context to support their position, liberals defend their point of view in the same way. They merely choose different verses, especially those that refer broadly to the norms of Love or Justice. The issue is not accepting or rejecting Bible passages but which ones and why. Since Leviticus is part of the canonized Scripture, we need to find a way to relate the proscriptions against homosexuality to our modern understanding of human sexuality and the Bible's deeper insights into the nature of human relationships. We will address this after we have examined the New Testament verses that deal with homosexuality.

Like the Old Testament, there are only a few New Testament passages, three to be precise, that refer to homosexual behavior. All of them appear in the Pauline letters: Romans 1:26-27, 1 Corinthians 6:9-11, and 1 Timothy 1:10. All scholars agree that Paul is the author of Romans and Corinthian letters, but disputes exist over whether he wrote First Timothy or someone else did so in his name. For the sake of the following discussion, resolving the authorship question is unimportant. What is significant is that all three appear in the canonized New Testament that the Church views as its sacred Scripture. Like the Old Testament, conservatives and liberals disagree in their interpretation of the New Testament passages as well, which should come as no surprise.

Beyond these three letters, no reference to homosexuality exists anywhere else in the New Testament. In the Gospels, Jesus does not counsel his followers about homosexuality one-way or the other. If he did, we have no knowledge of it. Thus, the written Scripture reveals that no teaching about the morality of homosexuality emanated directly from the mouth of Jesus. This has not kept scholars from speculating about what he might have believed. For liberals, Jesus' silence means that he did not disapprove. For conservatives, his silence does not imply that he approved. Rather, it means that he accepted the Jewish sexual morality of his day, which forbad homosexual behavior.

The truth is that we will never know what Jesus thought. As a result, in the face of Biblical silence, we will not attempt to read his mind on this matter. The lack of a direct mandate from the founder of the Faith complicates the current discussion on the morality of homosexuality in the Church. Christians must turn to other sources for insight. Since the three Pauline letters are the only texts within which the New Testament mentions homosexuality, we will concentrate on how conservatives and liberals interpret them in light of the current debate. This means that we must examine how Paul viewed homosexuality from the perspective of his Gospel of Christ and within the context of first century Greco-Roman culture. For the sake of the following discussion we will assume that 1Timothy reflects Paul's viewpoint even if someone else wrote it.

Paul's transformation theology provides us with clues to understanding where the issue of homosexuality fits into his moral imagination. To become a new creation in Christ requires changing from the old to the new self and community. This transformation involves giving up old pagan attitudes and immoral actions and developing new ones consistent with the new life in Christ. Paul demonstrates the nature of this transformation by listing the acceptable and unacceptable characteristics that embody both the old and new ways of living. As we stated earlier, Galatians 5:16-26 contains the best known of his lists of the fruits of the flesh and of the Spirit.

Virtually all of Paul's epistles incorporate morality lists even though he never develops an exhaustive inventory. He did not write his letters to create a systematic moral theology but rather to address specific problems that appeared in the growing but troubled congregations he founded. The one exception is the Church in Rome, which someone else started, allegedly Peter. Paul voiced his opinion candidly on all types of issues, ranging from major ones such as the relationship between Faith, Love and Law to lesser ones such as how men and women should dress while praying (See 1 Corinthians 11:4-10)

Paul's lists vary in length because of the occasional nature of his writings, which focus on the circumstances of each budding church. He added to or subtracted from the lists as he saw fit depending on the context and included only those moral instructions that he thought best suited each congregation's situation. Most of his lists contain general ethical instructions such as avoiding immorality, greed, theft, idolatry, and so on, but he expanded some of them to include specific issues as well.[6] As stated, the reference to homosexuality appears in only three Pauline letters.

For conservatives, these New Testament letters reinforce the Old Testament's sanction against homosexuality. In 1 Corinthians 6:9-10 Paul writes, "Fornicators, idolaters, adulterers, male prostitutes, sodomites, thieves, the greedy, drunkards, revilers, robbers—none of these will inherit the kingdom of God." In 1 Timothy 1:10, he includes sodomites on the list along with fornicators, murderers, slave traders, liars, perjurers, and others. The language is clear according to conservatives: The Bible condemns homosexuality.

Liberals reject using the Bible this way to declare as immoral all forms of homosexuality because it overlooks both the historical setting within which Paul addressed the homosexuality issue and the changes that have occurred in our understanding of the nature of human sexuality during the past century or so, especially that not everyone is born heterosexual. Scholars like Robin Scroggs focus on the Greco-Roman context and original words that Paul employed in order to gain clearer insight into the kind of homosexual activities that he condemned. In 1 Corinthians 6:9-11 and 1 Timothy 1:10 Paul describes the sin of homosexuality with the Greek words *malakoi* and *arsenokoitai*. According to Scroggs, within the context of ancient Roman civilization, these words referred specifically to the practice of pederasty, sex between an adult male and boy, or to acts of homosexual prostitution among men in pagan religions.[7]

Paul's third reference to homosexuality appears in Chapter 1:26-27 in the longest and most systematic of all his letters, Romans. This is the only writing in which he mentions female as well as male homosexual acts as unnatural. More than in any of his other letters, Paul elaborates his mature theology and ethics. He begins by observing that God's created order is not hidden behind some mysterious veil. It is visible for all to see. He writes (Romans 1:19), "What can be known about God is plain." This assumption is critical because it allows him to assert that no persons can claim they did not know what God expects of them.

From this point forward, Paul develops his dualistic theology of transformation. On the one hand, everyone sins and dies because of Adam's Fall. "Sin came into the world through one man, and death came through sin, and so death spread to all because all have sinned." (Romans 5:12) On the other hand, all can be saved through Christ. "While we were enemies, we were reconciled to God through the death of his Son." (5:10) "Therefore just as one man's trespass led to condemnation for all, so one man's act of righteousness leads to justification and life for all." (5:18)

Paul also emphasizes that no one can achieve moral perfection in this life, because everyone falls short of the glory of God. In Romans 3:10 he refers to Psalms 14 and 53 of the Old Testament, "There is no one who is righteous not even one." Next, he draws out the ethical implications of this assertion for human sinfulness. Prior to becoming transformed through Faith in Christ, sin leads to idolatry; and idolatry produces immoral behavior. Paul aims his harsh criticism at the worshippers of Rome's many pagan deities. "Claiming to be wise, they became fools; and they exchanged the glory of the immortal God for images resembling a mortal human being or birds or four-footed animals or reptiles." (Romans 1:22-23)

As a result of their idolatry, God delivers a harsh judgment not by obliterating them as in the case of Sodom and Gomorrah but by withdrawing support. Once God pulls back, so to speak, immorality takes over because the sinful spirituality of pagan worship causes it. During his extensive journeys throughout Asia Minor, Paul encountered many of the ancient world's polytheistic practices, which he mentions frequently in his writings. In Romans, he includes twenty-four of them. His reference to homosexuality is included in this list.

Here are the relevant passages.

> Since they did not see fit to acknowledge God, God gave them up to a debased mind and to things that should not be done. They were filled with every kind of wickedness, evil, covetousness, malice. Full of envy, murder, strife, deceit, craftiness, they are gossips, slanderers, God-haters, insolent, haughty, boastful, inventors of evil, rebellious toward parents, foolish, faithless, heartless, ruthless. (Romans 1:28-31)

"God gave them up in the lusts of their hearts to impurity, to degrading their bodies among themselves." (Romans 1:24) In particular, "women exchanged natural intercourse for unnatural, and in the same way also the men, giving up natural intercourse with women, were consumed with passion for one another." (Romans 1:26-27) We would be correct in concluding that Paul's view of homosexuality stems from his more general critique of pagan idolatry.

Clearly, Paul's intent is not to single out homosexual activity apart from the many other forms of immorality that he associates with Greco-Roman pagan culture and polytheistic worship. This would be consistent with his Jewish monotheistic background, his dualistic view of Adam's sin and Christ's saving sacrifice, and his new creation transformation theology. Assuming that the monotheistic God of ancient Israel made everyone heterosexual, pagan acts of temple prostitution, heterosexual and homosexual, distort the divine design of the universe. Pederasty and prostitution, as depicted in 1 Corinthians and 1Timothy, are contrary to the will of God. In Paul's moral imagination, none of the Greco-Roman world's immoral cultural and religious practices have any place at all in Christ's new eschatological community that awaits the Lord's return.

This completes our survey of the four Old Testament and three New Testament references that deal with the issue of homosexuality. On the basis of this analysis, how might we move beyond the deadlock between conservatives and liberals over how to interpret these passages? To begin, both sides can readily condemn the intended and actual homosexual rape described in the stories of Sodom and Gomorrah and the traveling Levite. Conservatives and liberals can find common ground in denouncing Lot for presenting his daughters for rape. Likewise, all Christians can deplore the actions of the Levite who offered his concubine's life to save his own. Christians everywhere can feel anguish over inhospitality toward strangers wherever it occurs.

In short, both Genesis 19 and Judges 19 describe immoral behaviors that every Christian ought to deplore. We can learn a great deal from these two stories. At the same time, for conservatives to focus only on homosexuality and liberals on inhospitality, and to end in a stalemate, is to miss the deeper meaning for the life of Faith. Both conservatives and liberals have common ground in rejecting the profound and multiple immoralities associated with these two stories. Neither one offers any insight into the nature of long term, loving relationships of any kind.

Next, the Leviticus Code lays out a vision of holiness that the Jews brought with them upon return to Jerusalem after decades of exile in Babylon. Liberals maintain that this Code has little relevance for modern Christians because it was designed by the ancient Levite priests to restore Jewish biological purity. They maintain, and correctly so, that no Christian, including conservatives, obeys all the Holiness laws or related penalties. If so, Christians would still have to slaughter animals for worship and execute each other for adultery or cursing parents. Liberals also argue, and correctly so, that it is hypocritical for Bible quoting conservatives to claim that particular laws of the Holiness Code reveal God's literal will while selectively ignoring others.

Conservatives respond that no matter what liberals say, the Old Testament is unequivocal in its rejection of homosexuality in all four of the passages where it is mentioned, irrespective of historical context. Liberals reply that is true. At the same time, they contend that all of the Jewish writers assumed that everyone was born heterosexual. From the context of their cultural assumptions, they would have concluded that any and all homosexual acts were immoral. None of the Old Testament authors had knowledge of the modern view of human sexuality. They possessed no awareness of the distinction between sexual orientation and activity. Nor did they understand that it is natural to be either heterosexual or homosexual. As a result, they probably could not even envision that homosexuals are as capable as heterosexuals of establishing long-term loving relationships.

Does this mean that we should reject the Holiness Code as some liberals suggest? The answer is no because many of the Code's statutes still remain applicable to the modern world. The blanket rejection of the Holiness Code is inappropriate because it trivializes the struggle of the ancient Jewish people to establish ethical precepts consistent with being people of God. While Christians no longer engage in animal slaughter during worship or advocate the death penalty for cursing one's parents, both conservatives and liberals still believe that adultery and bestiality are immoral. The Holiness Code is one important resource among many that Christians can use to nurture their moral imaginations without accepting or rejecting every, or only some, aspects of it.

Like the four Old Testament passages, the three New Testament Pauline references to homosexuality offer plenty of common ground on which Christians of all persuasions can stand. When Paul condemns homosexuality, he refers to sexual acts between an adult male and boy and to idolatrous pagan ritual prostitution. Christians everywhere can agree that these two forms of sexual behavior are innately immoral.

Thus, the seven Old and New Testament references to homosexuality set an important Scriptural backdrop for the contemporary examination of the morality of homosexuality. The Bible condemns homosexual rape, pederasty, and prostitution. To this we would add heterosexual prostitution and rape as well. Lot's offer to give his daughters to the men of Sodom and Gomorrah and the Levite's horrific act of handing over his concubine to be killed by the men of Gibeah are deplorable. It is inconceivable that any conservative or liberal Christian would use these two stories to defend heterosexual gang rape just because they appear in the Bible.

In sum, we do not have to remain deadlocked in disagreement over conservative versus liberal interpretations of the Bible's view of homosexuality. We can move forward by combining the best insights of both. At the same time, we must take seriously the modern scientific understanding of the origin and nature of human sexuality. Our challenge is to apply the best Biblical insights that emanated from a culture that assumed everyone was naturally heterosexual to one that assumes that one could be either naturally heterosexual or homosexual. In turn, this will lead us to a final consideration of the continuing relevance of the traditional celibacy-fidelity heterosexual norm.

Ethical Perspectives

How might we combine the Bible's best ethical visions to our modern understanding of human sexuality in order to increase goodness in the world? The four frameworks of moral reasoning provide us with a point of departure. Walter Wink writes, "The Bible has no sexual ethic" because it "knows only a love ethic."[8] He is correct in part. The Bible also knows of Moral Law, Character, and Justice-Liberation ethics. In combination, these four frameworks create the Bible's overarching moral imagination. As stated earlier, disputes among Christians over the morality of homosexuality exist because opponents support their disparate positions with different frameworks. By combining the strengths of all of them we can arrive at the optimal ethical position. We will start with the Faith and Love images and follow with Justice and Liberation. Then we will consider the Character and Moral Law perspectives.

A contemporary Christian sexual ethic begins with the affirmation that God's grace embraces all persons, irrespective of their natural sexual predispositions. References to Faith and Love saturate the Scripture from beginning to end and appear repeatedly throughout every historical time period. They are quintessential Transformation images. Everyone is heir to Christ's redeeming Love and may become a faithful servant of Christ's Church, which ought not exclude anyone because of sexual orientation.

This does not mean that any and all forms of sexual activity are morally acceptable. From the perspective of Christian Ethics, whether straight or gay, relationships that reduce human beings to sexual objects or merely exploit sexual activity for commercial purposes are inherently unloving. When one person uses another person only for momentary impersonal sexual gratification, sexual behavior is unethical. The Biblical condemnation of homosexual rape, homosexual prostitution, and pederasty fit this category. We would also add heterosexual rape and prostitution as well. To this list we can add adultery, pornography, straight and gay adult lifestyles that foster casual or transitory multi-partner sexual activity, or that promote promiscuous sexual behavior without sustained personal commitment or concern for the other person's well being.

However, we cannot classify as immoral sexual activities that occur within deeply caring relationships among persons who are by nature either heterosexually or homosexually oriented. What matters most is the quality of the relationship within which sexual activity occurs. In principle, if it is natural to be either straight or gay, then it is moral for both straights and gays to engage in expressing their Love for each other through sexual activity. It is arbitrary and unacceptable to claim that only straight-oriented but not gay-oriented persons can engage in sexual behavior. When sexual activity becomes an integral part of an ongoing relationship that is nurtured in Love and involves continual care for the other person, then it is moral.

This means that a contemporary Christian sexual ethic, based on Biblical ethical images, would encompass all persons irrespective of their sexual preferences. At the same time, it would be anchored in a vision of Christian Love that requires nothing less that the highest standard of personal responsibility: adult sexual activity within the context of long-term, loving commitments.

Does this position imply that the liberal view of homosexuality trumps the conservative one? The answer is no because it accepts the Biblical view that homosexual rape, pederasty, prostitution, and other forms of sexual dehumanization are immoral. At the same time, it recognizes that sexual exploitation is not limited to homosexuals but applies to heterosexuals as well. A constructive contemporary Christian view of sexuality moves beyond the naturalist heterosexual assumptions of the Biblical writers, which by definition leads to an "anti-all forms of homosexuality" position, and makes room for both straight and gay relationships that are based on Love, care and deep commitment.

For some critics, it is not enough to appeal to Love as the basis for justifying homosexual activity because they consider gay or lesbian sexuality to be deviant behavior that diminishes human dignity. Or they equate homosexuals with alcoholics, drug addicts, or gamblers in need of recovery or conversion to heterosexuality. At worst they label gays as perverted pedophiles who prey on children. For such critics, the correct Christian view is to "love the sinner while hating the sin."9 This position is not morally compelling because it perpetuates stereotypes that demean all gay and lesbian persons and that label all their relationships as unhealthy and abnormal, a viewpoint that the American Psychiatric Association rejected in 1973.

This does not mean, however, that the slogan—love the sinner but hate the sin—ceases to have relevance. It does. However, we need to reinterpret it in light of our understanding of Biblical Faith and the modern view of human sexuality. In the words of Paul, all fall short of the glory of God. All are sinners, heterosexual and homosexual alike. Both straights and gays can commit sexual sins that treat persons as merely dehumanized sex objects to be used only for momentary gratification or making money. Even so, Christians remain obligated to continue loving them as persons for whom Christ died but not their sins. Christian Faith combines forgiveness with repentance. Christianity calls for an end to all exploitative sexual practices and for the creation of only humanizing, loving sexual relationships.

On another level, this issue is not only about Love but also about Justice and Liberation. For James B. Nelson we are guilty of homophobia, the irrational fear of same-sex attraction, and heterosexism, systematic discrimination against gay and lesbian persons throughout our institutions.10 He compares homophobia and heterosexism to racism and sexism. Marvin M. Ellison writes, "Heterosexism and homophobia operate to maintain gender injustice in our churches and throughout this society."11 Newspapers around the nation report daily the mistreatments to which gay and lesbian people continue to be subjected. The 1998 killing of Matthew Sheppard in Wyoming dramatizes the degree to which anti-gay prejudices can erupt at any moment into violence against same-sex persons.

Whether liberal or conservative, Christians of all persuasions rightly deplore such acts of hatred. At the same time, violence is only the tip of the iceberg. At a far deeper level, ongoing injustices against gay persons continue to penetrate our social institutions in areas such as jobs, education, organizational membership and leadership, and so on. It goes without saying that ending these patterns of discrimination would bring greater Justice and Liberation to gay and lesbian persons who must daily confront the heavy hand of homophobia and heterosexism. Nelson and Ellison are right to remind us of how extensively they have infused all of our institutions, including the Church, and have led to a denial of rights and opportunities for gays, which straights take for granted.

One area in particular, the nature of the family, triggers more controversy than any other. The main issue that divides conservatives and liberals is whether the legal right to marriage should continue to be restricted to heterosexuals or be expanded to include homosexuals as well. Conservatives have remained staunchly opposed to any move that would legalize same-sex unions and have actively fought to pass laws that would continue to prohibit them. They maintain that historically marriage has always been limited to male-female relationships and that we should continue to respect this tradition.

Since much of the controversy turns on the meaning of the word marriage, some have proposed that we use different language to describe same-sex unions, such as domestic partnerships. This alternative offers some distinct advantages although not everyone agrees. Same-sex unions do not have to be called marriages in order for states to create parallel legal structures that would give gays and lesbians access to the same rights and protections that straights enjoy by being legally married.

In one sense, the debate comes down to the question, "What's in a word?" In another sense, even though disagreements exist on how to answer this question, a deeper issue involves the legal sanctioning of same-sex unions by whatever name they are called. When the Biblical perspectives of Love and Justice, as we have described them throughout this book, are applied to our modern understanding of human sexuality, such a public initiative would be morally justifiable. In short, when it comes to the public sanctioning of loving relationships, gays and lesbians should have access to the same legal rights as straights.

The states of Hawaii and Vermont have taken the first steps in this direction by enacting legal statutes that parallel those of traditional marriage and that offer homosexuals equal public status and protections that accrue to heterosexual couples when they marry. How far other political jurisdictions will go in creating similar structures either by expanding the definition of marriage, or evolving an alternative but parallel language, is unclear, even as the forces of change push society in this direction.

In addition to questions about the nature of marriage, another family related aspect of the sexuality debate involves the nurturance of children. For conservative voices like the Ramsey Colloquium, homosexuality weakens family values and adversely affects the normal development of children.[12] When the family is damaged, so is society. Those who take this position point out and rightly so that the high rate of divorce, which steadily hovers around fifty percent of all marriages, exacts a considerable toll on children. We should work to reverse this trend by supporting initiatives that stabilize marriages and safeguard children. Support for legalizing homosexual unions only serves to undermine this effort.

At one level, this position has appeal because few would disagree with the contention that stable and loving families provide the best environment for raising children. At another level, this argument wrongly displaces responsibility for the troubled heterosexual family structure onto gay people. If fifty percent of all marriages end in divorce, the problem lies not with homosexuals but with the heterosexuals who are in those ill-fated marriages. To claim that support for homosexual unions contributes to the deterioration of heterosexual family relationships is to unjustly perpetuate a stereotype. In this sense it represents a step backwards and not forward toward creating more goodness in the world.

More importantly, it deflects from the real issue, which is not the form of sexual expression but the quality of the relationships that exist among people whatever their natural sexual orientation. Being heterosexual does not guarantee a good relationship. Nor does being homosexual assure a bad one. Both straight and gay people can be in good or bad relationships. Serious dysfunctions can damage all types of unions and are not confined only one family form.

In 1995 a report from the American Psychological Association concluded, "results of research to date suggest that children of lesbian and gay parents have normal relationships with peers and that their relationships with adults of both sexes are also satisfactory."[13] Recent research by the American Academy of Pediatrics reveals that children who are raised by loving homosexual parents fare as well as those who are raised by loving heterosexual parents. As a result the AAP advocates that same-sex couples should have full rights to adopt children.[14] If this is so, then from the perspective of both Love and Justice, it stands to reason that homosexual couples should be able to join in legal partnerships or marriage, whichever term one prefers, in order to provide their children with the same statutory privileges and protections that married heterosexual couples have for their children.

Next, we turn to the question of how Character development relates to human sexuality. As shown earlier, the Bible is saturated with images of high ethical expectations. The Torah, the Wisdom writings, and the prophets repeatedly remind the ancient Israelites that God expects them to become and remain a righteous people. The New Testament Gospel writers use the heart to symbolize that good works stem from good motivations. For the Apostle Paul, becoming a new creation in Christ results in spiritual and moral transformation characterized by humility, joy, peace, patience, kindness, faithfulness, gentleness, self-control, and so on. When combined with Love and Justice, Biblical visions of virtue provide Christians with insight into the Character traits that nurture and sustain human relationships whether they are straight or gay.

We can also tie the Moral Law framework to the morality of human sexuality but with modifications. Once again, the Old and New Testaments provide the primary reference point. The Holiness Code and Paul's letters contain proscriptions against specific homosexual practices that are exploitative and dehumanizing. We can deplore the homosexual rape images in the stories of Sodom and Gomorrah and of the Levite's concubine and endorse the Pauline proscriptions against pederasty and prostitution.

At the same time, we need to move beyond the Bible's assumptions that everyone is heterosexual at birth and that homosexuality is a perversion of nature. We ought to reject out of hand the patriarchal cruelties that led Lot of offer his daughters to be raped and the Levite's concubine to be murdered. We should affirm that all forms of sexual abuse, whether homosexual or heterosexual, are morally unacceptable. This implies that we would do well to add to the Biblical Moral Law tradition new moral propositions that embody the highest standards of Christian Love, Justice, and Character development in light of the modern scientific understanding of human sexuality.

Finally, we come to the question of the status of the celibacy-fidelity heterosexual norm. In truth, it is both acceptable and at the same time unnecessary limited by permitting only one possibility. A single standard by definition applies to only one type of family structure and not others. While the celibacy-fidelity heterosexual norm continues to remain relevant, given our changing understanding of human sexuality and the diversity of family patterns that characterize post-industrial society, it is unnecessarily restrictive. No doubt many Christians remain committed to sexual abstinence before marriage and sexual fidelity within marriage. We should applaud them.

At the same time, the fifty percent divorce rate indicates that for many heterosexual couples, Christians among them, the celibacy-fidelity norm is frequently honored in the breach. At the beginning of the twenty-first century the average length of marriage stands at seven years. During the past quarter century, household patterns have steadily diversified into a growing number of single parent families, unmarried couples living together with or without children, blended families, and serial marriages. One-third of all children are no longer born within heterosexual marriages. For these arrangements, the single celibacy-fidelity heterosexual norm offers little moral guidance.

In addition, for homosexuals who cannot marry or partner legally, the celibacy-fidelity heterosexual norm is meaningless. We would be right to remove the double standard that sanctions sexual activities between loving heterosexuals but not homosexuals. If persons can be naturally heterosexual or homosexual and if both heterosexuals and homosexuals are equally capable of entering and sustaining faithful long-term relationships, then it is both loving and just to allow that heterosexuals and homosexuals have access to legal marriage (or partnership) and adoption rights.

To conclude, a sexual ethic relevant to our time integrates the strengths of Christianity's four frameworks of moral reasoning, Faith and Love, Moral Law, Character, and Justice and Liberation. It starts with the affirmation that God's Love as revealed in Christ embraces everyone regardless of their sexual orientation and calls for an end to all forms of prejudice and discrimination against gay and lesbian people. It requires the highest standards of Character development and sexual conduct based on shared responsibility and long-term commitment to provide ongoing care.

It forbids rape, prostitution, pornography, the promiscuous and commercial use of another person as a temporary sex object, and all forms of sexual abuse, exploitation and dehumanization. It makes room for both heterosexual and homosexual marriages, or legal partnerships, and supports the right of all persons to adopt and raise children whatever their sexual preference. In sum, it calls for the sustained transformation of our moral imagination and of all our attitudes and behaviors based on the Biblical vision that God's kingdom as revealed in Christ includes everyone, which in the end contributes to increasing the total amount of goodness in the world.

Notes

1. Tony Marco, "Self Class Protections for Self-Alleged Gays: A Question of 'Orientation' and Consequences," copyright 1991-1994, internet website: http://www.leaderu.com/morco/special/spc 1 1 b.htm.

2. John Boswell, *Christianity, Social Tolerance, and Homosexuality,* Chicago: University of Chicago Press, 1980.

3. See Victor Paul Furnish, "The Bible and Homosexuality: Reading the Texts in Context," in *Homosexuality In the Church,* edited by Jeffrey S. Siker, Louisville, Kentucky: Westminster John Knox Press, 1994, p. 33.

4. Chandler Burr, "Homosexuality and Biology," in *Homosexuality In the Church,* edited by Siker, p. 132.

5. This view is shared by New Testament scholars like Robin Scroggs, *The New Testament and Homosexuality,* Philadelphia: Fortress Press, 1983 and Walter Wink, editor, *Homosexuality and Christian Faith: Questions of Conscience for the Church,* Minneapolis: Fortress Press, 1999.

6. See Scroggs, *The New Testament and Homosexuality,* p. 103.

7. Scroggs, *The New Testament and Homosexuality,* Chapter 7.

8. Wink, *Homosexuality and the Christian Faith: Questions of Conscience for the Church,* p. 44.

9. William Muehl, "Some Words of Caution," in *Moral Issues and Christian Response,* edited by Paul T. Jersild and Dale A. Johnson, fourth edition, New York: Holt, Rinehart and Winston, Inc., 1988, p. 164.

10. James B. Nelson, *Body Theology,* Louisville: Westminster/John Knox Press, 1992.

11. Marvin M. Ellison, "Common Decency: A New Christian Sexual Ethics," in *Moral Issues and Christian Response,* edited by Dale T. Jersild, and others, sixth edition, New York: Harcourt Brace College Publishers, 1998, p. 65.

12. The Ramsey Colloquium, "The Homosexual Movement: A Response," *First Things,* Volume 41, March 1994, pp. 15-20.

13. "Lesbian and Gay Parenting," American Psychological Association Public Interest Directorate, 1995, website: http://www.apa.org/pi/parent.htm.

14. As reported by Jeremy Manier, "Doctors Support Gay Adoption," *Chicago Tribune,* February 4, 2002. The AAP report indicates that between 1,000,000 and 9,000,000 children are already being raised in homosexual families and that many states have passed laws that allow gays and lesbians to legally adopt children. Thus, the idea of gay adoptions is not novel.

Index

A

Abraham, 22, 23, 44
Acts, Books of, 25, 30, 115, 116, 136n. 2
Adaptation (evolution), 35
Agape, 58
Agent, 103
Alaric, 51
Alexander the Great, 23, 112
Alexandria, 95
Ambrose of Milan, 95, 96–97, 148
American Academy of Pediatrics, 217
American Psychiatric Association, 201, 215, 217
Amos, Book of, 91, 110
Ananias, 115
Anderson, W. French, 185, 187, 188
Anglicanism, 122
Animal abuse, 176
Antiochus IV, 112
Aquinas, Thomas, 34, 52, 73, 75–76, 76, 97–98
  integration of four frameworks and, 143
Aristotle, 96, 97
  Aristotelian metaphysics, 34
Artificial Insemination by Husband (AIH), 82
Assyrians, 45, 91, 112
Audience of study, xii

Augustine of Hippo, 34, 51, 61, 73
  integration of four frameworks and, 143
  pessimism of, 54
Axiological laws, 83–84

B

Babylon, 23, 91, 112
  wisdom tradition of, 89–90
Bandstra, Barry L., 62n. 1, 107n. 1, 136n. 1
Barth, Karl, 128
Benkert, Karoly M., 200
Bible
  as book of transformation, 23–28, 139
  challenge of science to, 34–36
  faith-love framework, 60–61
  frameworks of moral reasoning and, 21–28
  homosexuality and, 198, 203–213
  infallibility of, 35
  literal truth and, 82
  See also New Testament; Old Testament
Biotechnology. *See* Genetic modification
Birth control, 81–82
Bisexuality, 196
Black Power and Black Theology (Cone), 132
Blade Runner, 183

Bonhoeffer, Dietrich, 57–59, 144
Boswell, John, 198
Brave New World (Huxley), 183
Brightman, E. S., 83
Brunner, Emil, 59
Burr, Chandler, 201

C
Calvin, John, 78–79, 100, 102, 148
    integration of four frameworks
        and, 143
    pessimism of, 56
Capital punishment, 157–173
    behavioral sciences and, 159–161
    definitions of, 157–158
    detterence and, 159–160
    economic analysis of, 160–161
    empirical perspectives of, 159–161
    ethical perspectives of, 161–173
    justice and, 162–166
    love and, 166–173
    psychological arguments and, 160
    race and, 164
    revenge and, 161–162
    Texas and, 163
    wrongful convictions, 163, 167
Capitalism, 35, 81, 100, 124
Carmody, Denise Lardner, 31
Carmody, John Tully, 31
Casti connubii, 81
Catholic Church, 79
    authority and, 80
    birth control and, 80–82
    dualism of, 99
    liberation and, 124–125
    moral law and, 80–82
    See also Counter-Reformation
Celera Genomics, 177
Celibacy, 197
Celibacy-fidelity heterosexual norm,
    197, 202, 218
Character Ethics, 5, 13–14, 89–108
    genetic modification and, 179

heart as metaphor, 14
homosexuality and, 218
Law of the Covenant and, 14
New Testament and, 92–95
Old Testament and, 89–92
Reformation and, 98–102
strengths and limitations of, 18
virtue and, 13–14
Character formation, 104
*Children of Light and the Children of
    Darkness, The,* 130
Chosen people, 65–66
Christ and Culture (Niebuhr), 54
Christian church
    adaptability of, 26–27
    adaption of Jewish heritage, 29–30
    eschatological expectations, 27
    hierarchical structures, 117–118
    inclusiveness of, 150–153
    pacifism of, 50
Christian ethics
    common elements of, 6–7
    diversity and, 3
    modern social science and, 60
    as a specific form of ethics, ix
    See also Transformation ethics
Christian Realism, 128–131, 149
Christianity
    Medieval era, 32, 51–52, 72–73,
        97, 120
    modernism and, 33–36, 55 (*See
        also* Reformation)
    outsider *vs.* insider status, 31
    Patristic era, 32, 50, 71, 95, 117,
        118–119
    post-Constantine era, 50–51
    transformations of, 31
Circumcision, 28, 30, 85n. 2, 150
City of God, The (Augustine), 51
Clement of Alexandria, 95–96, 117–
    118
Clericalism, 99
Cloning, 12

See *also* Genetic modification
Cold War, 36
Colossians, letters to, 136n. 4
Community
    Christian, 27–28
    pre-industrial *versus* industrial, 35
Cone, James, 132
Conservative religion, 79, 201, 203–213
Constantine, 31, 73, 96
Corinthians, letters to, 69, 94, 98, 147, 208, 209, 211
Cornelius, 30
Council of Trent, 79
Counter-Reformation, 79
Covenant, 14, 23, 91
    code of, 66–68
    Mosaic, 65
    Old *vs.* New, 24, 69
Creation story, 23, 34
Cyrus, 112

D
Daniel, 121
Darwin, Charles, 34, 80
David, 44–45, 89, 112
Deuteronomy, Book of, 11, 44, 45, 46, 62n. 1, 90, 109, 110
    code of, 68
DeWolf, L. Harold, 83
Didache, 71–72, 117, 142
Diggers, 121, 122–123
Divine Institutes, The (Lactantius), 119
Divine Law, 76, 77, 143
Divorce, 219
DNA (deoxyribonucleic acid), 175–179
Dodd, C. H., 27

E
Ecclesiastes, Book of, 89
Edict of Milan, 31

Elizabeth I, 122
Ellison, Marvin M., 215
Enlightenment, 33
Ephesians, letters to, 47
Eternal law, 76–77, 79
Ethos, 101
Eugenics, 178, 183
    Nazis and, 184
Evangelicism, 25, 82
Evil, 4
Evolution, Darwin's theory of, 35
Exodus, Book of, 10, 11, 65, 66–67, 161, 162
Experience, 29–37
Ezekiel, Book of, 46
Ezra, 23

F
Faith, 7–8
    doctrine of faith alone, 79
    internal and external tie, 146–148
    justification by, 56, 59
    rules and, 8
    supernatural virtue and, 98
    Will of God and, 8
    See *also* Faith-Love Ethics
Faith-Love Ethics, 5, 7–9, 43–63
    Medieval christianity and, 47–51
    New Testament and, 47–51
    Old Testament and, 43–47
    Reformation and, 52–57
    strengths and limitations of, 17
Feminism, Christian, 133–134
Fidelity, 197
Fletcher, Joseph, 58–59, 147
Flood, 44
Frameworks of moral reasoning, four
    Bible and, 21–28, 139
    as description of fundamental images, xi
    experience and, 29–37
    historical settings of, 21–39

inclusion and, 150–153
multiple use of, 141–143
reason and, 29–39
strengths and limitations of, 17–19
theological origins of, 21–39
tradition and, 29–37
transformation and, 3–20, 143–155
See also Character Ethics; Faith-Love Ethics; Justice-Liberation Ethics; Moral Law Ethics
Francis of Assisi, 52, 55
Free will, 98
Freed, Edwin D., 25
Freud, Sigmund, 200
Fundamentalism, 35, 79, 82

G
Galatians, letters to, 9, 28, 30, 51, 54, 72, 94, 116, 208
Galileo, 33, 35
Gattaca, 191
Geisler, Norman, 82–83
"Generalized Other," 146
Genesis, Book of, 22, 43, 44, 201–204, 205, 211
Genetic enhancement, 187
Genetic modification, 175–194
background issues, 175–179
diagram, 177
ethical considerations, 178–194
nature and, 180–182
theology and, 182–194
therapy, 178
Gentiles, 30
Germ-line therapy, 186
Gomer, 45, 142
Goths, 31–32, 73
"Graded absolutism," 82–83
Greco-Roman rationalism, 34
Greece
wisdom tradition of, 89–90
Gustafson, James M., 105–106

H
Haltigar, Bishop, 74
Hanukkah, 113
Harnack, Adolf, 127
Hauerwas, Stanley, 104
Hawaii, 216
Hebrew scripture. See Old Testament
Hebrews, letters to, 93
Henry VIII, 122
Heterosexuality, 196
Hodge, Charles, 35
Holy Spirit, 114
Homosexuality, 195–221
adoption and, 217–219
conservative interpretations of, 201, 203–213
definitions, 195–196
ethical perspectives, 213–220
family and, 216–219
liberal interpretations of, 201, 202, 203–213
marriage and, 202, 216–217
origin of word, 200
Hosea, Book of, 45–46, 91, 142
Hughes, J., 188
Human Genome Project, 176–177
Human law, 76, 77, 79
Human nature, 54–57, 127
dualism, 76
Human Rights Declarations for men, 152
Humanae vitae, 81
Hus, John, 39n. 12

I
"Ideal type," x
Identity issues, 146–149
See also Sexual identity
Image, x
See also Moral imagination
In Vitro Fertilization Embryo Transplantation (IVF-ET), 82, 193n. 1

Inclusiveness, 150–153
"Individual conscience," 33
Individualism, 100
Industrialism, 36, 102
Infallibility, papal, 80
Institutes of the Christian Religion (Calvin), 101
Instruction for Human Life in Its Origin and on the Dignity of Procreation, 81
Isaiah, Book of, 46
Israel, ancient, 62n. 1, 85n. 1
  Character Ethics and, 89–92
  Kingdom of God and, 24–25
  liberation and, 110–114
  mission of chosen people, 65–66
  as regional political power, 23
  See *also* Old Testament

J
Jeremiah, 46, 91, 92, 142
Jeroboam II, 91
Jesus
  as exemplar revealing Will of God, 6–7
  healing powers of, 49
  heart as metaphor, 14
  mercy of, 49
  moral law and, 70–85
  new order and, 47
  optimism of, 55
  as personification of God, 48
  prophetic identity, 114
  resurection of, 47
  as sword bearer, 121
  transformation and, 24
Jim Crow laws, 149
Job, Book of, 89
Johann, Robert, 102–103
John, Gospel of, 28, 48, 49
John, Revelation to, 25
John Paul II, 81
John XXIII, 80, 125

Joshua, Book of, 23, 109, 110
Josiah reforms, 68
Judah, 91
Judas Maccabee, 23
Judges, Book of, 204, 205, 211
Just War, 51, 73, 75, 158
Justice
  capital punishment and, 162–166
  eternal *vs.* earthly, 16
  homosexuality and, 215
  inclusion and, 150–153
  See *also* Justice-Liberation Ethics
Justice-Liberation Ethics, 5, 14–17, 109–138
  equality and, 16
  genetic modification and, 179
  New Testament and, 114–117
  Old Testament and, 109–114
  strengths and limitations of, 18–19
Justification by Faith alone, doctrine of, 32
Justin, 50

K
Kant, Immanuel, x
  deontological thought of, xi
Kingdom of God, 24–25, 127
  justice and, 16
Kings, Book of, 23, 110

L
Labor issues, 80–81, 124–125, 149
Lactantius, 119
Laissez faire, 35
Laity, 99
Law of the Covenant, 14
  See *also* Covenant
Leo XIII, 76, 124, 125, 126
Levellers, 121, 122–123
Leviticus, Book of, 11, 46
  holiness code, 11, 67–68, 205–207, 211–212
Liberal religion, 79

Liberation, 15–16
　cycles, 112–113
　homosexuality and, 215
　See also Justice-Liberation Ethics
Liberation theology, 124
Lilburne, John, 122
Logos, 96
Love, 9
　capital punishment and, 166–173
　genetic modification and, 179
　homosexuality and, 214–215
　inclusion and, 150–153
　Jesus and, 9
　as social activity, 147
　transformation of, 150
　See also Faith-Love Ethics
Luke, Gospel of, 46, 48, 49, 93,
　　114–117, 136n. 2, 142, 166
　Lazarus story, 115
Luther, Martin, 32, 52–53, 78, 99,
　　148
　integration of four frameworks
　　and, 143
　paradoxical approach of, 54
　pessimism of, 54–55

M
Maccabee, Joseph, 111
Maccabee, Judas, 112
Manicheanism, 34
Mark, Gospel of, 46, 48, 115, 142
Marriage, 28
Marsilius of Padua, 119–120, 122
Marter et magistra, 125
Martyrs, 50
Marxism, xi–xii, 35
Matthew, Gospel of, 25, 46, 48, 49,
　　69, 71, 93, 115, 142, 166
　bridesmaid parable, 27
　heart as metaphor, 14
　Sermon on the Mount, 28, 92–93,
　　114
McFaul, Thomas R., 223

McVeigh, Timothy, 173n. 1
Mead, George Herbert, 144–149
Mendel, Gregor, 175
Mercy, 166–167, 169
Mesopotamia
　wisdom tradition of, 89–90
Methodism, 55–56
Micah, Book of, 110
Mill, John Steward
　utilitarian ideas of, xi
Millenarian movements, 26
Modernism, 33–36, 55
　industrialism and, 102
　Reformation and, 99–100
Monasticism, 99
Moral and Medicine (Fletcher), 60
Moral career, 103
Moral imagination, x
　Bible and, 30–31, 198
　frameworks of moral reasoning
　　and, 30–31
　as goal of transformation ethics, 6
　integration and, 154–155
　as integrative method, xii, 139–
　　156
　motivations and consequences, xi
　philosophy and, 83
　science and, 83
　self and society and, xii
　theology and, 83
Moral Law Ethics, 5, 9–13, 65–87,
　　198
　absolute, 83
　coherency and, 9–10
　Counter-Reformation and, 79–80
　early Christianity and, 71–72
　Geisler and, 82–83
　homosexuality and, 218
　Medieval era and, 72–77
　Muelder and, 83–85
　New Testament and, 69–72
　Old Testament and, 65–69
　prescription and, 9–11

procedural, 12–13, 83–85
Reformation and, 78–79
social change and, 11
strengths and limitations of, 17–18
subjectivism, 83
Moral Man and Immoral Society
(Niebuhr), 129
*Moral Responsibility: Situation
Ethics at Work* (Fletcher), 60
Moses, 23, 65–66, 109, 111, 121,
141
Mount Ebal, 109
Mount Gerizim, 109
Muelder, Walter, 83–85
Muntzer, Thomas, 78, 121, 122
Mutually Assured Destruction
(MAD), 36

N
Natural law, 76–77, 79, 81
Natural selection, 35
Nazism, 58
Nehemiah, 23
Nelson, James B., 215
Neo-Platonic philosophy, 34, 96
New Testament
canonization of, 22
Character Ethics and, 92–95
dualism, 51
Faith-Love Ethics and, 47–51, 47–
61, 60–61
four frameworks and, 142–143,
150–151
justice and, 16
Justice-Liberation Ethics and, 114–
117
moral law and, 69–85
Moral Law Ethics and, 69–72
perspectives on homosexuality,
207–213
theological origins of in Old
Testament, 22–28

Niebuhr, H. Richard, 54, 59
Niebuhr, Reinhold, 124, 128–131,
143, 149
Nietzsche, Friedrich, xi
1984 (Orwell), 183
Noah, 44
Noblesse oblige, 120, 149
Nuclear bomb, 36
Nuremberg Code, 184
Nygaard, Richard L., 170

O
Octagesimo adveniens, 125, 132
Old Testament
Character Ethics and, 89–92
codes, 66
Faith-Love Ethics and, 43–47
faith-love framework, 60–61
four frameworks and, 141–142,
149
Justice-Liberation Ethics and, 109–
114
moral law and, 65–66
Moral Law Ethics and, 65–69
perspectives on homosexuality,
203–207
as theological origin of New
Testament, 22, 50
wisdom traditions, 89, 148
Origen of Alexandria, 34, 95–97,
148
Origins of Species, The (Darwin),
34, 80
Overton, Richard, 122

P
Pacem in terris, 125
Paradigm, x
Parousia, 26, 27
Paul, 24–25, 47–48, 51, 61, 69, 71,
85n. 2
authenticity of letters, 136n. 4

character tradition and, 93–94
Damascus road conversion, 25
dualistic theology of transformation, 210
evangelicism of, 27–28, 30
homosexuality and, 207–209
inclusiveness of, 150–151
liberation and, 116
as New Testament integrator, 142
pessimism of, 54
Paul VI, 81, 125, 126, 132
Penitential texts, 73, 75, 77
Penultimate sphere, 58, 144
Personalistic moral law, 84
Peter, 30
Peters, Ted, 191
Pius IX, 80
Pius XI, 81
Plato, 96
Pompey, 113
Post-industrialism, 36
Poverty, 114–118
Predestination, 100, 101
Premeditated murder, 158, 169
Priesthood of all believers, 32, 99
Property, private, 100–101, 122–123
Protestantism, 32–33, 39n. 12, 79
  liberation and, 126–136
  See also Reformation
Proverbs, Book of, 89, 90
Psalms, 210

Q
Quest for the Historical Jesus, The (Schweitzer), 24

R
Ramsey Colloquium, 217
Rational-empirical method, 33–36
Rauschenbusch, Walter, 124, 126–127, 149
Reason, 29–39
  natural virtue and, 98

revelation and, 37–38
Red Sea, 136n. 1
Reformation, 32–33
  Character Ethics and, 98–102
  Faith-Love ethics and, 52–57
  Justice-Liberation Ethics and, 120–121
  modernity and, 99–100
  Moral Law Ethics and, 78–79
Relativism, 60
Reproductive technologies, 193
Rerum novarum, 124–125
Revelation, 37–38
Revenge, 161–162
Rifkin, Jeremy, 194n. 2
Ritschl, Albrecht, 127
Rochester Theological Seminary, 126
Romans, letters to, 47, 48, 53, 54, 69, 121, 166, 207, 209, 210
Rome
  Roman Empire, 50
  sack of, 32
Ruether, Rosemary, 133–134
  integration of four frameworks and, 143
Rule of Benedict, 73–75, 77
Russell, Letty, 133

S
Sacramental system, 73, 79
Sanger, Margaret, 81
Sapphira, 115
Schweitzer, Albert, 24
Science, modern, 33–36, 79–80
  rational-empirical method, 33–36
Scroggs, Robin, 209
Second Coming, 25–27, 26–27, 47
Segregation, racial, 149
Self-determination, 103, 104
Self-examination, 57
Serial killings, 158
Sermon on the Mount, 28

Sexual activity, 196
Sexual identity, 200–203
Sexual orientation, 196
Sexuality, 81, 199–203
  versus Sex, 195
Sheppard, Matthew, 215
Situation ethics, 58–60, 102–103
Slavery, American, 149, 151
Smith, Adam, 35
Social change, 11
Social Gospel, 126–127, 143, 149
sola Scriptura, 53
Solomon, 44–45, 89–91, 107n. 1,
  112
Somatic therapy, 178, 185–186
Stark, Rodney, 31
Stem cell research. *See* Genetic
  modification
Stoicism, 34, 96, 97
Summa Theologica (Aquinas), 52,
  76, 97, 143
Syllabus of Errors, 80
Synoptic Gospels, 106

T
Telos, 76, 79, 81, 97
Ten Commandments, 23, 66
Terrorism, 151–152, 173n. 1
Tertullian, 37
Thessalonians, Letter to, 25
Tillich, Paul, 59
Timothy, 117, 207, 208, 209, 211
Titus, 117
Torah. *See* Old Testament
Tower of Babel, 23, 43–44
Tradition, 29–37
Transformation ethics, x, 31
  as Bible based, 139
  capital punishment and, 157–173
  continuum of, 4
  diagram, 145
  dualism and, 4

foundations of, 1
frameworks of moral reasoning
  and, 3–20, 143–155
genetic modification, 178–194
integration and, 150–155
life as transformation, 176
relativism and, 4
Treatise on Good Works (Luther), 53
Trinity, 96
Troeltsch, Ernst, 98, 101

U
Ultimate sphere, 58, 144
United Nations, 152

V
Vatican II, 125, 143
Vermont, 216
Vice, 98
Virtue
  cardinal, 98
  as habit, 13–14, 103
  natural *vs.* supernatural, 98
  theological, 98
Vocation, 99, 103

W
Walter, James J., 182
Walwyn, William, 122
Weber, Max, x, 101–102
Wesley, John, 55–56
  quadrilateral, 29
Western *vs.* Eastern, 32
"Who Is the Rich Man that Shall Be
  Saved?" (Clement), 118
Will of God, 6
  faith and, 8
William, James, x
Winstanley, Gerrard, 123
Wogaman, J. Philip, 31, 54
Women issues, 204–205
Wycliff, John, 39n. 12

About the Author

Thomas R. McFaul is Professor of Ethics and Religious Studies at North Central College in Naperville, Illinois, located in the western region of metropolitan Chicago. For more than three decades he has taught a broad range of courses to both undergraduate and graduate students. His teaching interests incorporate both theoretical and applied ethics including such diverse fields as comparative world religions and religious ethics, philosophical ethics, technology and ethics, bioethics, business ethics, and urban ethics.

He also possesses a deep interest in studying the future and teaches courses that help students think about how to think about the future as well as the future itself. This book grows out of his extensive academic background and concentration in Christian ethics and integrates many of the themes that cut across the spectrum of his courses. He has authored, co-authored, or edited other books and many articles.

In addition, Dr. McFaul has served in several academic administrative positions that range from department chair to director to dean to vice president. He has extensive curriculum development experience, and for many years has helped create new courses and programs. His lifelong commitment to an interdisciplinary approach to learning has led him to look for ways to combine multiple viewpoints that stretch beyond the boundaries of academic disciplines while integrating their best insights. Transformation Ethics follows this framework of learning. In addition to being a Professor of Ethics and Religious Studies, he also serves as North Central College's Coordinator of Cultural Events.